IMAGES
of America

PRAIRIE DU CHIEN

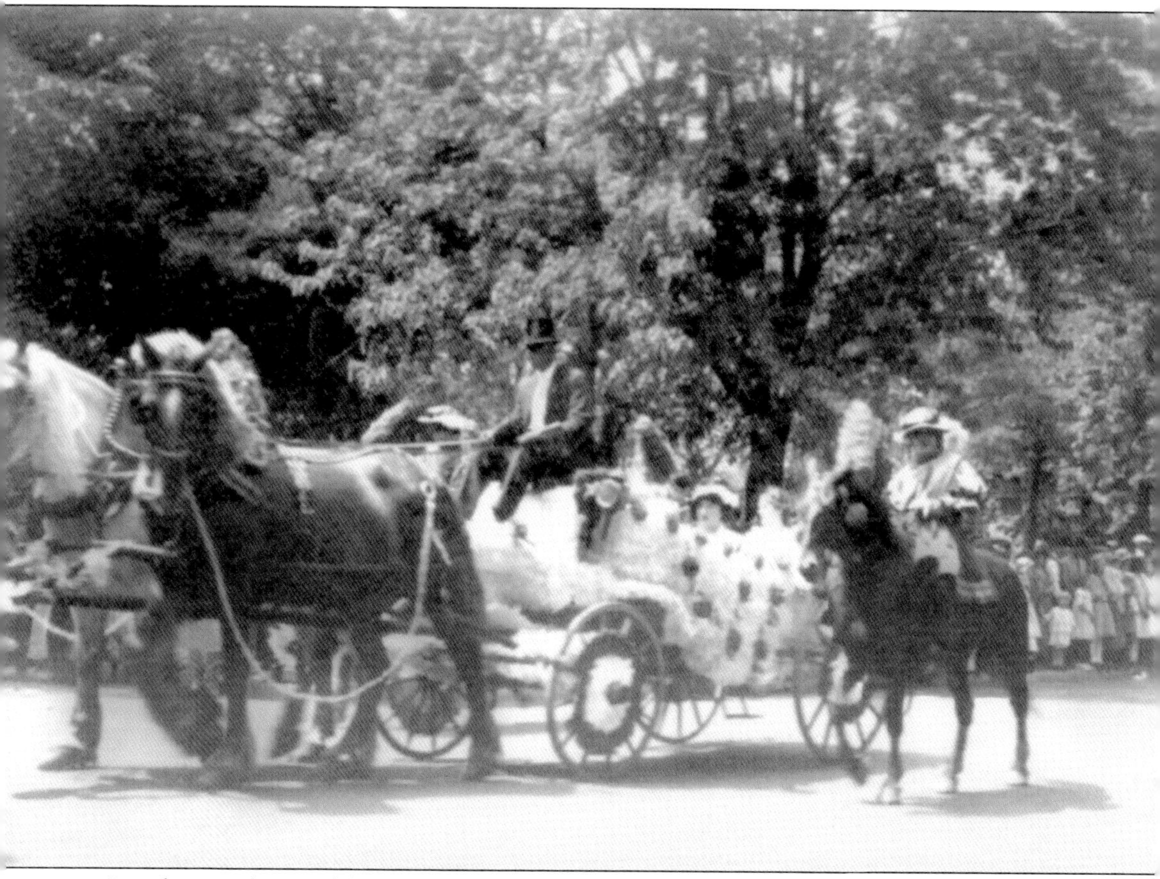

Parades are about celebration. They can reflect patriotism or commend community pride. They can commemorate a person's life. In Prairie du Chien, residents also organized parades to celebrate and commemorate history. In 1932, Prairie du Chien marked the 250th anniversary of Jacques Marquette and Louis Jolliet's entrance into the Mississippi River with a parade of floats and a pageant.

ON THE COVER: This is the Villa Louis Days Parade in May 1947. From 1935 through 1951, the City of Prairie du Chien owned the Villa Louis, the Dousman family estate. Each May, to mark the opening of the house for tours, a parade of bands and floats marched down Blackhawk Avenue. (Courtesy Tony and Chris Trentin.)

IMAGES
of America

PRAIRIE DU CHIEN

Mary Elise Antoine

ARCADIA
PUBLISHING

ISBN 978-0-7385-8356-3

Published by Arcadia Publishing
Charleston, South Carolina

Printed in the United States of America

Library of Congress Control Number: 2010934708

For all general information, please contact Arcadia Publishing:
Telephone 843-853-2070
Fax 843-853-0044
E-mail sales@arcadiapublishing.com
For customer service and orders:
Toll-Free 1-888-313-2665

Visit us on the Internet at www.arcadiapublishing.com

To my sisters, who grew up in Prairie du Chien surrounded by its history. To my children, so they better know their heritage.

Contents

ACKNOWLEDGMENTS

When I was a young girl, my family lived with my grandmother in her house; we lived on one side and she on the other. Many a morning, I would get up, dress, and eat breakfast. I would then go out our kitchen door, walk across the back porch, and open the door to Granny's kitchen. There we would sit and "have tea and toast." Granny's part of the house was filled pictures and memories of her family that she often looked at while we talked and she told me stories about Prairie du Chien and its residents. Some afternoons, I would dress in a nice skirt and blouse and join her as she shopped and called upon her acquaintances.

When I was 10, we moved three blocks away to "the other side of town." There I met my neighbor Florence Bittner. She regaled me with more stories about Prairie du Chien, including some I would never have heard from my grandmother. Both women, though, exuded an unspoken belief in the importance of remembering and preserving our past that impressed me and influenced my direction in life.

Some of the information I gleaned from Granny and Florence, supplemented by stories told by other lifelong residents of the community, has found its way into this book. The rest of the story of Prairie du Chien comes from my interest that was sparked by these two women and years of research.

This information alone would not have made this book possible; I needed photographs. The images you will see have been preserved by the descendants of residents of Prairie du Chien. When I asked to make their photographs part of this book, all responded with overwhelming generosity. These images make the fascinating history of Prairie du Chien come to life. Thank you to all. You will see the names of the many people and institutions that made this possible as you read. All other images are from my personal collection.

I thank Nick and Matt for their technical assistance and Virginia for helping clarify the story I wanted to tell. Thank you to the editorial staff at Arcadia Publishing for their understanding editing. I often get carried away when sharing the rich heritage of my community.

May Ona and Connie be pleased. I tried to follow your footsteps.

To everyone, I wish you enjoyment.

Author's Note: When people ask me about a good history of Prairie du Chien, I refer them to *Prairie du Chien: French, British, American* by Peter L. Scanlan, the 1884 *History of Crawford and Richland Counties*, and *Old Crawford County* edited by John G. Gregory. I tell them that Dr. Scanlan's book is excellent and is based upon good documentary research. I can tell, though, by the looks on their faces that this is not quite what is wanted. Scanlan's book is very detailed and focuses on the history prior to 1840. There is no publication for the reader that gives the concise overview history of Prairie du Chien.

While I make no claim to be as fine a historian as Dr. Scanlan, I wrote this book based upon careful research. I chose images of the community created and taken by the people who lived in Prairie du Chien. Together they convey a sense of what Prairie du Chien was—and is—and hopefully give the readers the history of Wisconsin's second oldest community that they desire.

Introduction

"La Prairie des Chien" was the name given by the French to the 9-mile plain just north of the confluence of the Wisconsin and Mississippi Rivers. A prairie of unmatched beauty, the Mississippi River, dotted with islands, flowed southward in front of the prairie, while towering bluffs to the east framed the flat grassy plain. The location of the prairie drew people. The French, competing with Great Britain in the fur trade, found the grassland to be the gathering place of the tribes with whom they wished to trade, and so they built a fortified post on a point close to the shore. When Great Britain vanquished France and gained her North American territory and the fur trade, the British also saw the importance of the prairie as a trading center.

Neither country encouraged settlement on the plain, but the constant political maneuvering of European countries and the young United States affected the daily lives of ordinary people. Some left their homes farther down the Mississippi to make a new home on the prairie where they could farm in peace. Other French-speaking men coming from Canada and Mackinac settled on the prairie as the fur trade expanded further up the Mississippi River.

Prairie du Chien was so far removed from the seat of national government that when the prairie became part of United States territory, the first Congress was not fully aware of the small settlement on the Mississippi River. It was Lt. Zebulon M. Pike who reported that the United States should build a fort at Prairie du Chien, and in 1816 the U.S. Army arrived to take command of the prairie and the entire upper Mississippi River drainage. Prairie du Chien was a strategic location as the United States strove to exert its authority over the fur trade region and the many Native Americans who inhabited the land. For 40 years, Fort Crawford dominated the area. The tribes of the upper Mississippi came to Prairie du Chien to express their loyalty to the United States and sign treaties giving their lands to the American government.

The shores of the prairie gently sloped into the eastern channel of the Mississippi River, offering a perfect landing for steamboats. From the arrival of the *Virginia* in 1823 to the days of the *Delta Queen*, Prairie du Chien was a major steamboat port. The broad flat prairie invited development when viewed by the first visitors to travel up the river, and so the next steamboats brought land speculators who bought up the French farm lots and surveyed the grassy land into plats and lots. Subsequent boats brought men and families from the eastern United States, who purchased the lots and built homes and businesses. As the Midwest became more settled, the farmers on the plains and loggers in the northern woods needed to get their produce quickly to eastern markets. Milwaukee businessmen saw this potential and organized a company to build a railroad connecting Lake Michigan to the Mississippi River. Several sites were contemplated for the river terminus. Prairie du Chien was chosen because of the ease of building tracks along the Wisconsin River and the thriving steamboat port. When completed, the railroad brought men and women who had crossed the Atlantic Ocean and traveled the Great Lakes with a dream of a life in the country with vast lands and opportunities.

Great speculation abounded that Prairie du Chien would grow to be the major port on the upper Mississippi River. But location now worked against the community. The Falls of St. Anthony further north on the Mississippi could power gristmills, and the land was open as far as the eye could see. At Prairie du Chien, the water flowed flatly, and the picturesque bluffs hemmed the prairie, limiting expansion. Minneapolis-St. Paul would grow to become what Prairie du Chien had hoped to be. The settlement became a bucolic village set in the midst of natural beauty. The railroads, steamboat lines, and ferries all promoted the glories of the river and bluffs and the history to be experienced in a stop at Prairie du Chien. Some living in the community also saw the potential in preserving the majestic river and bluffs that Marquette and Jolliet and Zebulon Pike had experienced. The buildings that stood as reminders of the Prairie du Chien that had been a power on the upper Mississippi were slowly disappearing and crumbling. Through publications, events, and preservation efforts, the early history of Prairie du Chien came alive for residents and visitors.

Having withstood the adversities of time, economic changes, and the power of the Mississippi River, Prairie du Chien retains the natural beauty and history that have drawn people for over 300 years.

One

A Frontier Settlement

After passing through a space of about six hundred and seventy miles of desert, this village comes upon one as if by enchantment, and the contrast is more striking as it bespeaks a certain degree of civilization.

—J. C. Beltrami, 1823

On June 17, 1673, Fr. Jacques Marquette and Louis Jolliet beheld the Mississippi River. They were the first Europeans to document travel on the upper Mississippi. Their journey led to the settlement of the prairie just north of their entry into the waterway. For the next 100 years, French explorers and fur traders used the prairie as a place of rendezvous.

In the 1770s, French from the Illinois Country built homes at la Prairie du Chiens and were joined by French Canadians. Great Britain had gained control of the North American fur trade, and hostilities between the British and the United States affected the prairie. After the American Revolution, Prairie du Chien became the westernmost settlement in United States territory. But when war was declared again between Great Britain and the United States in 1812, most of the residents of the prairie allied themselves with the British.

In 1816, American soldiers returned to Prairie du Chien and constructed Fort Crawford. The soldiers were to ensure the loyalty of the residents of the prairie and curb the power of the fur traders. Additionally, the military was to maintain peace among the Indian nations of the upper Mississippi and secure land, so treaties were negotiated at Prairie du Chien.

Whether under French, British, or American control, Prairie du Chien was distinctly French in culture. There were three separate villages on the grassland. The Main Village was on an island. Across the *marais* (slough) was the Village of St. Friol, and on the north end of the prairie was the Upper Village. Each village faced the waters of the Mississippi River. Behind the two mainland settlements, stretching to the bluffs, were 43 farms lots; all were measured in arpents. Most of the residents spoke French, and they built their homes of logs in the *pièce sur pièce* style.

As a frontier settlement in a changing America, Prairie du Chien experienced the tensions between the military and the fur traders. Confrontations marked the drive of men wanting the land the Native Americans claimed as theirs. One by one, the tribes of the upper Mississippi relinquished their claims, and the land surrounding Prairie du Chien was opened for settlement.

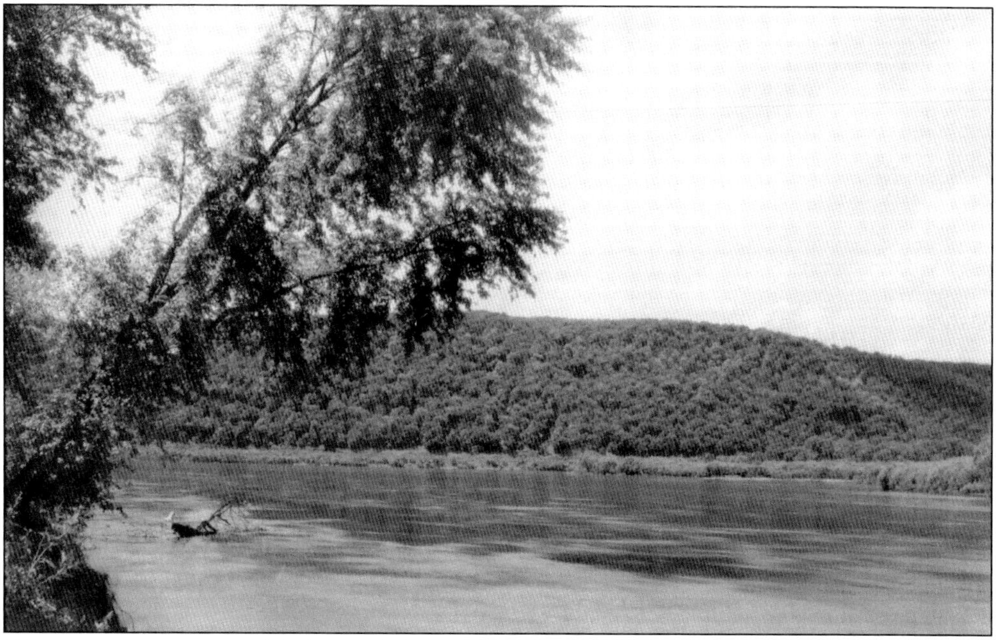

The two canoes carrying Fr. Jacques Marquette, Louis Jolliet, and their five companions glided onto the Mississippi River on June 17, 1673. Marquette later wrote that he beheld the river "with a Joy that I cannot Express." Marquette's diary and map mark the first recorded European contact with the upper Mississippi River. (Courtesy Martner Collection.)

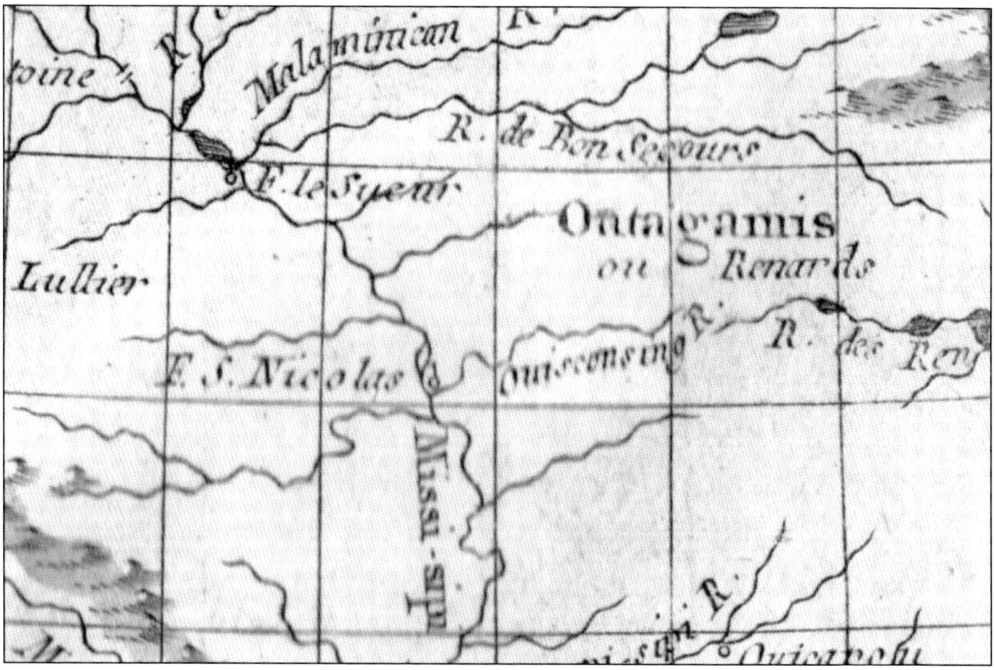

Explorer-fur trader Nicolas Perrot was commandant at Green Bay. In that capacity, he traveled the Mississippi several times, constructing a string of forts and ousting British traders from the region. On the lower end of the prairie, Perrot built Fort St. Nicolas, a post used during the trading season. French, then British, traders used the fort.

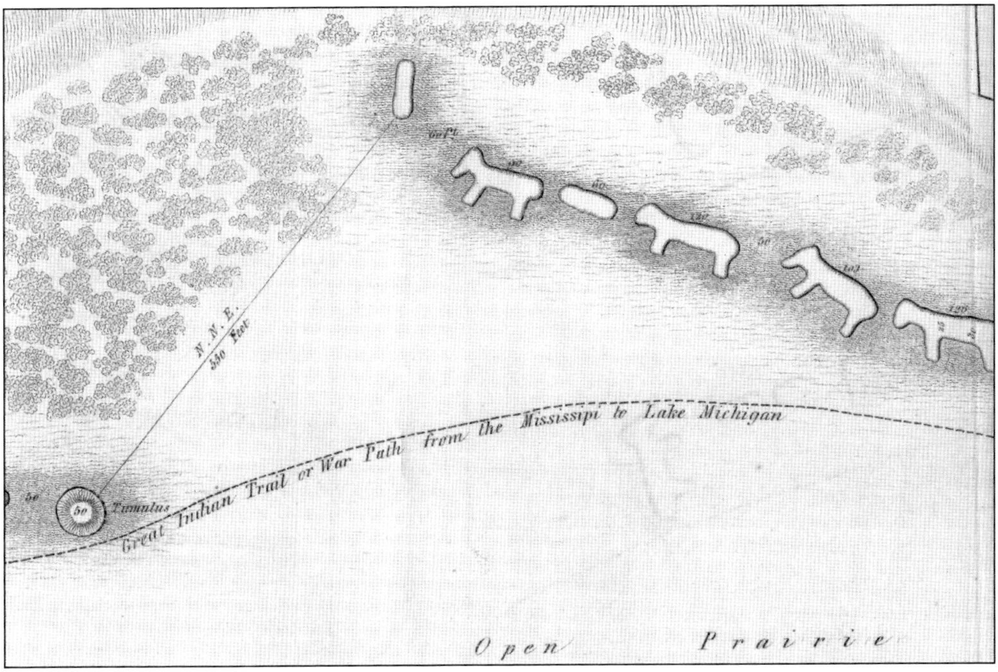

French explorers took little note of the many conical, linear, and animal-shaped mounds on the prairie and atop the bluffs along the Mississippi River. Not until the 19th century would men record and speculate about the mounds and the people who had built them centuries before.

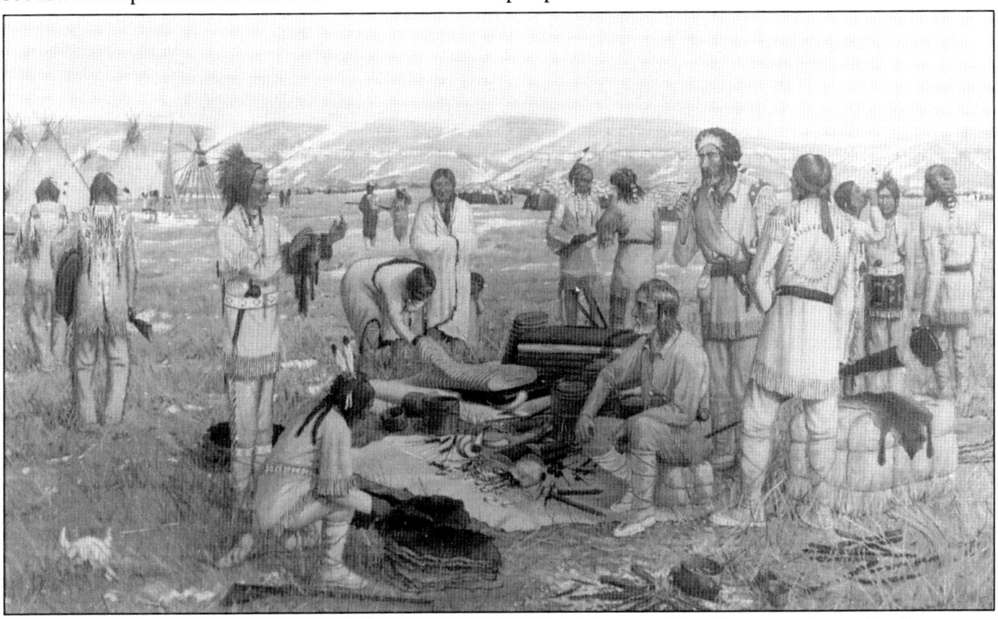

After the close of the Fox Wars, the prairie became a seasonal gathering place. Each spring, tribes from throughout the upper Mississippi arrived at the prairie with canoes filled with beaver pelts and furs. French traders from Michilimackinac, the Illinois Country, and New Orleans had brought bales of goods, and commerce occurred for weeks. In 1766, Jonathan Carver described this activity at "Prairie Les Chiens," thereby recording the name of the place. (Courtesy Ken and Louise White.)

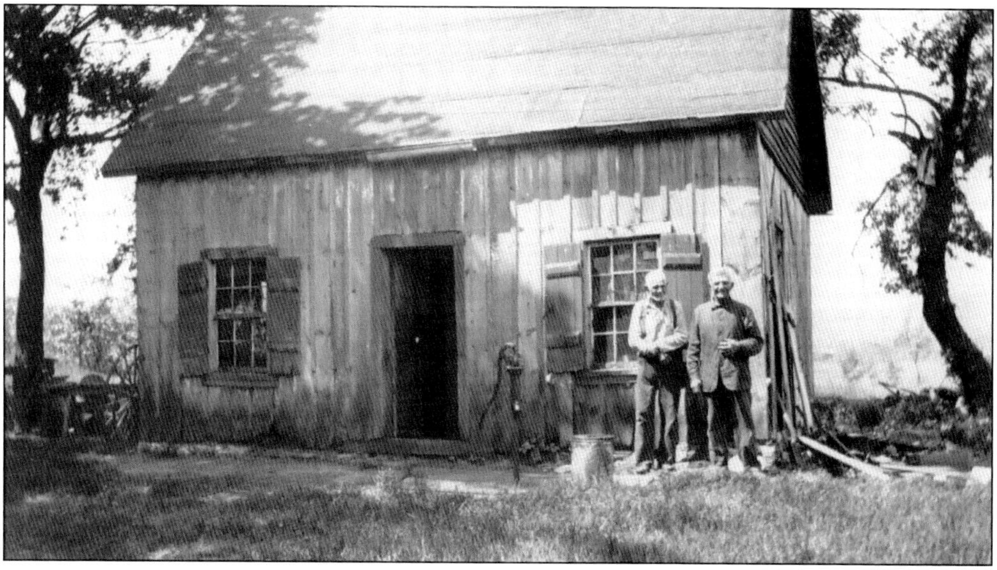

In the early 1770s, Frenchmen from Kaskaskia and Cahokia settled at Prairie des Chiens. They selected sites on the island west of the prairie and built homes. The Illinois French brought their pattern of settlement and architecture with them. Their houses were built by setting grooved posts into a sill, and split timbers or small logs were slid between the uprights. Spaces were then chinked, and the houses were covered with siding.

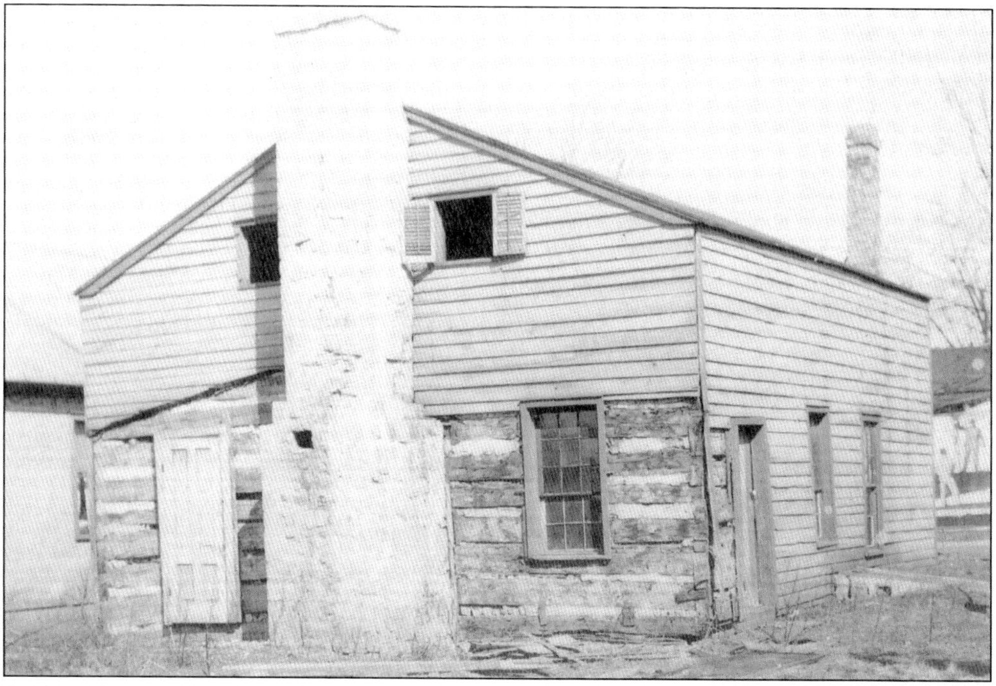

Within 10 years, French-speaking men and families from Mackinac settled on the prairie. Their building tradition came from Quebec. The homes they constructed were also made of hewn timbers, but were laid up horizontally. Though small, the houses were comfortably furnished with fine accessories transported from trading houses in St. Louis and Quebec. (Courtesy Martner Collection.)

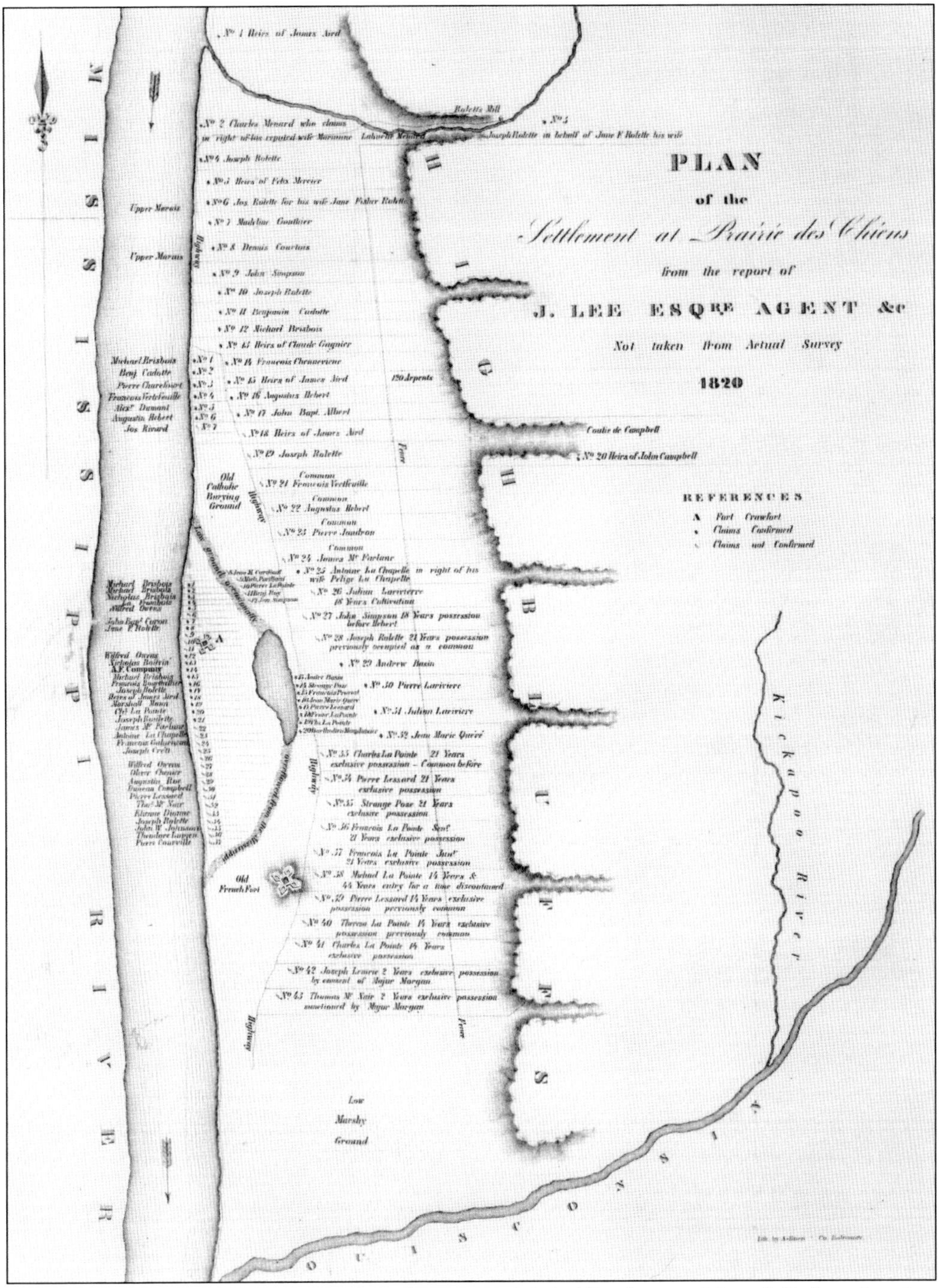

By 1811, thirty to forty houses stood on the prairie. Michel Brisbois and Joseph Rolette lived in the Main Village where the Michilimackinac Company had a trading house, and Nicholas Boilvin operated an Indian agency. On the prairie were the Village of St. Friol and the Upper Village. The homes of Strange Powers, Pierre Lariviere, and Francois Vertefeuille were just as comfortable as those of the traders. More families lived on and farmed the long, narrow farm lots measured in arpents stretching to the bluffs.

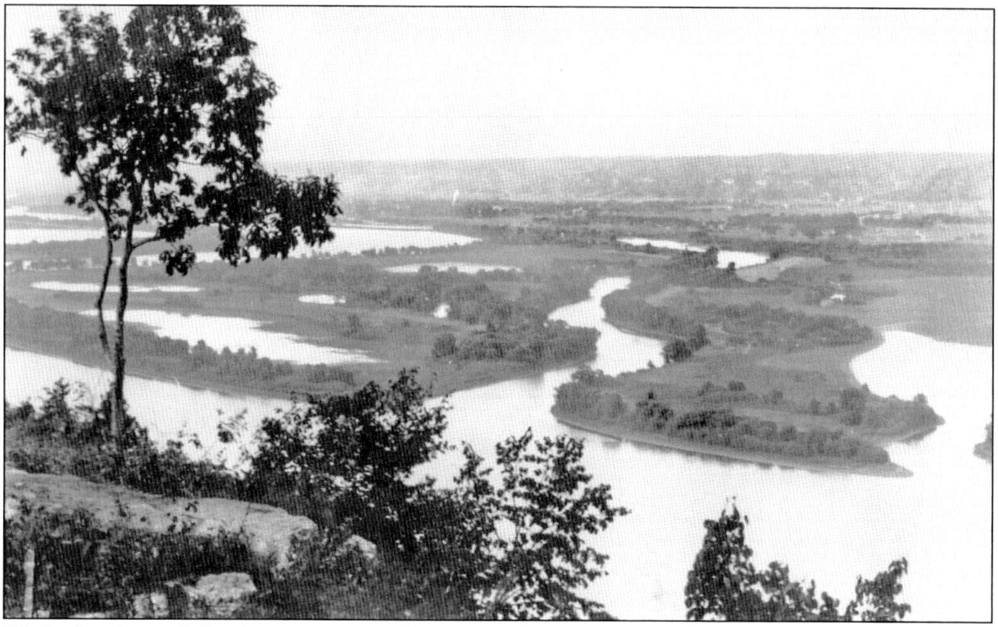

With the close of the American Revolution, Prairie du Chien had become part of the United States. While Lewis and Clark undertook their "Corps of Discovery," in 1805 Lt. Zebulon Pike led a reconnaissance of the upper Mississippi. At Prairie du Chien, Pike found British flags flying and the Native Americans wearing British peace medals. Pike recommended a fort be built on a bluff overlooking the Wisconsin and Mississippi Rivers.

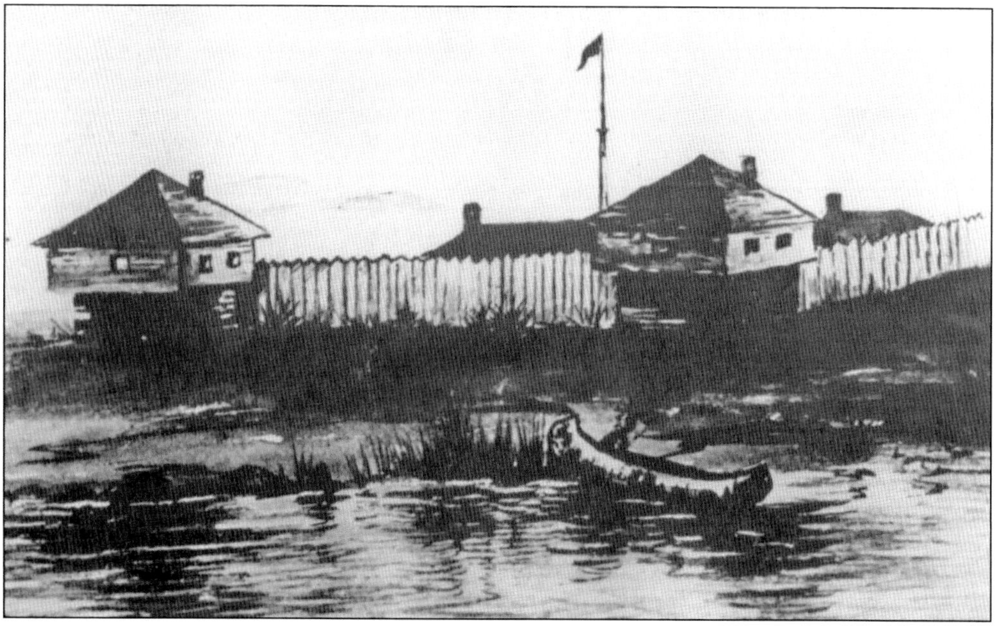

When war broke out between the United States and Great Britain in 1812, both knew that whoever controlled Prairie du Chien controlled the upper Mississippi and its natural wealth. The United States built Fort Shelby at Prairie du Chien. When the British sent a force to attack the fort, most of the residents assisted the British. If the British won, the residents of Prairie du Chien knew their economic future would be secure. (Courtesy Wisconsin Historical Society WHi-42230.)

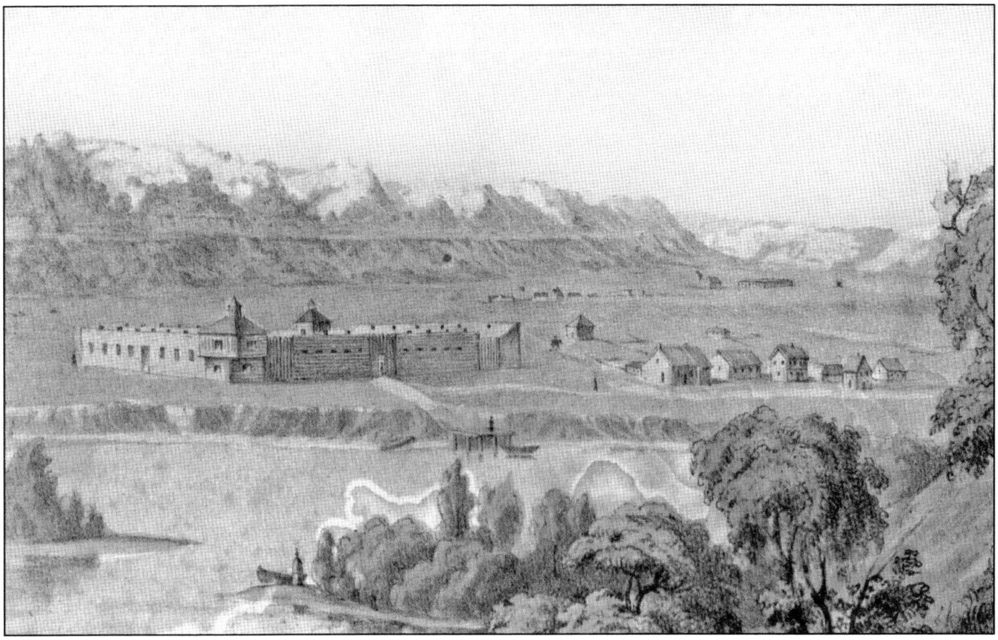

The American forces lost the Battle of Prairie du Chien but returned in 1816. Considering the residents traitors, Col. Talbot Chambers ordered the people to move their homes and cemetery, as they were located where he wanted to build a fort. Fort Crawford, named for Secretary of War William Crawford, was an earth and log structure able to hold six companies. It secured the upper Mississippi River and gave the United States a commanding presence.

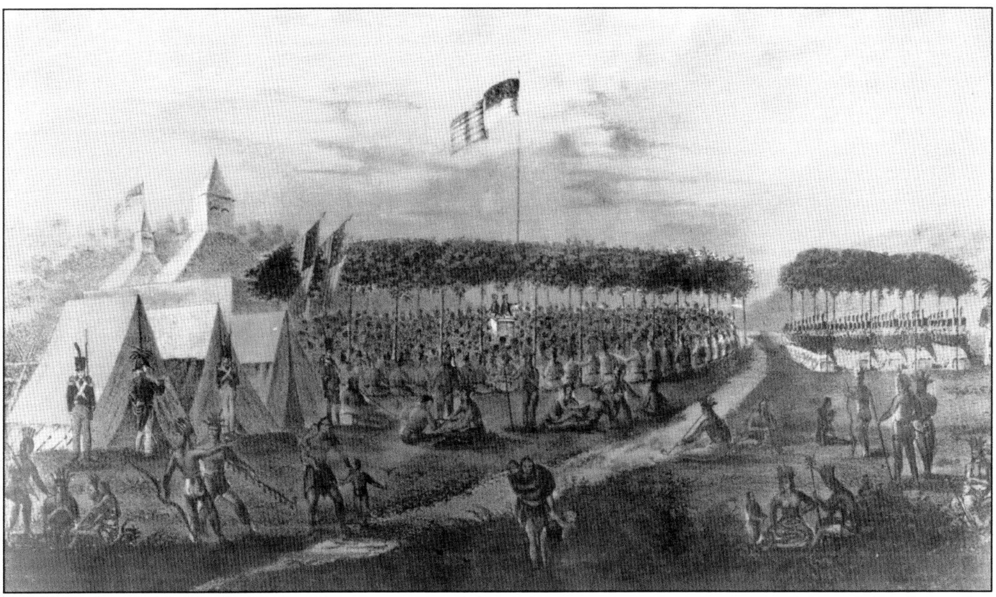

In an attempt to address hostilities between tribes and tension caused by miners and squatters on Native American lands, the United States invited thousands of Indians representing all the tribes of the upper Mississippi to gather at Prairie du Chien in August 1825. After 14 days of discussion, led by William Clark and Lewis Cass, a treaty was signed that all hoped would bring peace.

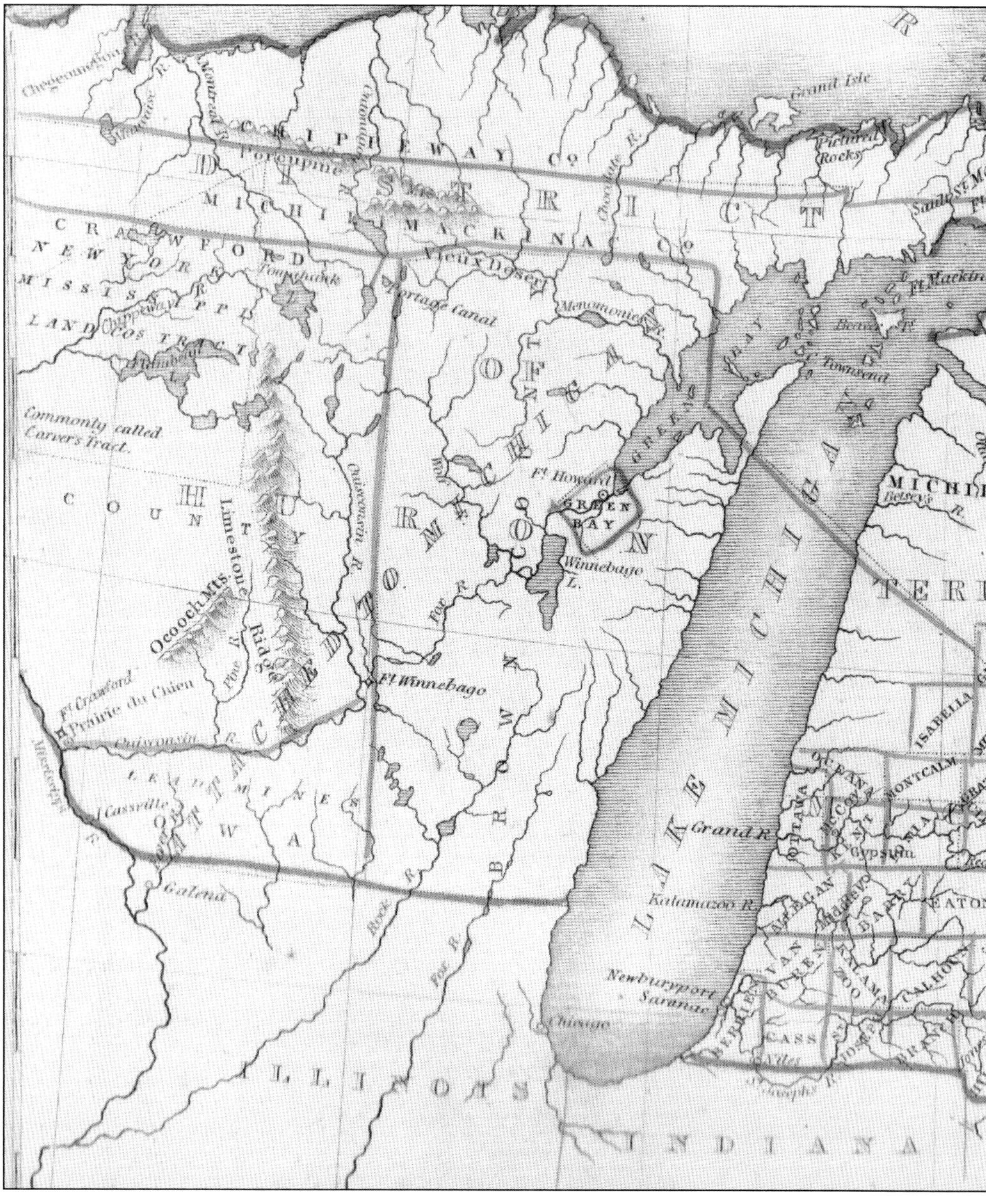

When Illinois became a state in 1818, the vast tract of land to the north was transferred to Michigan Territory. This was divided into three counties. The western county was named Crawford. As the only settlement in Crawford County, Prairie du Chien became the county seat. Men who had demonstrated loyalty to the United States were appointed county officers.

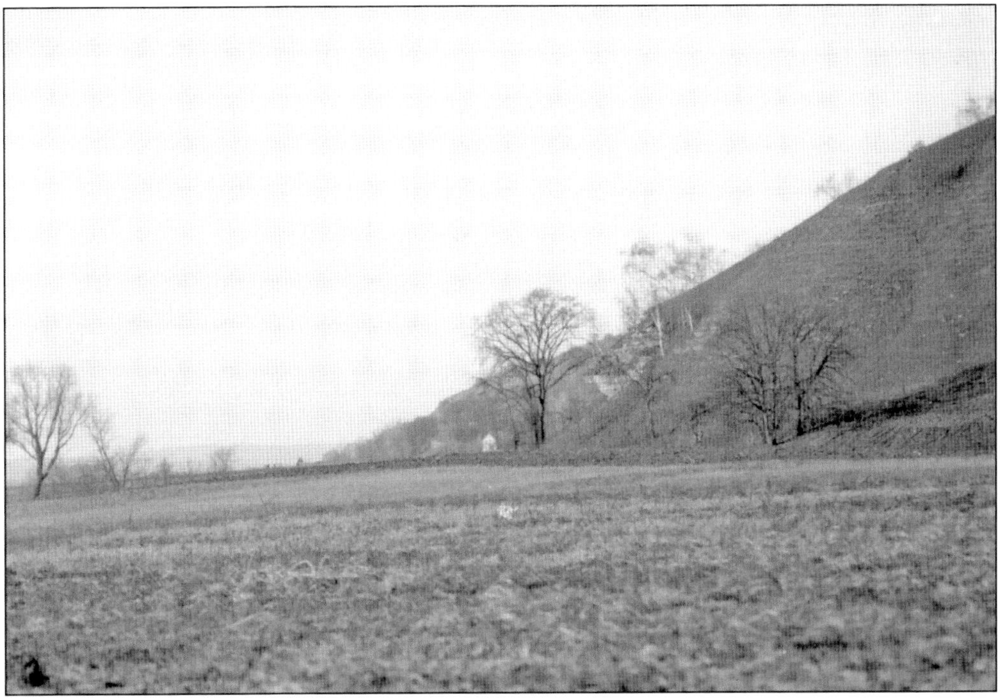

The 1825 treaty and soldiers could not stop men from coming onto Winnebago land to mine lead, and conflicts ensued between the white settlers and the Native Americans. In the spring of 1827, Red Bird was chosen to lead a strike back against the settlers. For reasons that are unclear, Red Bird and his followers attacked the Gagnier family, who farmed on the prairie. Registre, head of the Gagnier family, and an old soldier were killed. As part of the uprising, Winnebago attacked a keelboat. Hostilities came to an end with the surrender of Red Bird and his companions. By the 1829 Treaty of Prairie du Chien, the Winnebago and other tribes relinquished claims to land in the lead country.

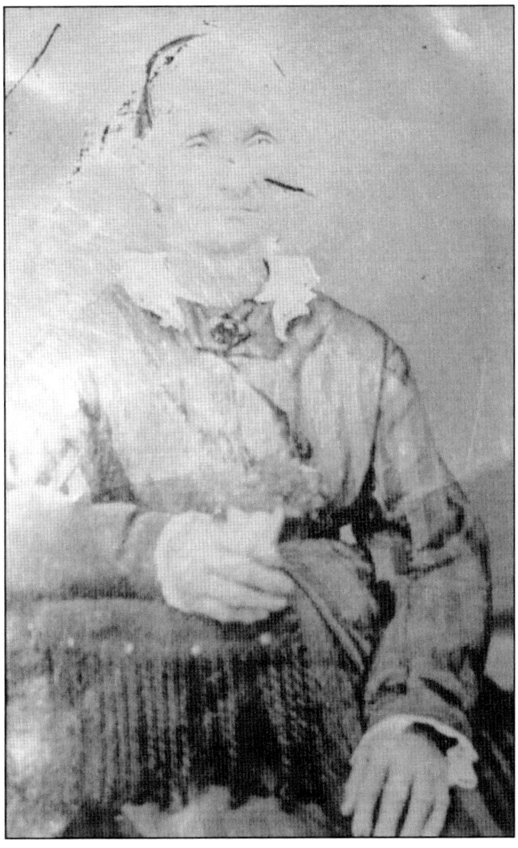

In the raid, 10-month-old Marie Louise Gagnier had been scalped and her neck cut. Under her grandmother's care, Marie Louise (pictured) recovered, married twice, raised 12 children, and lived to age 67 with a silver plate covering the scalp wound. (Courtesy John Haltmeyer.)

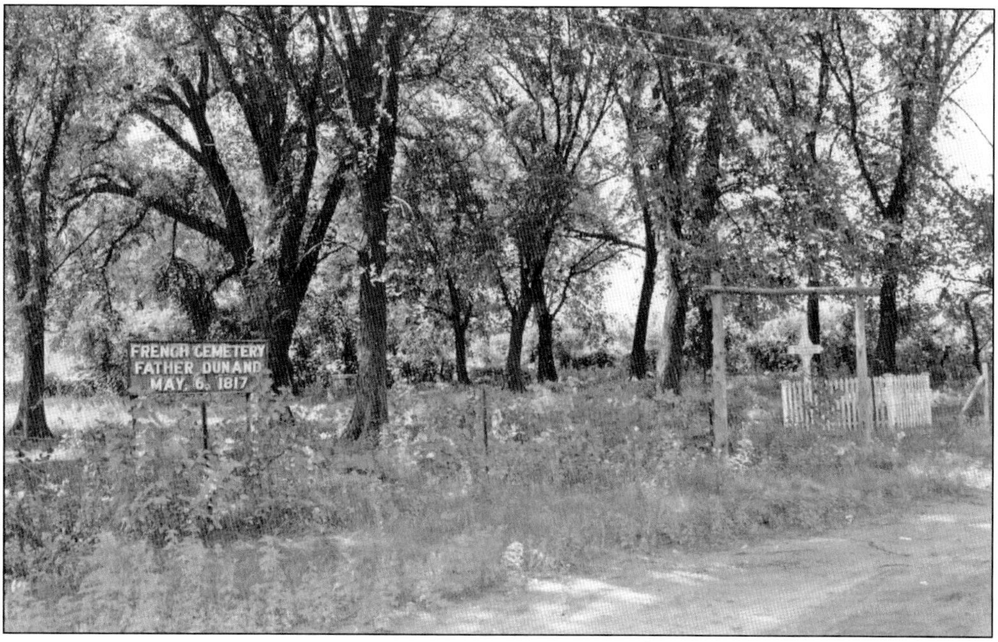

When Colonel Chambers ordered the people of Prairie du Chien to dig up their dead and bury them elsewhere, they chose a high point on the prairie between the Village of St. Friol and the Upper Village. In 1817, Father Dunand came to Prairie du Chien. The first Catholic priest to minister to the residents, he blessed the cemetery. This was the only Catholic burying ground at Prairie du Chien until 1840.

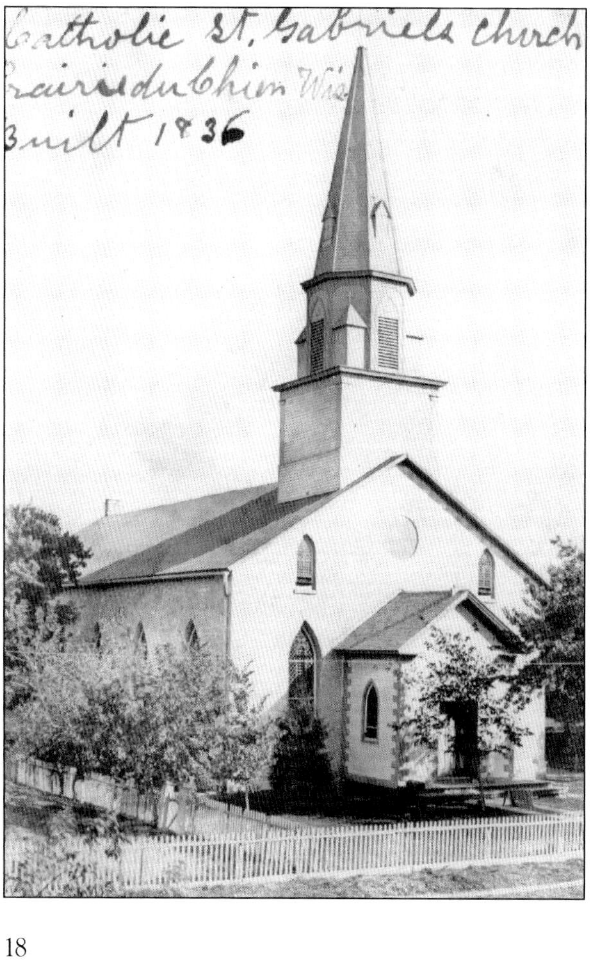

Fr. Samuel Mazzuchelli came to Prairie du Chien in 1832 and again in 1835. Mazzuchelli's plans for a stone church so impressed Strange Powers that he donated 4 acres of land. The cornerstone was laid in 1839, and work progressed slowly. Named St. Gabriel's, the "chaste Gothic" structure designed by Mazzuchelli was completed about 10 years after it was begun. (Courtesy Wisconsin Historical Society WHi-42036.)

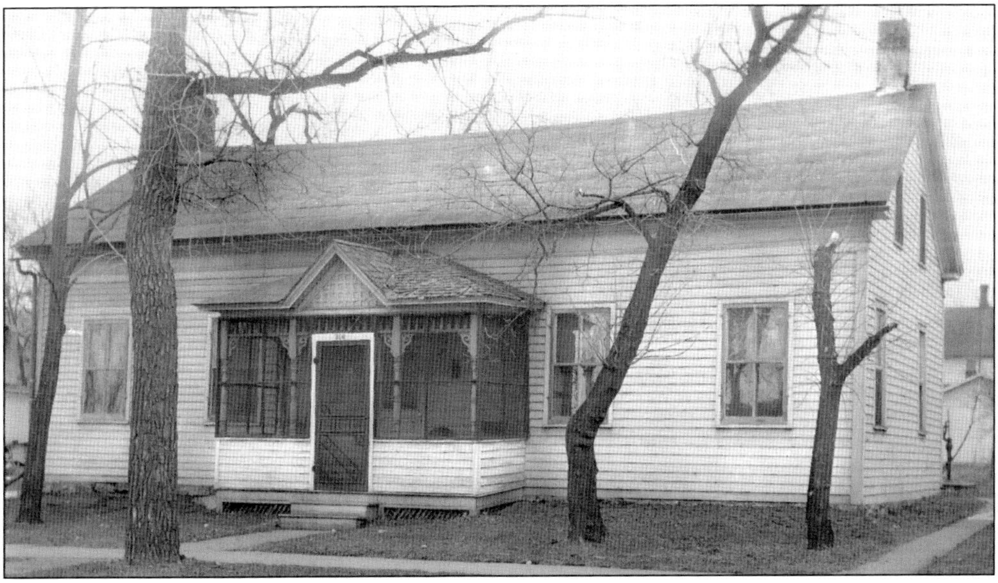

Fr. Augustin Ravoux was appointed the first permanent pastor of St. Gabriel's parish in 1840. Within a few months, Fr. Joseph Cretin succeeded Ravoux. Ravoux returned to Prairie du Chien in 1843, living with Father Cretin in a small house near the church. Here Father Ravoux printed *Wakantanka ti ki Chanku* (Path to the House of God), a catechism in the Sioux language for use among the Lakota.

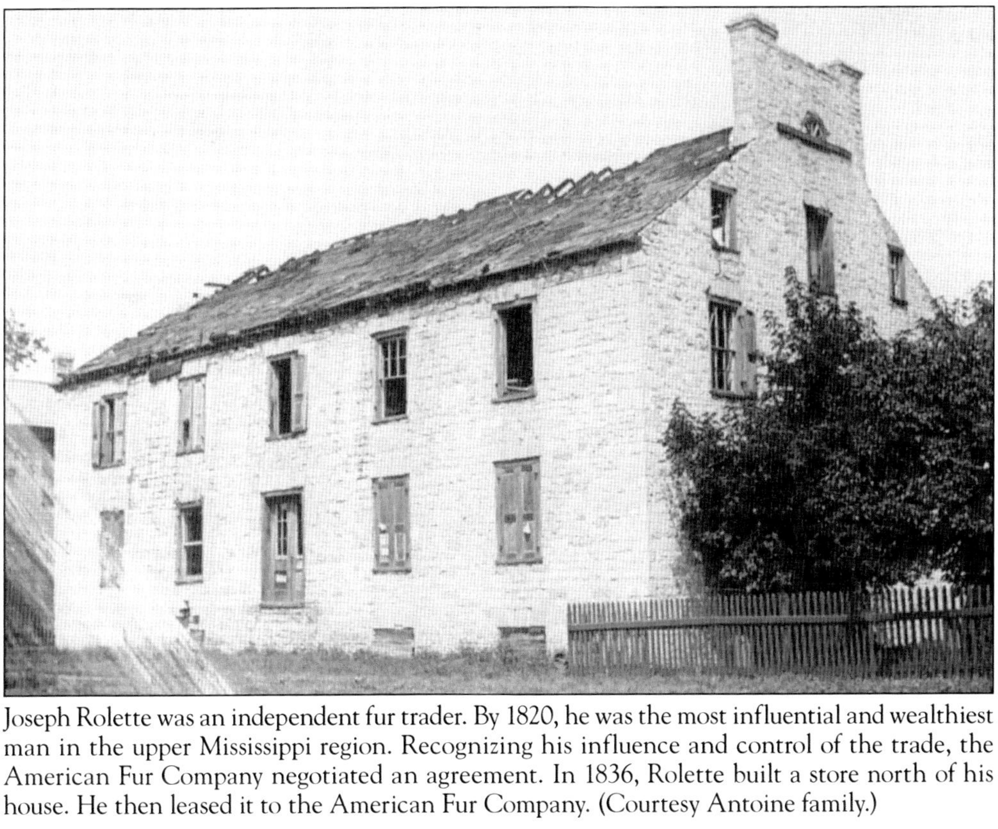

Joseph Rolette was an independent fur trader. By 1820, he was the most influential and wealthiest man in the upper Mississippi region. Recognizing his influence and control of the trade, the American Fur Company negotiated an agreement. In 1836, Rolette built a store north of his house. He then leased it to the American Fur Company. (Courtesy Antoine family.)

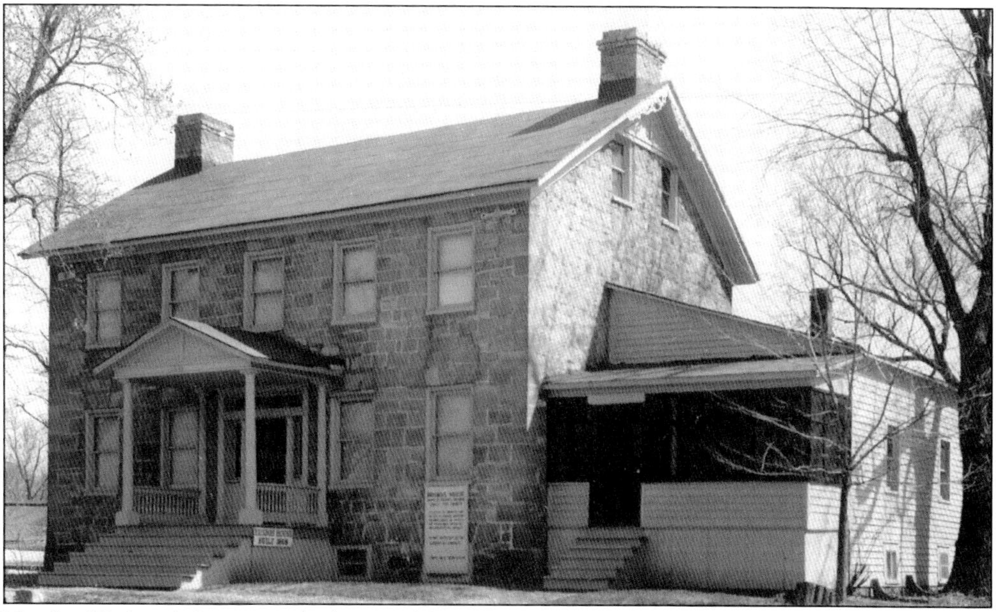

North of Rolette's Store was the home of the Michel Brisbois family. Brisbois helped the residents gain title to the prairie in 1781. He raised his niece, Jane Fisher, who married Rolette in 1818. By 1836, their marriage had failed. In articles of separation, Rolette agreed to build her "a stone dwelling house." When Jane married Hercules L. Dousman, she gave the house to her cousin B. W. Brisbois. (Courtesy Ken and Louise White.)

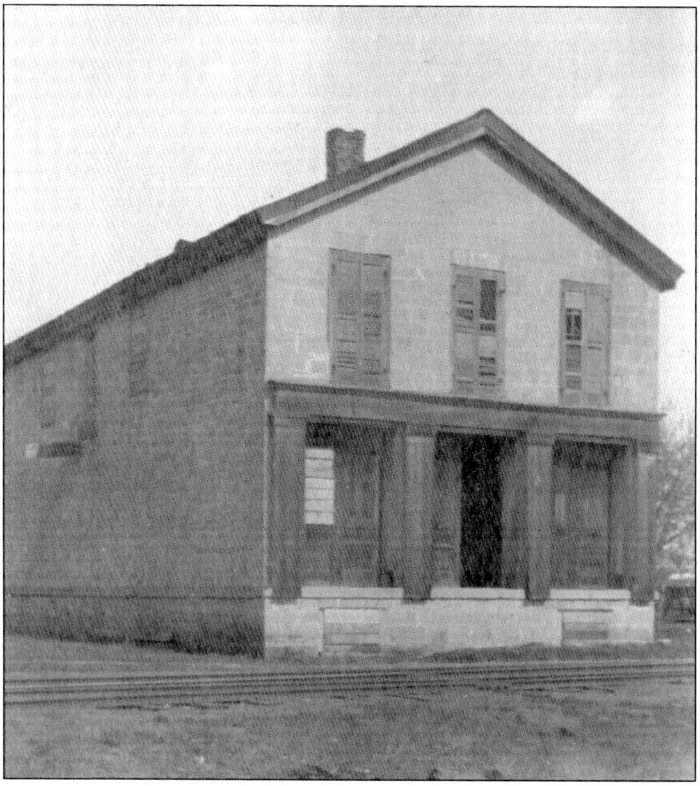

Main Village Lot No. 14 had been the site of trading houses since about 1790. Two log structures had been used by the Mackinac Company, the U.S. Fur Factory, and the American Fur Company. In 1850, B. W. Brisbois replaced the buildings with a stone store. Brisbois still traded goods for furs, though money was more the medium of exchange. (Courtesy Martner Collection.)

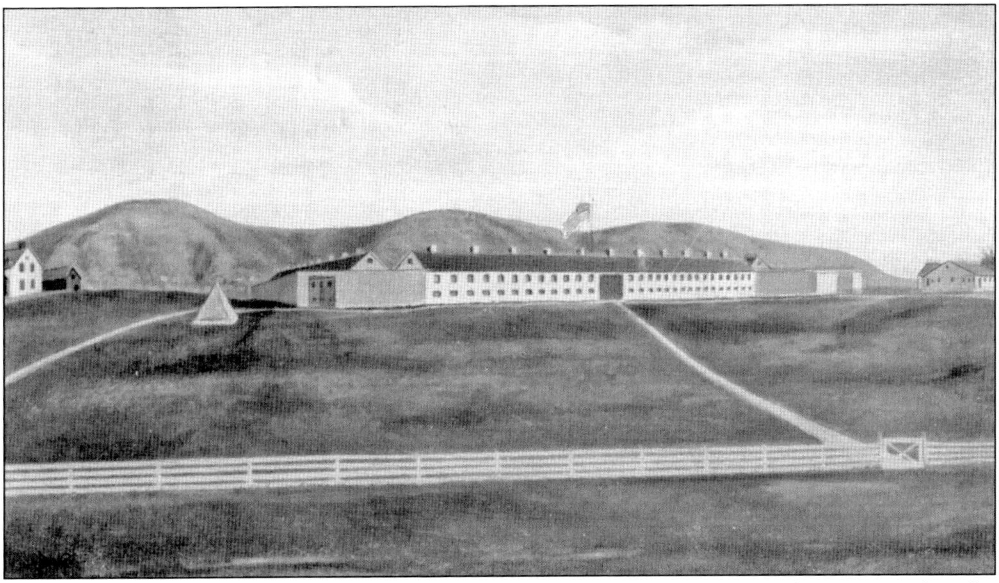

Fort Crawford had been so badly damaged by floods that it was abandoned in 1826. After the Winnebago Uprising, troops returned to build a new fort sited on high ground. Lt. Jefferson Davis oversaw much of the construction of the second Fort Crawford. The barracks were built of limestone. Barns, a blacksmith shop, and a farm ensured the fort was self-sufficient. (Courtesy Virginia Antoine.)

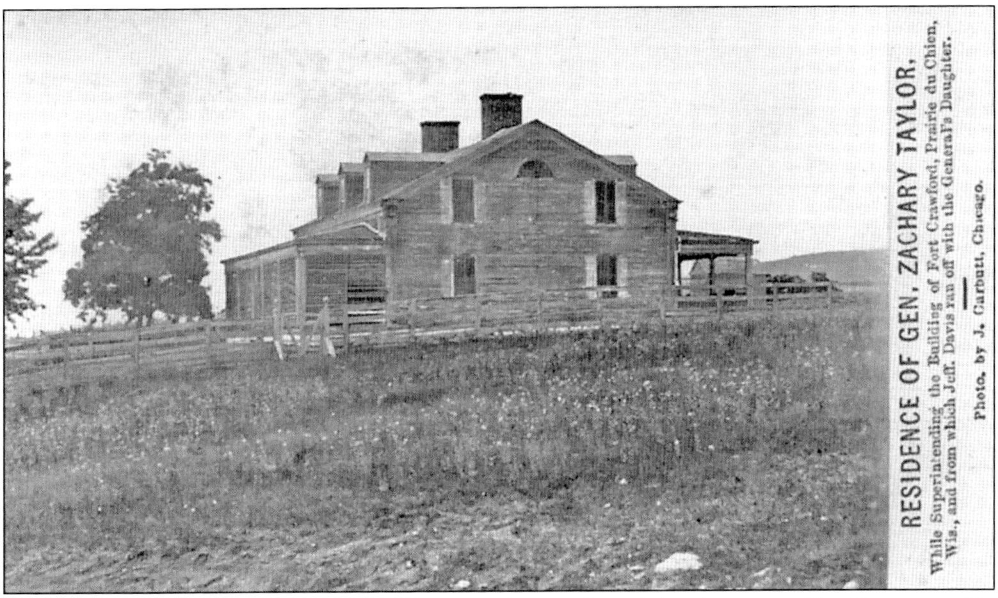

James Lockwood came to Prairie du Chien in the employ of the American Fur Company. He built his home and store separate from the French traders. Having studied law, Lockwood was appointed associate judge for Crawford County in 1830. At this time, he sold his home to the U.S. government for use as the commandant's home. Zachary Taylor, who commanded Fort Crawford in 1829–1830 and again from 1832 to 1837, lived in this house. (Courtesy Cliff and Michele Krainik, Warrenton, Virginia.)

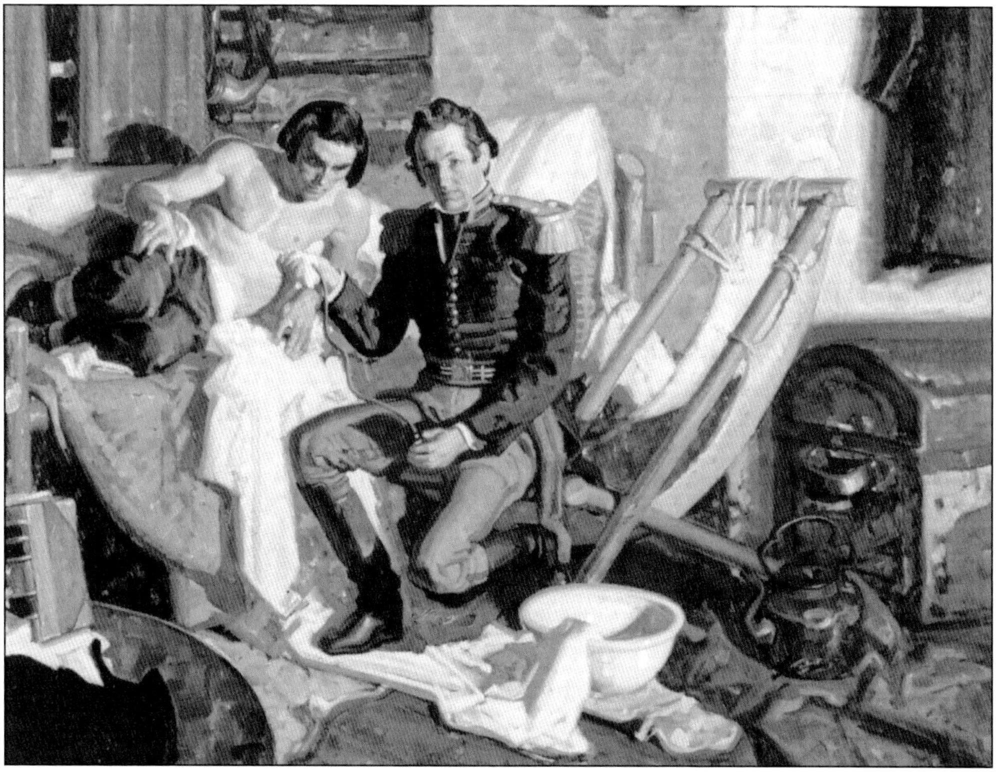

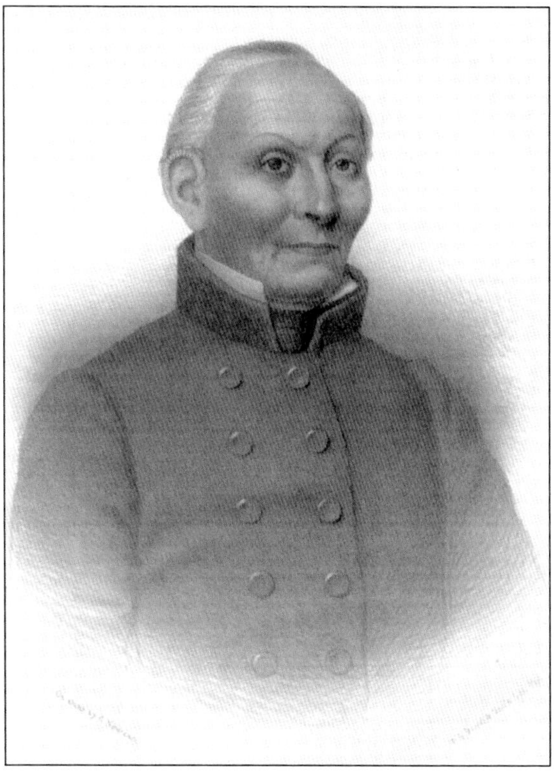

Dr. William Beaumont served as Fort Crawford post surgeon from 1828 to 1832. Alexis St. Martin had been shot in the stomach while Beaumont was stationed at Fort Mackinac. Beaumont is seen here caring for St. Martin. When the hole from the shot never healed, Beaumont used St. Martin to perform experiments on human digestion. While at Fort Crawford, Beaumont continued his experiments. (Courtesy Prairie du Chien Historical Society—Peckham Collection.)

Refusing to recognize the 1804 treaty with the Sac, Black Hawk and his band sided with the British during the War of 1812. In May 1832, they attempted to return to their traditional village. American troops chased Black Hawk and his band for four months. The war ended at the battle on the Bad Axe River when the band tried to cross the Mississippi and was slaughtered.

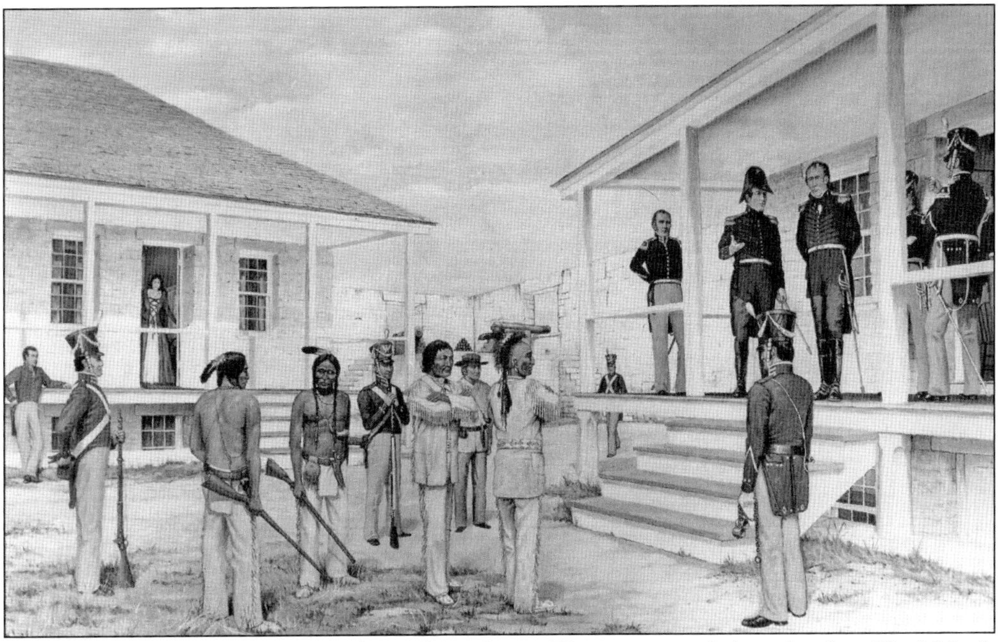

Black Hawk escaped the battle on the Bad Axe River. Wearing suits of white deerskin, Black Hawk and White Cloud, a Winnebago prophet, surrendered to Joseph Street, the Winnebago agent at Prairie du Chien. Under the guard of Lt. Jefferson Davis, Black Hawk and 10 others traveled to Jefferson Barracks south of St. Louis. After captivity and a forced tour of the eastern United States, Black Hawk returned to his family. (Courtesy Wisconsin Historical Society WHi-4514.)

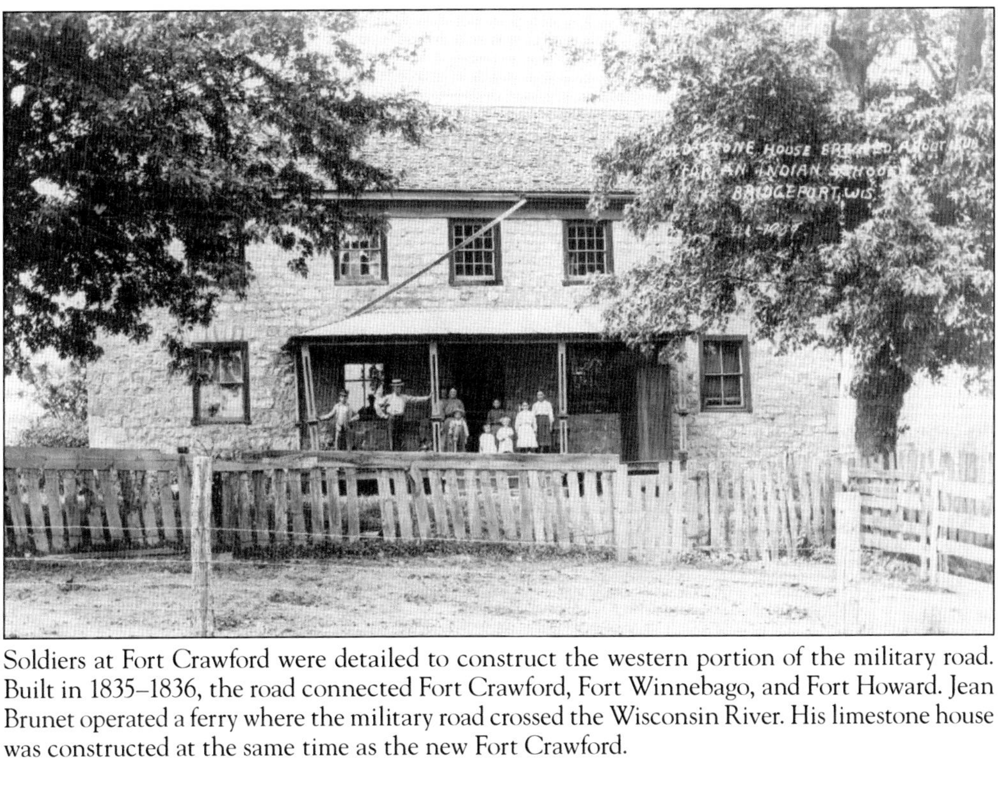

Soldiers at Fort Crawford were detailed to construct the western portion of the military road. Built in 1835–1836, the road connected Fort Crawford, Fort Winnebago, and Fort Howard. Jean Brunet operated a ferry where the military road crossed the Wisconsin River. His limestone house was constructed at the same time as the new Fort Crawford.

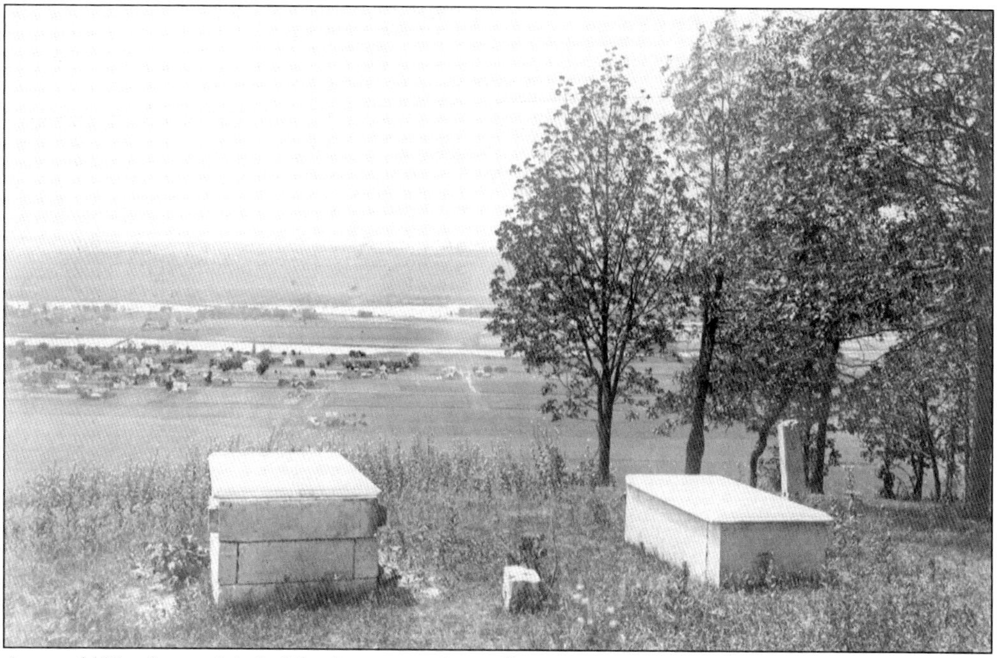

As an old blind man, Michel Brisbois wrote his will, requesting he be buried on a bluff overlooking Prairie du Chien. One story states he made the request so that he could look down on the prairie he loved. Another story was that Michel made the request so he could look down on Joseph Rolette. (Courtesy Martner Collection.)

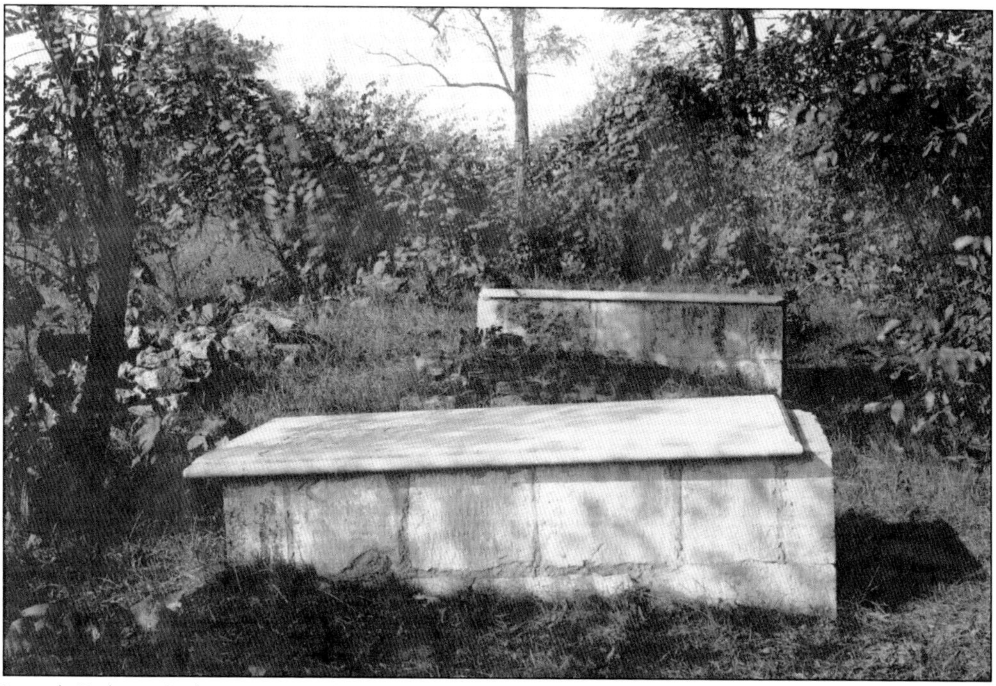

Joseph Rolette died in 1842. He had been sick and cared for by his daughter Elizabeth, who was also ill. Rolette was buried in the old Catholic burying ground. Five months later, Elizabeth was laid to rest next to him. (Courtesy Prairie du Chien Historical Society—Peckham Collection.)

Two

Expansion Begins

We [Prairie du Chien] *are at this time ahead of what Milwaukee and Chicago were 20 years ago . . . it is not deemed visionary to suppose that in less that 20 years we shall be equal to what they are now.*

—Alfred E. Brunson, 1857

Prairie du Chien was changing. Michel Brisbois, Joseph Rolette, and their contemporaries were gone. The fur trade had moved west, and by 1857 the Indian nations of Wisconsin had been confined to reservations. Speculators and entrepreneurs saw potential in Prairie du Chien with its open land and access to the Mississippi River. Examining the layout of the prairie, they chose to establish a "new" Prairie du Chien away from the French-speaking inhabitants. Their vision called for an American community. With the economy shifting, the Frenchmen sold their farm lots. William Beaumont, James Lockwood, and others purchased the parcels south of Fort Crawford. Speculators from New York formed Prairie du Chien Land Company No. 1, then No. 2. The farm tracts were surveyed into blocks and lots. In 1836, Alexander MacGregor had initiated a ferry between Prairie du Chien and Iowa. With a landing that accommodated steamboats and a ferry, the south end of the prairie was prime for development. Settlers from New England and New York started arriving in the 1830s. They constructed homes in the styles of architecture popular in the eastern United States.

With the Native Americans on reservations, there no longer was a need for a military presence at Prairie du Chien. The United States War Department permanently closed Fort Crawford in 1856.

As one of the early arrivals to the prairie, Rev. Alfred Brunson witnessed the community's growth. In 1857, he published a promotional tract *Prairie du Chien. Its Present Position and Future Prospects*. Brunson emphasized the location of the community at the end of the Wisconsin River and position on the Mississippi River as a natural and most accessible route, commanding most of the trade and travel to and from southwest Wisconsin, northeast Iowa, and Minnesota.

That same year, the Milwaukee and Mississippi Rail Road arrived at Prairie du Chien and created the expansion Brunson promoted. The railroad brought immigrants from Europe to the prairie. Businesses and buildings sprang up to meet the needs of residents and travelers. A new Prairie du Chien was replacing the Prairie du Chien of the fur trade and military eras.

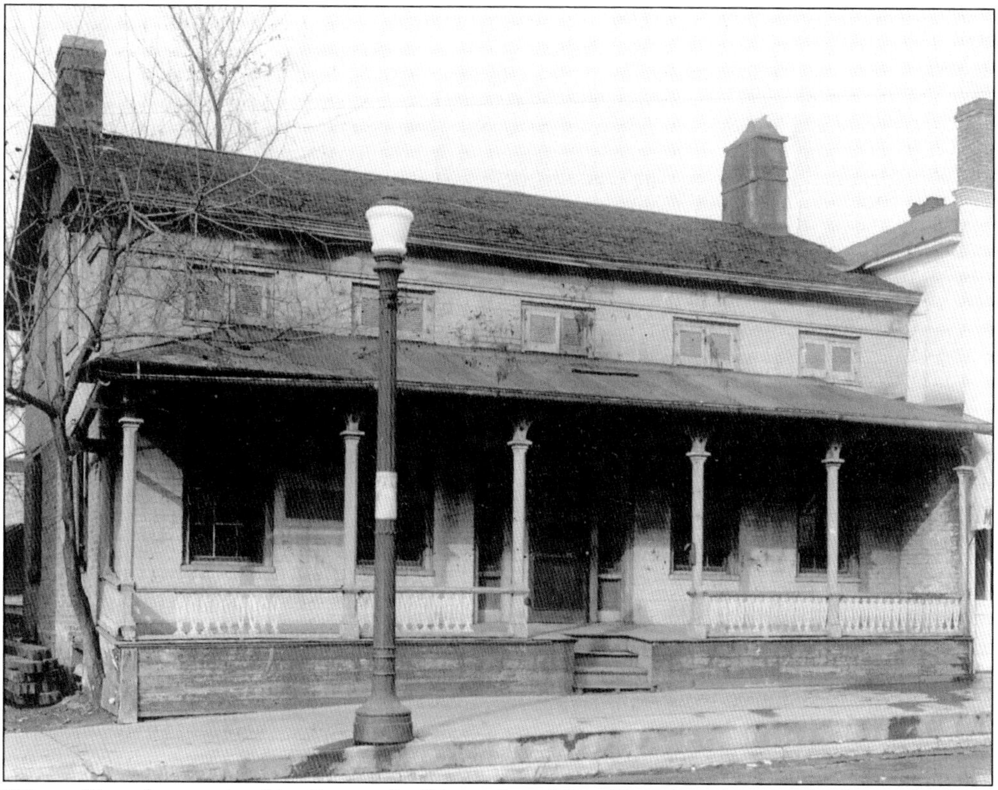

Wiram Knowlton arrived in Prairie du Chien from New York. Purchasing the house built by W. H. C. Folsom, Knowlton established a law practice. He served on the Wisconsin territorial council and, with statehood, was elected as a circuit court judge. During the Mexican War, Knowlton raised a company of volunteers assigned to Fort Crawford for frontier duty. *The Prairie du Chien Courier*, edited by Daniel Johnson, used Knowlton's home for its office. During the winter of 1860–1861, John Muir worked for the newspaper. (Courtesy Prairie du Chien Historical Society—Peckham Collection.)

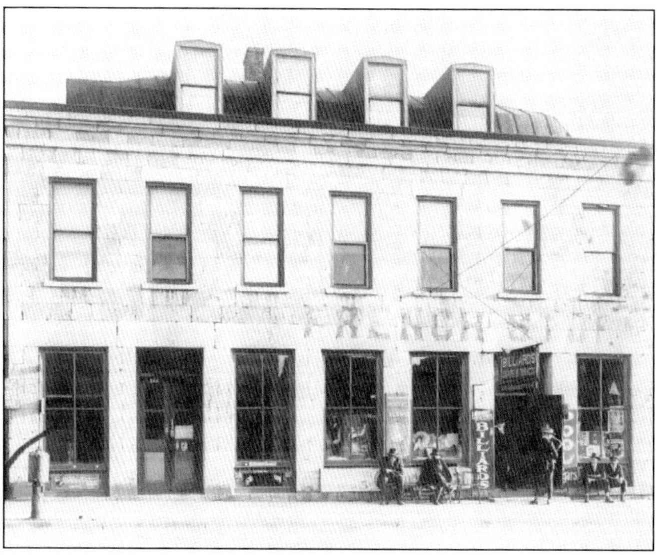

One of the earliest general merchandise stores to operate in Prairie du Chien was owned by two Frenchmen. Jules Famechon emigrated from France to St. Louis. Making connections, he continued up the Mississippi to Prairie du Chien, where he met Augustus Gaillard. They formed a partnership in 1849 and operated The French Store. Five years later, they built a large stone building on Bluff Street. (Courtesy Prairie du Chien Historical Society—Williams Collection.)

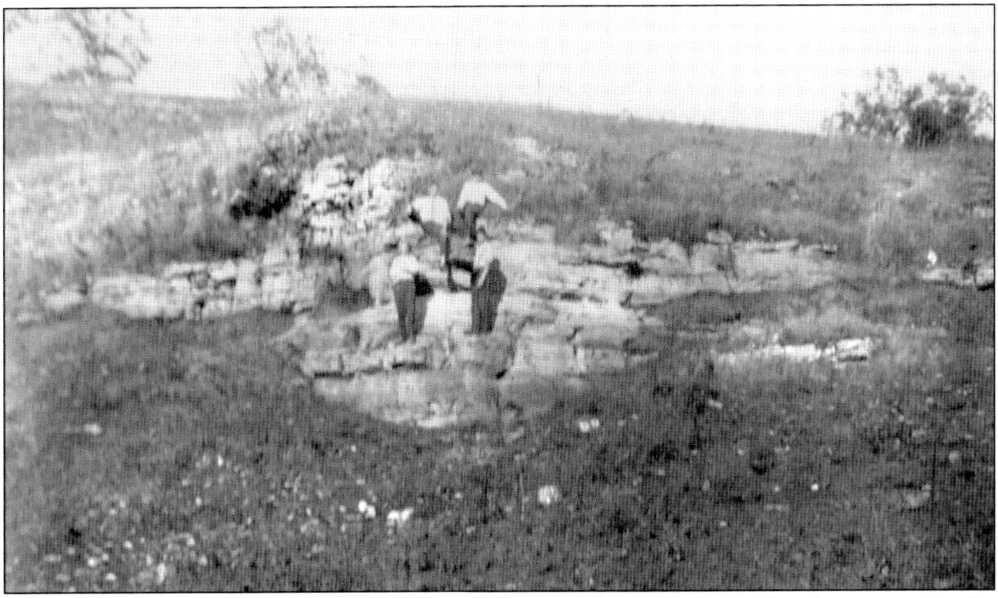

Quarries had been opened in the bluffs east of Prairie du Chien, providing limestone for the second Fort Crawford and St. Gabriel's Church. In the building boom of the 1840s and 1850s, quarries said to be "without number" operated, with one providing stone for the capitol building in Madison. (Courtesy Prairie du Chien Historical Society—Grelle Collection.)

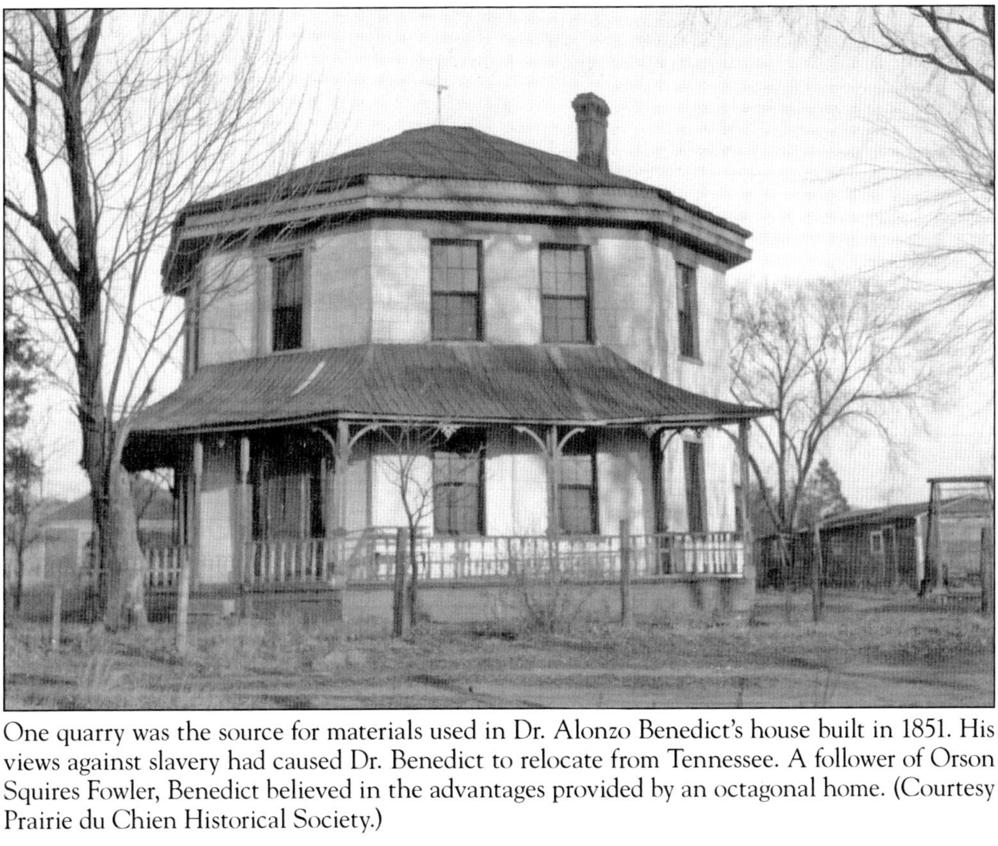

One quarry was the source for materials used in Dr. Alonzo Benedict's house built in 1851. His views against slavery had caused Dr. Benedict to relocate from Tennessee. A follower of Orson Squires Fowler, Benedict believed in the advantages provided by an octagonal home. (Courtesy Prairie du Chien Historical Society.)

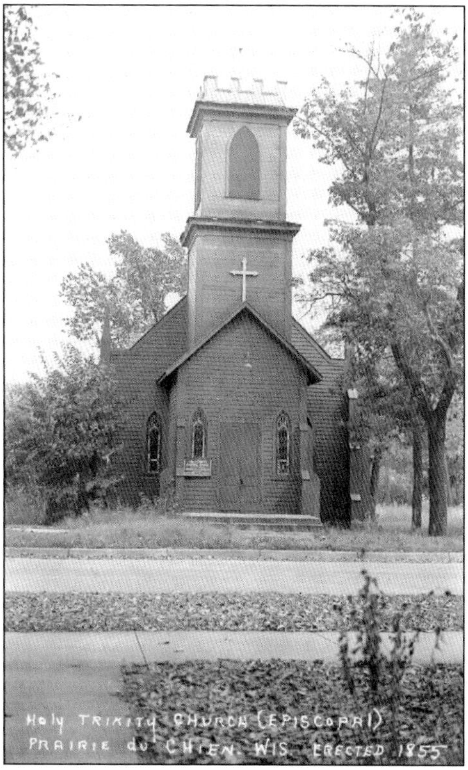

In 1836, the Reverend Richard Fish Cadle came to Prairie du Chien and found many Fort Crawford officers and their families eager to organize an Episcopalian church. He held services and requested aid in creating a vestry. In 1856, the War Department announced permanent closure of Fort Crawford, and the congregation needed a place to gather. The Prairie du Chien Land Company donated land for the vestry, and a temporary wooden church was built until a stone structure could be erected. The wooden church still stands.

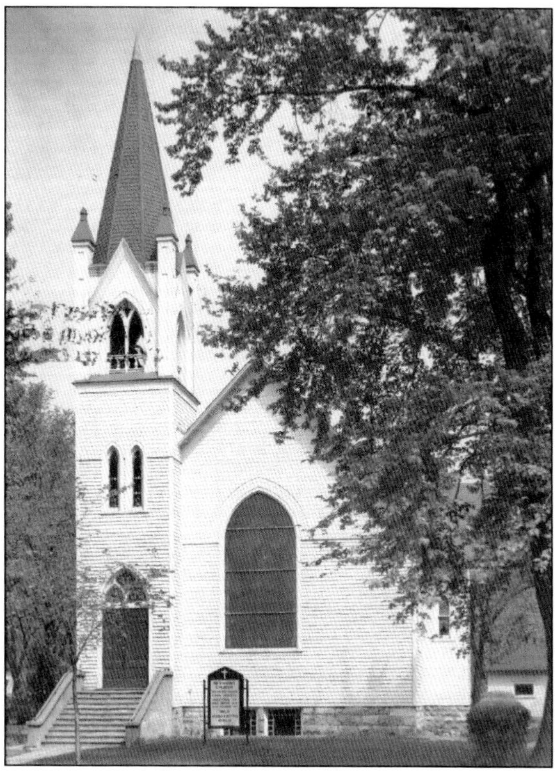

The Reverend Alfred Brunson came to Prairie du Chien to "minister to the sad plight of the Indians," riding circuit from Rock Island to the Falls of St. Anthony. Brunson organized the Methodist Society, holding services wherever possible. In 1843–1844, the Methodist Episcopal Society built a church, thereby giving the name Church Street to the thoroughfare on which St. Gabriel's and this edifice had been built. Brunson immersed himself in politics, and in 1872 he wrote his autobiography, *A Western Pioneer.* (Courtesy Prairie du Chien Historical Society—Peckham Collection.)

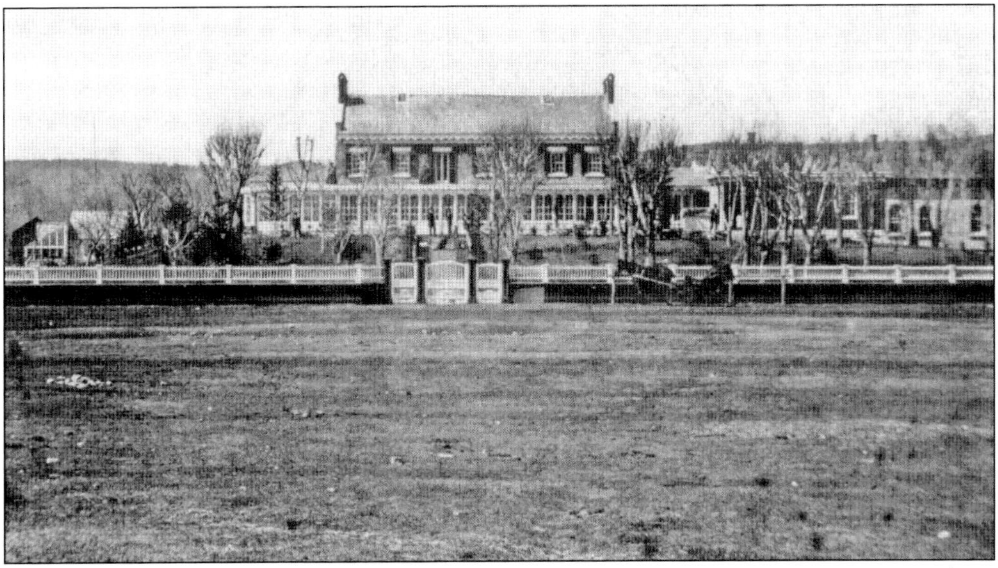

Hercules L. Dousman came to Prairie du Chien as a clerk for the American Fur Company, working for Joseph Rolette. An astute businessman, Dousman became partner, then major shareholder, of the Western Outfit of the Company. In 1843, he built a stylish home atop the mound where the first Fort Crawford had stood. The following year, Dousman brought his new wife, Jane Fisher Rolette, the widow of his former fur-trading partner, to the House on the Mound. (Courtesy Wisconsin Historical Society WHi-41982.)

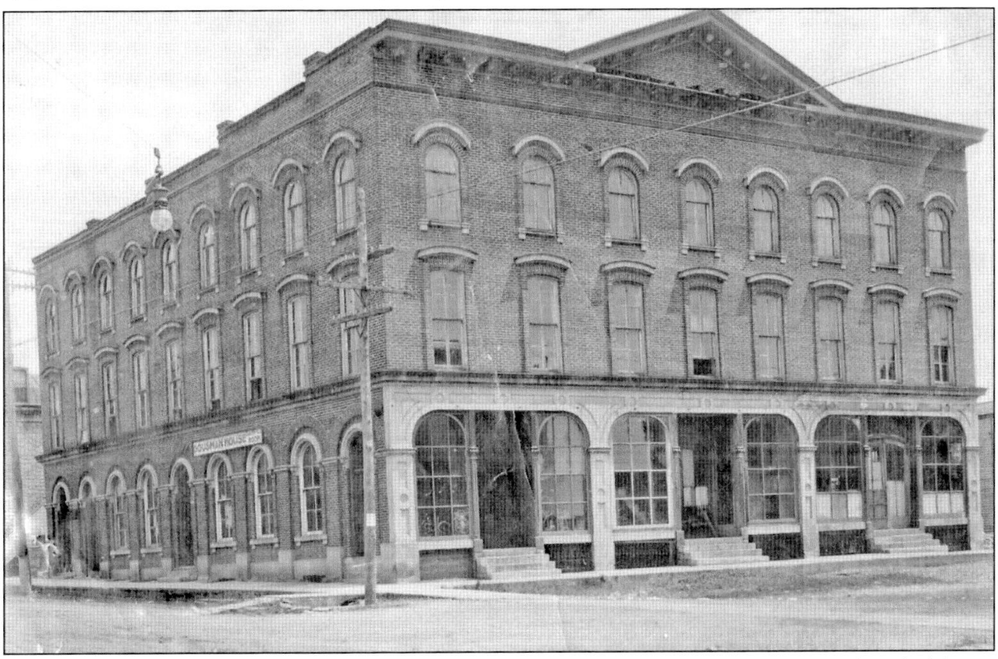

Dousman acquired Farm Lot No. 32 and several lots in the Village of St. Friol. A shareholder in the Milwaukee and Mississippi Rail Road, Dousman knew of the plans to make the prairie the railroad's western terminus. In the year before the railroad's arrival, Dousman began to develop the western portions of his lots. He contracted with Green and Upson of Milwaukee to construct a block of stores on Main Street. (Courtesy Martner Collection.)

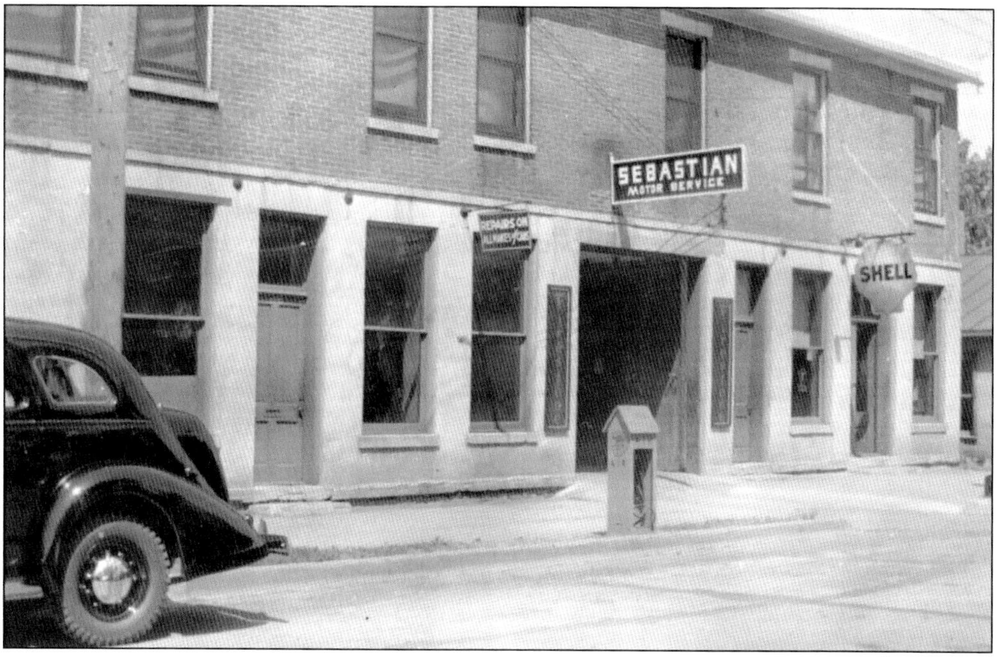

On Church Street, Dousman built another brick office building, called the Law Block, in 1858. Dousman rented two floors of offices to the lawyers who resided in Prairie du Chien and presented cases before the judges of Crawford County. (Courtesy Prairie du Chien Historical Society—Ohr Collection.)

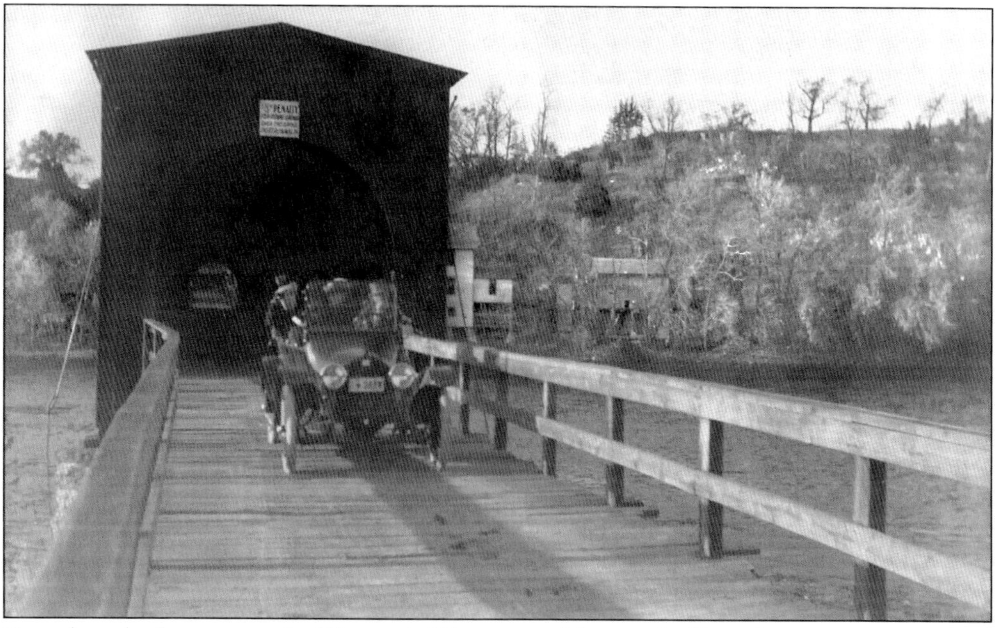

To replace the ferry across the Wisconsin River, several Prairie du Chien businessmen organized a company in 1854 to construct a bridge. The covered bridge was completed just in time for the arrival of the Milwaukee and Mississippi Rail Road. The company charged tolls, producing dividends for investors. The bridge continued to operate until 1931 when the State of Wisconsin built a new bridge to the west.

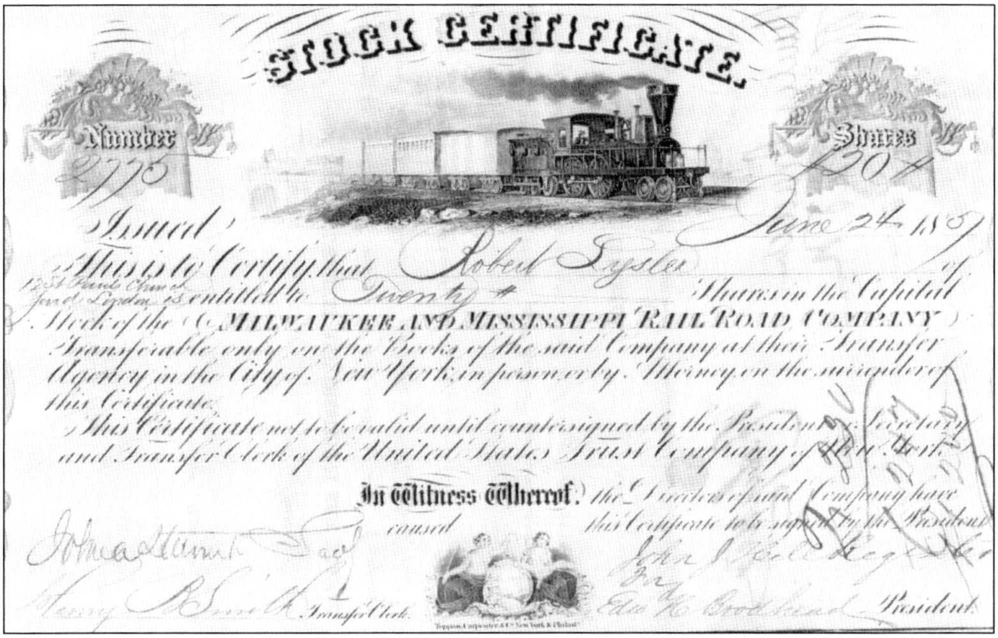
Stock Certificate.

Number

Shares

Issued

This is to Certify that

of

is entitled to

Shares in the Capital Stock of the Milwaukee and Mississippi Rail Road Company

Transferable only on the Books of the said Company at their Transfer Agency in the City of New York in person or by Attorney on the surrender of this Certificate.

This Certificate not to be valid until countersigned by the President or Secretary and Transfer Clerk of the United States Trust Company of New York.

In Witness Whereof, the Directors of said Company have caused this Certificate to be signed by the President

Transfer Clerk.

President.

Hundreds of residents waited along the tracks with great anticipation for the arrival of the first train of the Milwaukee and Mississippi Rail Road. Festooned with flags, the train, filled with dignitaries, arrived at 5:00 p.m. on April 15, 1857. An arriving steamboat answered the engine whistle, and 200 guns from a company of artillery announced the train. To symbolize the connection, an eight-gallon keg of Lake Michigan water was emptied into the Mississippi River.

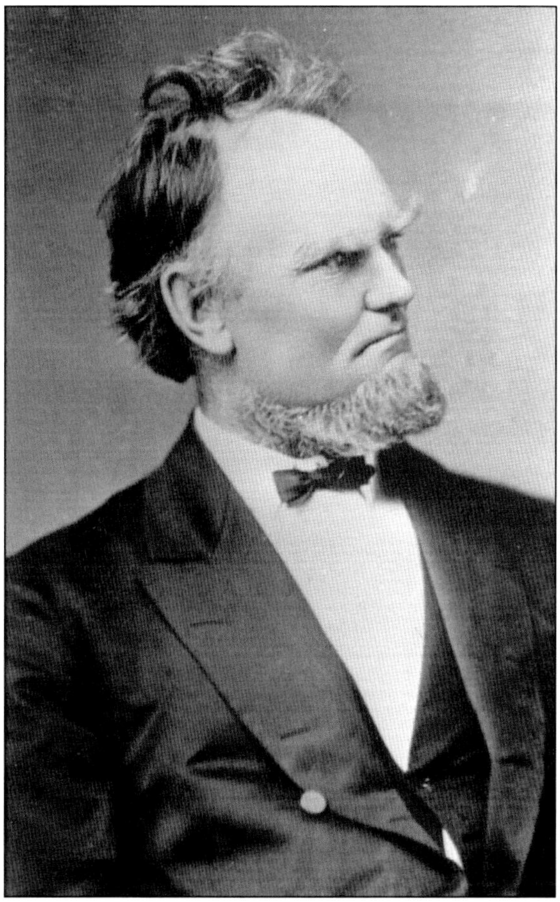

John Lawler came to Prairie du Chien employed as the station agent for the Milwaukee and Mississippi Rail Road. Within two years, he was promoted to general station agent. One of his responsibilities was to oversee the movement of passengers and freight from Prairie du Chien to St. Paul. This required transferring everything to packet boats. As usage increased and the railroad was reorganized as the Milwaukee and Prairie du Chien Rail Road, Lawler purchased more steamboats. He began to consider other means of transporting people and goods.

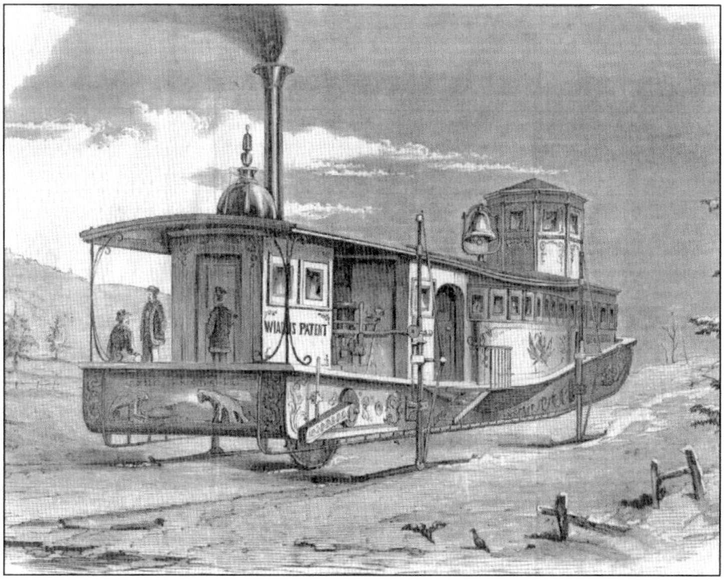

Once the Mississippi River froze, all river traffic ceased until spring. Norman Wiard of Janesville felt he had developed a solution. In 1859, he constructed a 20-passenger car to travel on the Mississippi in winter. Designed with continuous runners and skates, the ice car was propelled by a steam-driven corrugated hollow wheel that bit into the ice as it turned and pushed the boat.

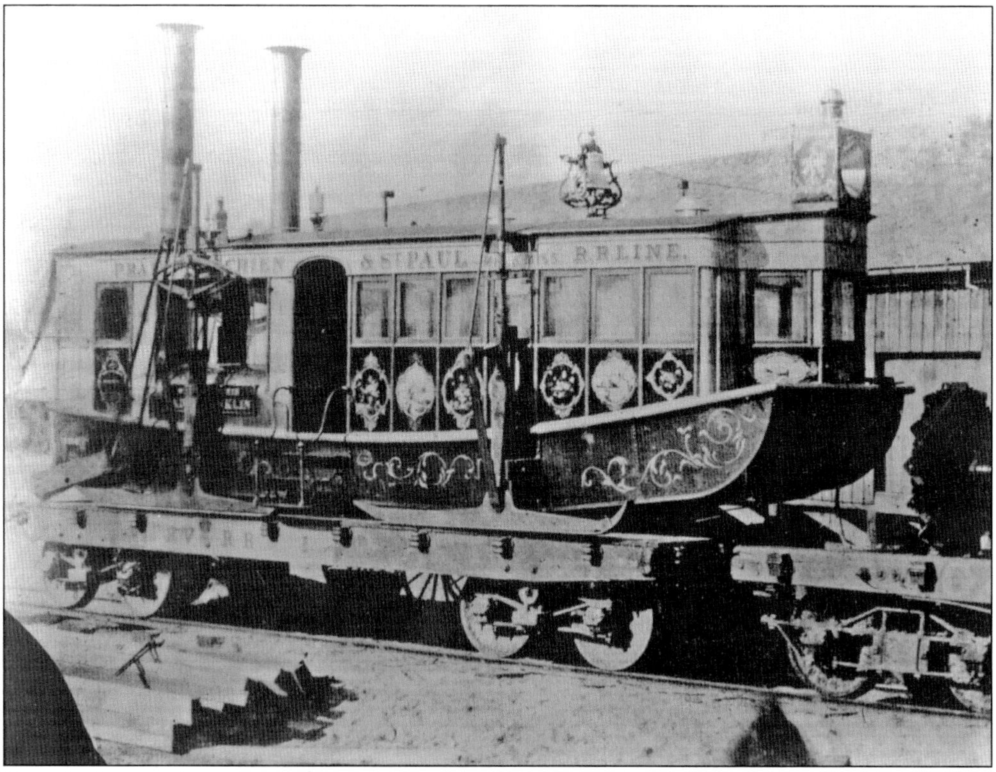

Wiard, along with John Muir, came to Prairie du Chien with the *Lady Franklin* in 1860. He reported that the trial run from Prairie du Chien to Lafayette [*sic*] and back took four hours and 10 minutes. The following winter, one of the runners broke when the boat was removed from storage. The *Lady Franklin* remained in Prairie du Chien as an object of curiosity. Wiard turned to inventing steam-powered cannon.

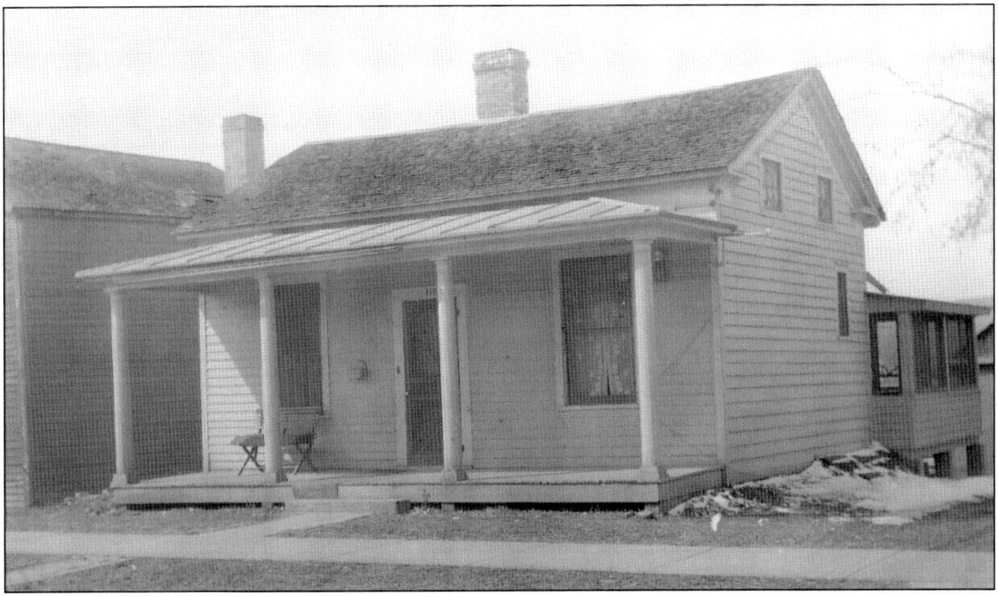

The winter of 1860–1861 also brought Ulysses S. Grant to Prairie du Chien. Grant worked as a clerk at the Galena, Illinois, store owned by his father and operated by his brothers. That winter, Grant traveled, servicing customers in southwest Wisconsin, northeast Iowa, and southeast Minnesota. He purchased hides and sold leather, harnesses, and supplies. While in Prairie du Chien, Grant boarded in this house owned by a family friend. (Courtesy Prairie du Chien Historical Society—Peckham Collection.)

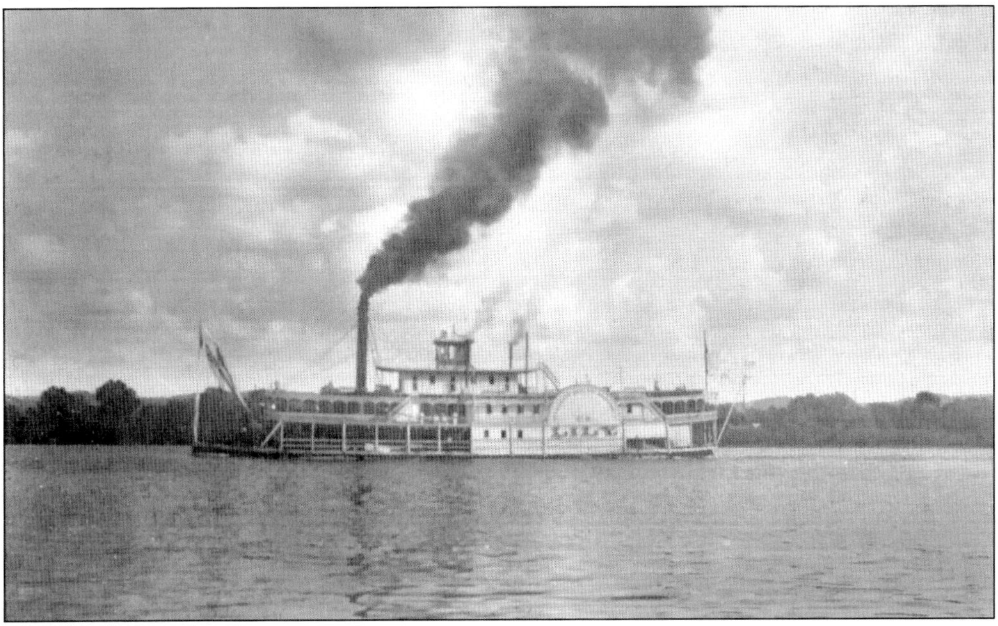

In 1863, the McGregor Western Railway was formed. John Lawler became vice president, and he devised a more efficient means of transshipment for passengers and goods across the Mississippi River. Forming the Northwest Packet Company, he had transfer barges constructed. Each barge was fitted with tracks to accommodate four freight cars, and then barges were towed by steamboat across the Mississippi. (Courtesy Martner Collection.)

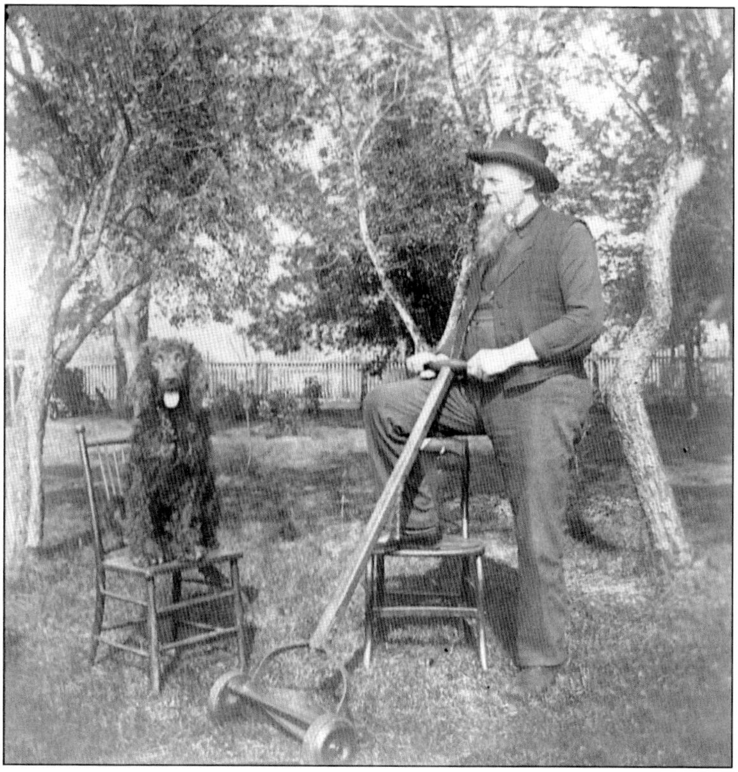

A locomotive engineer, John Ackerly directed the transfers for John Lawler. Four freight cars at a time would be pushed down the grade, over an apron, and onto the barges. Until the Pile Pontoon Bridge opened, Ackerly shifted thousands of cars without an accident or loss. After 50 years of service, he retired at Prairie du Chien. (Courtesy Martner Collection.)

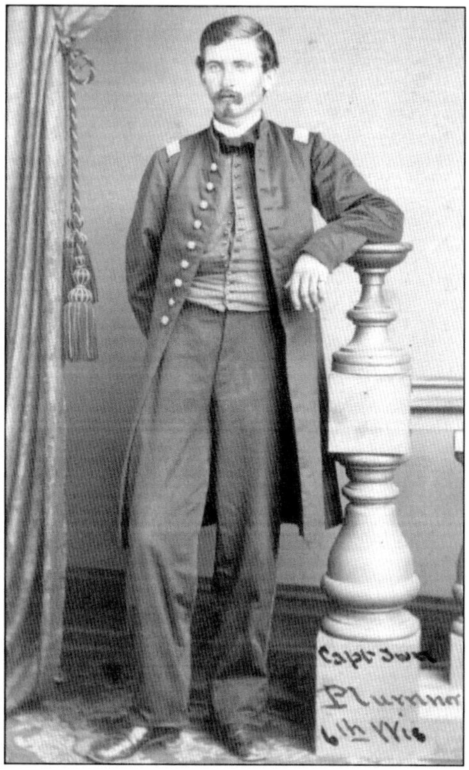

A few days after the firing on Fort Sumter, residents gathered at Union Hall to pledge their support of the Lincoln government. In early May 1861, the first company of Crawford County men under the three-year call organized at Prairie du Chien. The men left on the train for Madison and mustered into service as Company C, 6th Wisconsin Regiment of Volunteers. Philip Plummer was first lieutenant. Plummer was so highly regarded by his men that they presented him with a sword. (Courtesy Wisconsin Historical Society WHi-58530.)

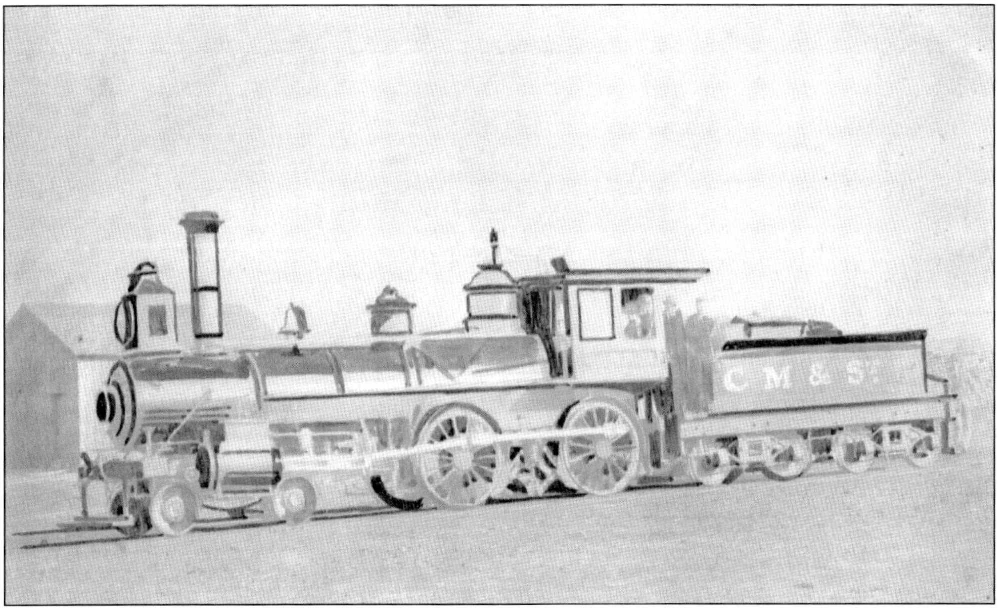

In May 1862, about 300 Confederate prisoners arrived at Prairie du Chien. They had been captured at the battle for Island No. 10. Too sick to make the journey to Chicago, they traveled by steamboat to Prairie du Chien, were transferred to the Milwaukee and Mississippi Rail Road, and continued to a prison at Camp Randall in Madison. No. 49, with James Ackerly as engineer, operated at this time. (Courtesy Martner Collection.)

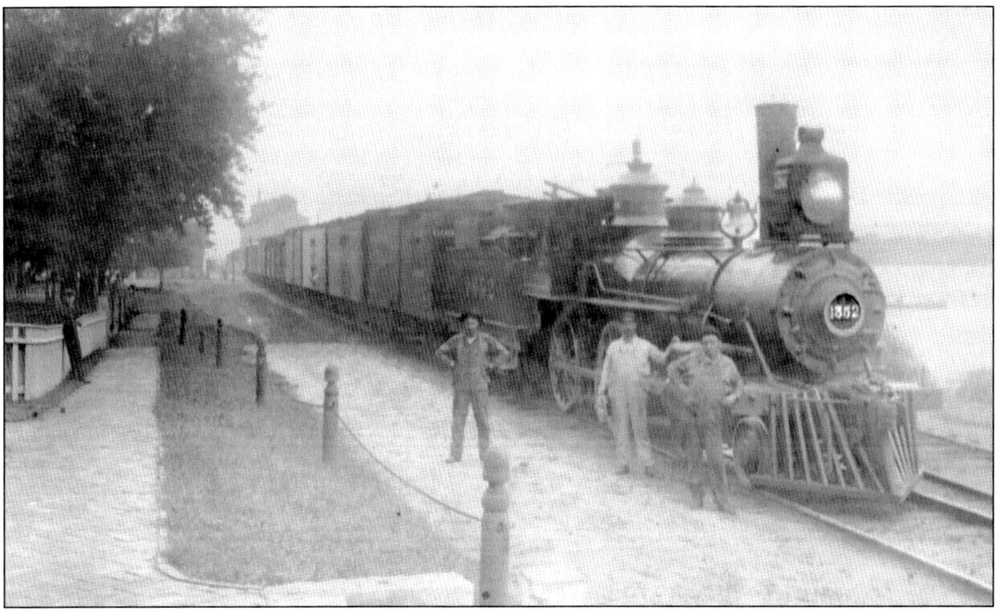

In 1864, the water level of the Mississippi was so low it was not possible for packet boats to reach the lower landing, so the railroad could not transfer passengers and goods to and from trains. The company's business had also outgrown its facilities. Reorganized as the Milwaukee and Prairie du Chien Rail Road, the enterprise moved its terminus to the upper landing. The railroad extended its tracks and erected a 200,000-bushel capacity elevator, a freight house, and platforms for trains, ferries, and steamboats. (Courtesy Bob Ziel.)

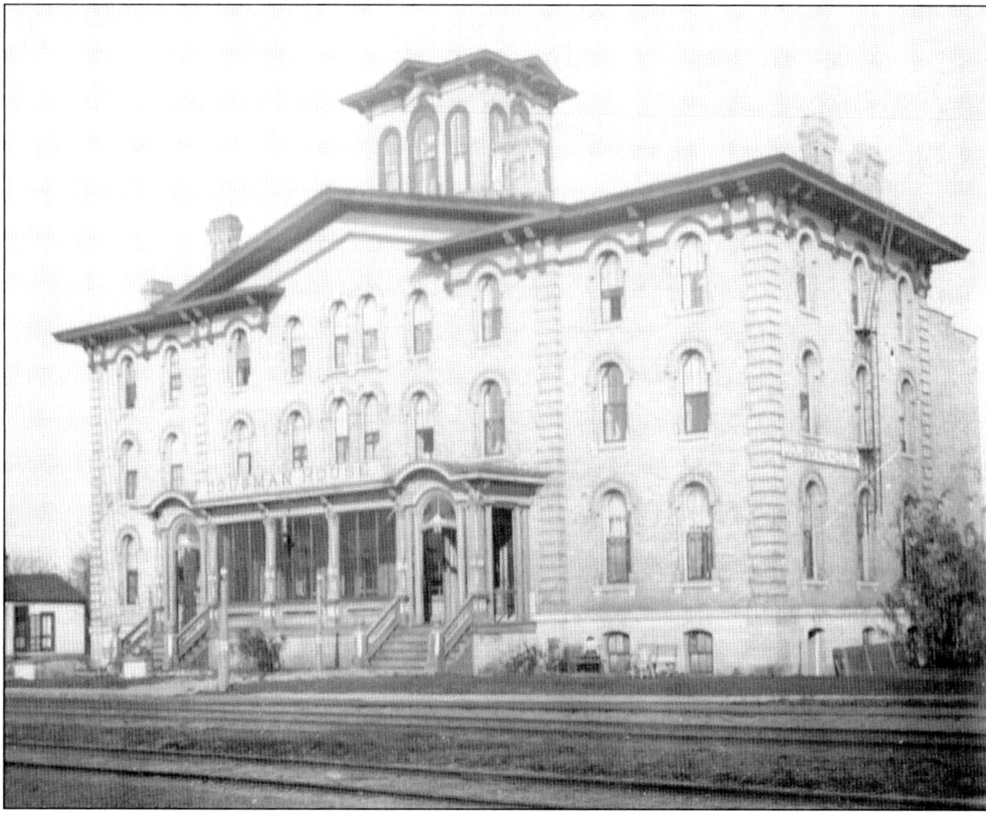

The railroad knew passengers would need a place to stay during layovers in Prairie du Chien, so it decided to build a hotel next to the passenger station on land donated by Hercules L. Dousman. Completed in 1864 at a cost of $45,000, the Railway House was hailed as one of the most impressive hotels in the Midwest. Built of Milwaukee cream brick, the hotel's 51 rooms were individually heated with stoves. A unique system of indoor toilets served each floor. About 1885, the name was changed to the Dousman House. (Courtesy Bob Ziel.)

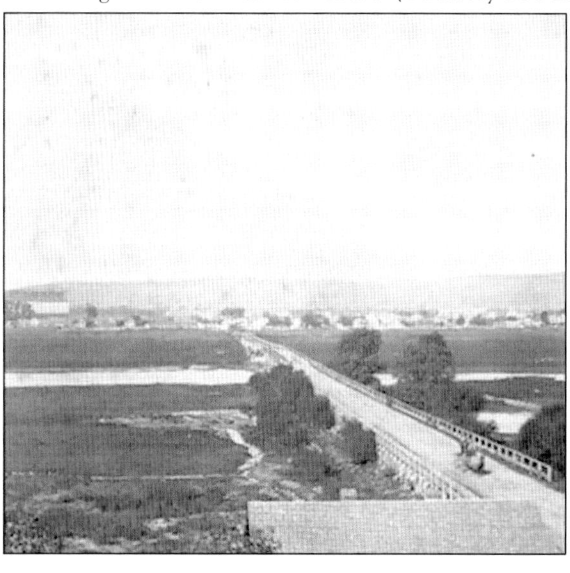

With the relocation of the train station to the island and construction of the Railway House, the old Main Village teemed with activity. So, in 1864, a bridge was erected connecting the commercial centers that fronted Water Street on the island and Main Street on the mainland. Horse and foot traffic flowed along Bluff Street and the newly graded Bridge Street. (Courtesy Cliff and Michele Krainik, Warrenton, Virginia.)

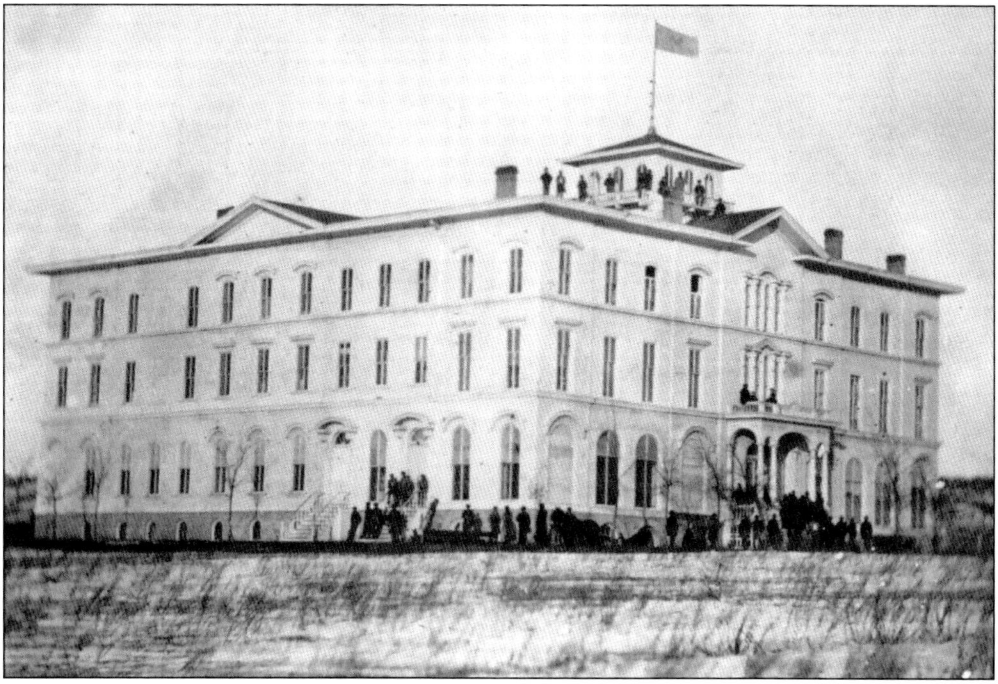

The moving of the railroad terminus caused the Brisbois Hotel to close. Cordelia Harvey, widow of Governor Harvey, received permission to establish three hospitals in Wisconsin to care for wounded soldiers. In November 1864, the Swift Hospital opened in a frame structure that had been the Brisbois Hotel. Until it closed in September 1865, the Swift Hospital cared for over 2,000 enlisted men from Wisconsin, Iowa, and Minnesota. The great number caused the old Fort Crawford Hospital to be pressed into use. (Courtesy Wisconsin Historical Society WHi-42359.)

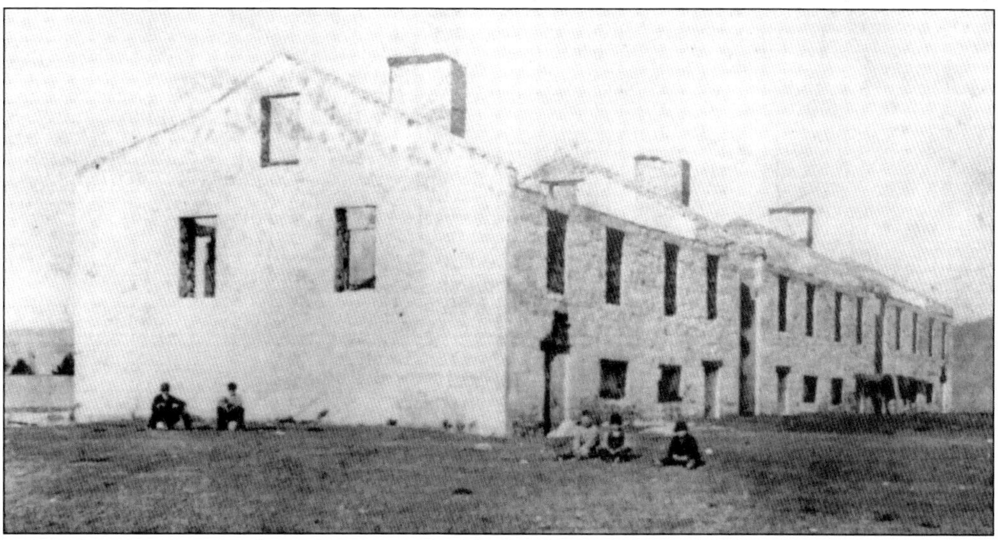

After almost 40 years of use, Fort Crawford had fallen into complete disrepair. The U.S. War Department decommissioned the Fort Crawford Military Tract. An auction was held in 1866 to sell all of the property. On it were the ruins of the officers and enlisted men's barracks, the house and outbuildings used by the fort's commandant, and a cemetery. (Courtesy Wisconsin Historical Society WHi-42276.)

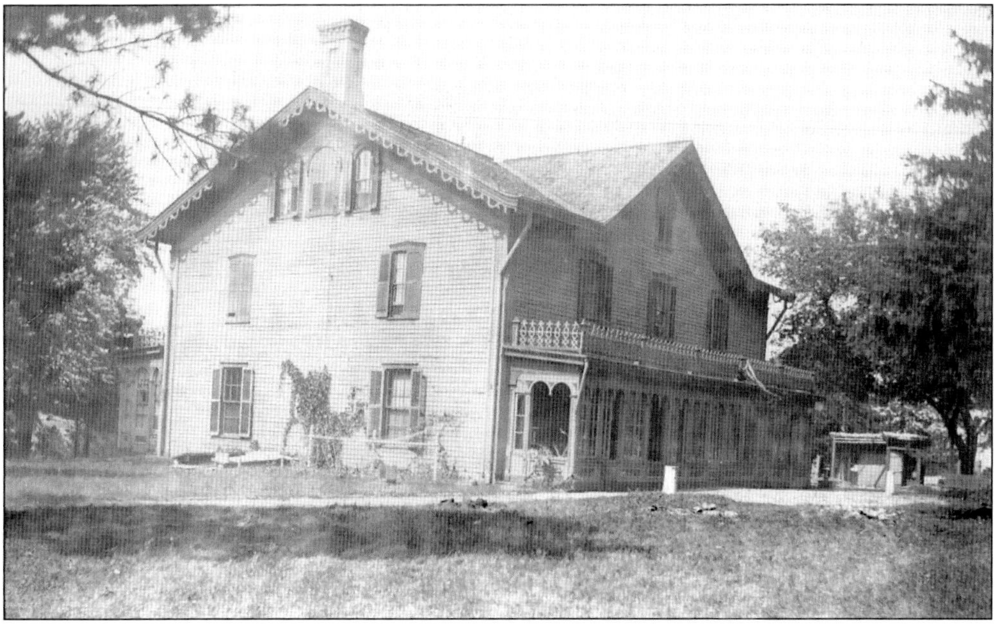

John Lawler purchased the western portion of the Fort Crawford Military Tract that contained the barracks and the commandant's compound. Lawler refurbished the commandant's house and made it his family home. (Courtesy Antoine family.)

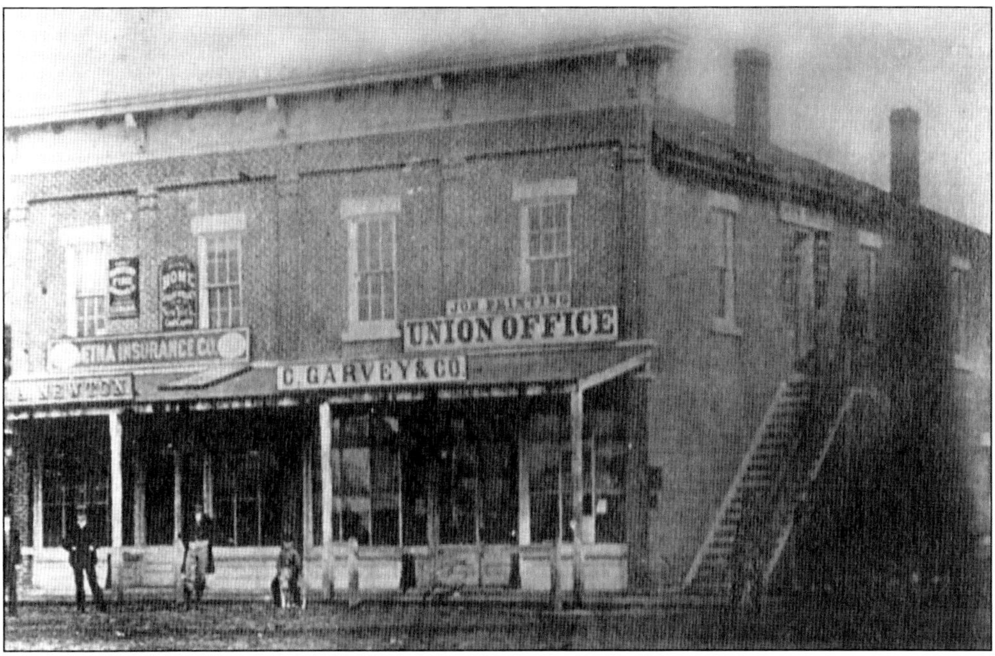

The railroad brought many immigrants from Europe to Prairie du Chien, and some of them chose to make the community their new home. Christopher and James Garvey had left Northern Ireland, and in 1867 they opened a dry goods store. Their business was so successful that within a few years they would erect their own building on the other side of the street. William Newton sold groceries and dealt in hides and pelts. James Green, an ardent supporter of President Lincoln, began *The Union* newspaper in 1864. (Courtesy Antoine family.)

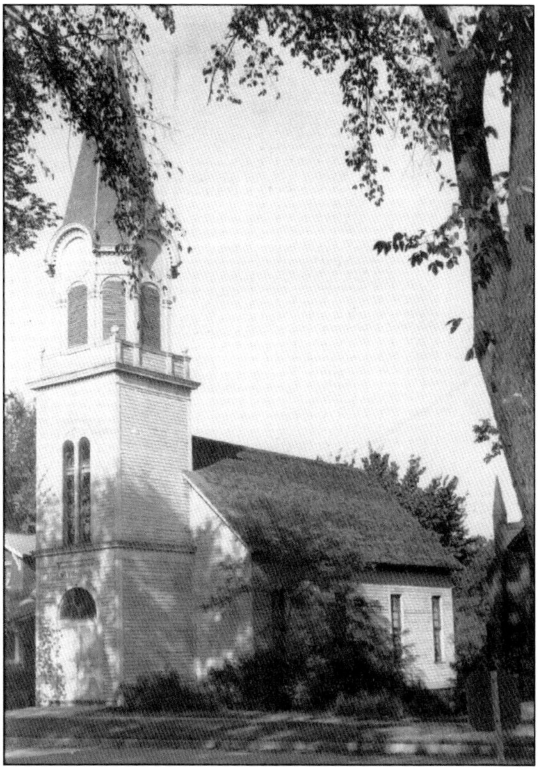

Many Germans settled at Prairie du Chien, bringing new trades and skills to the community. They also brought new religious denominations. Some joined St. Gabriel's Church, but missionary Rev. Mr. Himmler found a large number of immigrants from the region of Mecklenburg. They had an affiliation with the Lutheran faith, and he organized them into St. Peter's Evangelical Lutheran congregation in 1862. They built a church next door to the Episcopal Church in 1871. (Courtesy Virginia Antoine.)

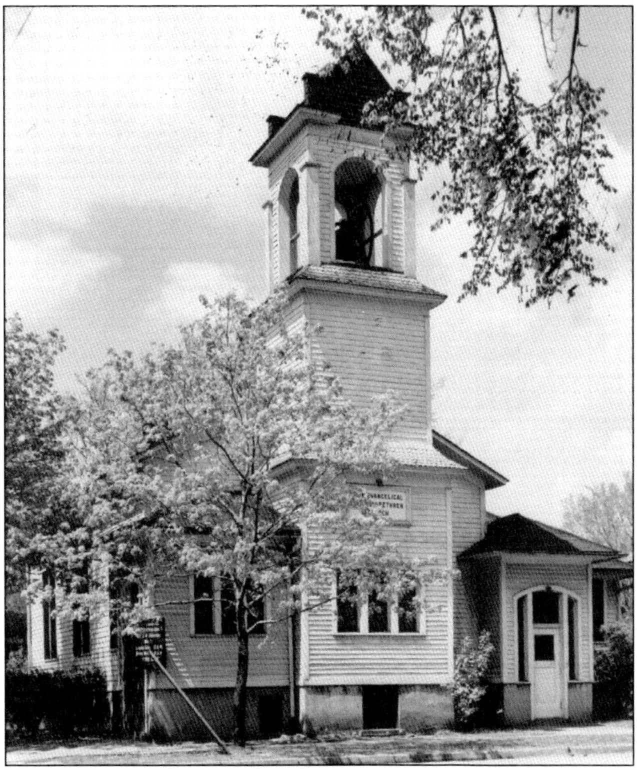

In the 1850s, a group of Germans purchased farmland on Dutch and Shanghai Ridges. By 1860, a few families had moved to Prairie du Chien. They were Pietists, and the Evangelische Gemeinschaft sent Rev. Peter Speich to minister to them. They met in the home of Christian Poehler, slowly raising funds to build a church. In 1866, the Zion Church in Prairie du Chien quietly held its first services. (Courtesy Prairie du Chien Historical Society—Peckham Collection.)

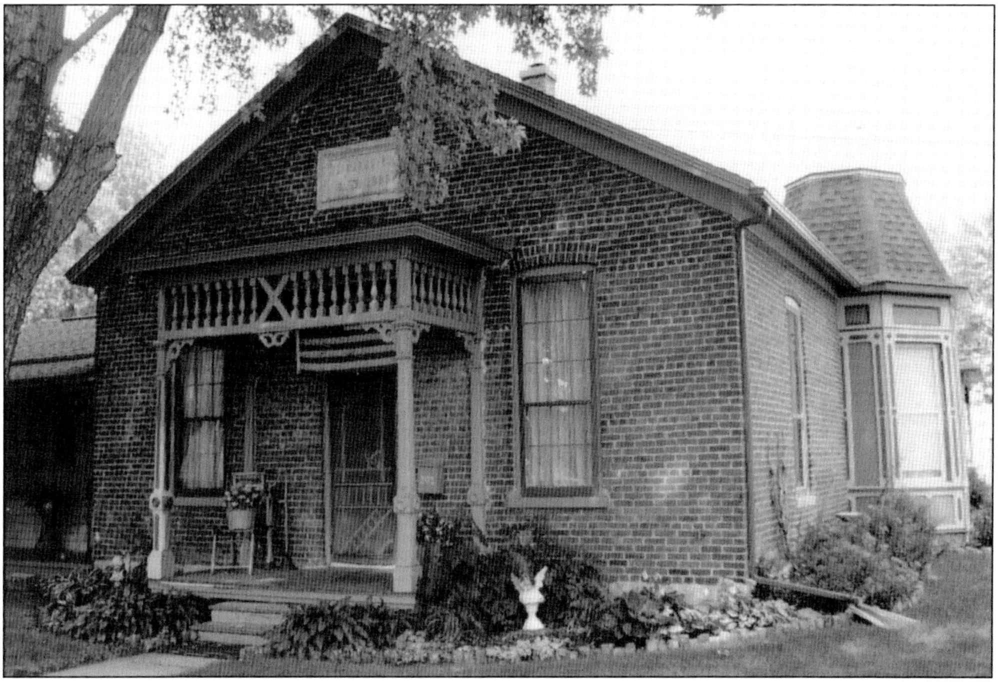

A number of German citizens wanted to continue their culture. In 1866, they met for the purpose of organizing an Independent German School. A constitution was adopted, stating that German would be taught without regard to any religious creed. In 1868, the association constructed a one-story brick school. Tuition was $1 for members and $1.50 for non-members. The school operated until 1878.

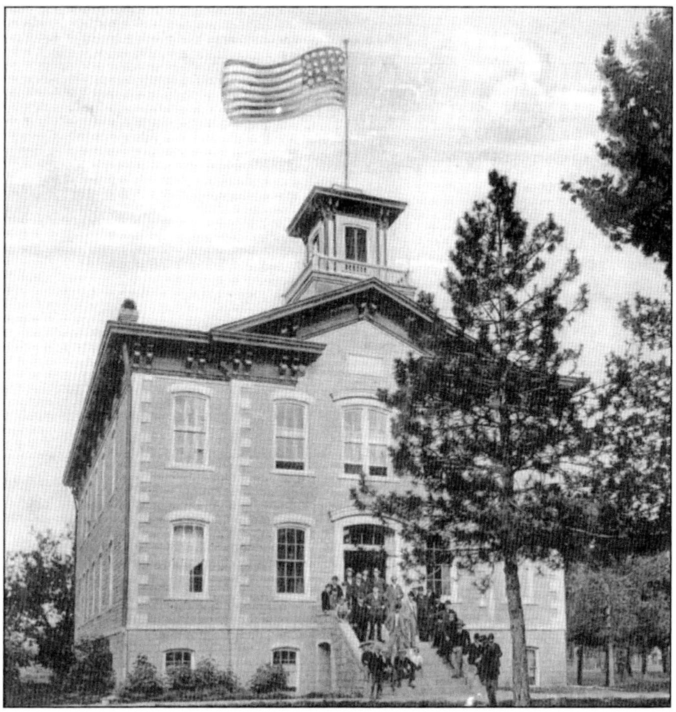

As Wisconsin readied to become a territory in 1836, the Crawford County Commissioners voted to build a courthouse. B. W. Brisbois donated a square of land fronting Church Street. William Wilson won the bid to construct a courthouse and jail. In June 1866, the commissioners decided to build a new courthouse and jail on the same site. Michael Menges and Nicholas Bertholt won the contract, which required that the structure be built of limestone quarried in Bridgeport. County officials moved into the new building on July 10, 1868. (Courtesy Virginia Antoine.)

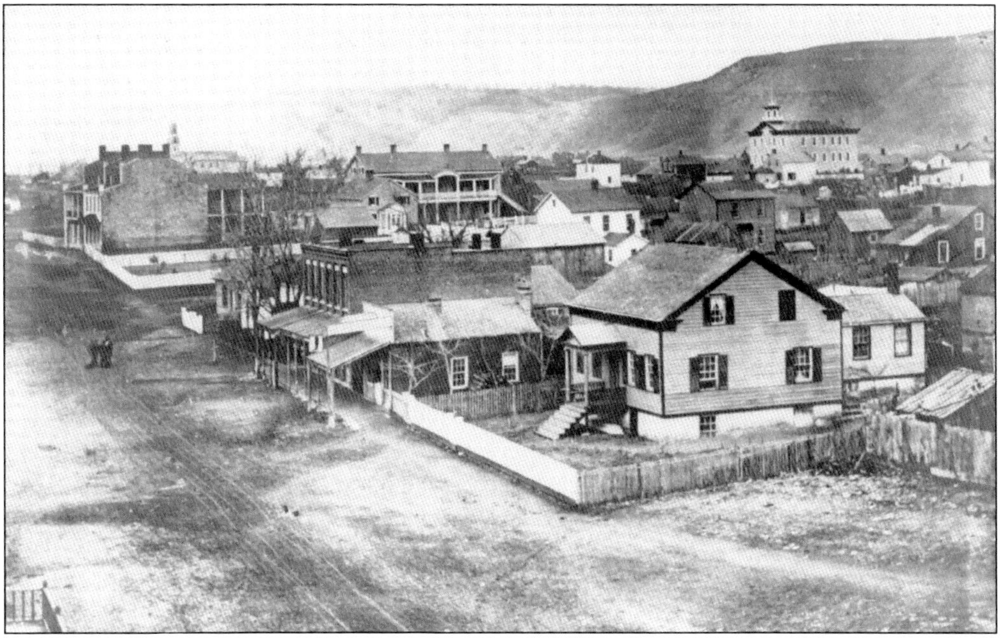

An Indian trail wound along the east bank of the Mississippi River from one end of the prairie to the other. Residents of the Village of St. Friol and the Upper Village assembled their log homes facing the trail, which became Main Street. By 1870, commercial buildings, such as the Brillion Hotel and the Famechon House, stood in the midst of modest residences.

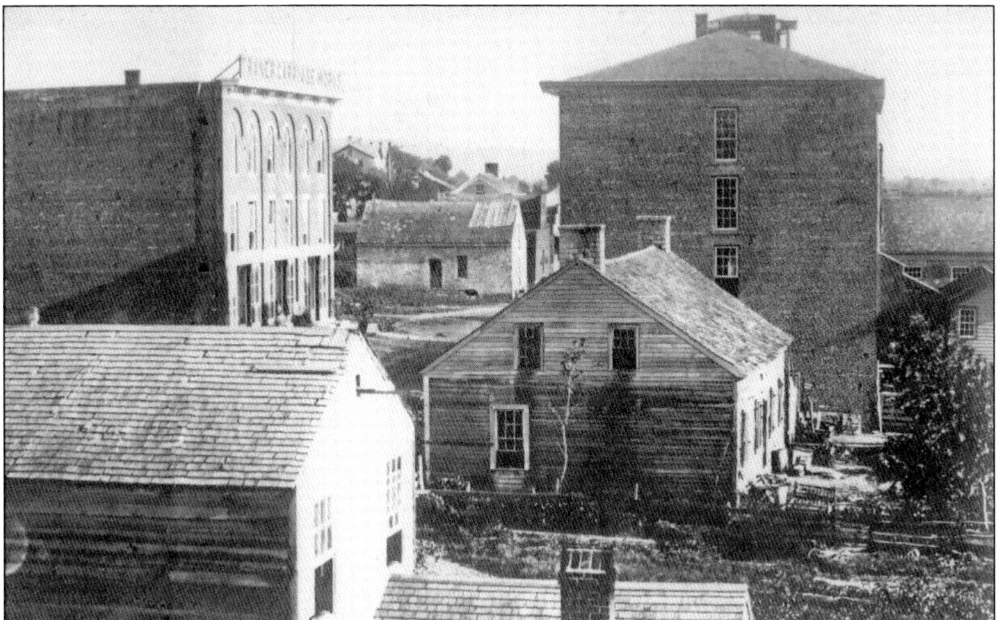

The change that occurred in the character of Prairie du Chien was most noticeable on south Main Street. The Union Block, built in 1856, housed the Traner Carriage Works. Across the street was the Kane Hotel. Built in 1839 as the Phoenix, and enlarged in 1856 under new management, the Kane towered over the French-Canadian log house of Antoine Boisvert. (Courtesy Martner Collection.)

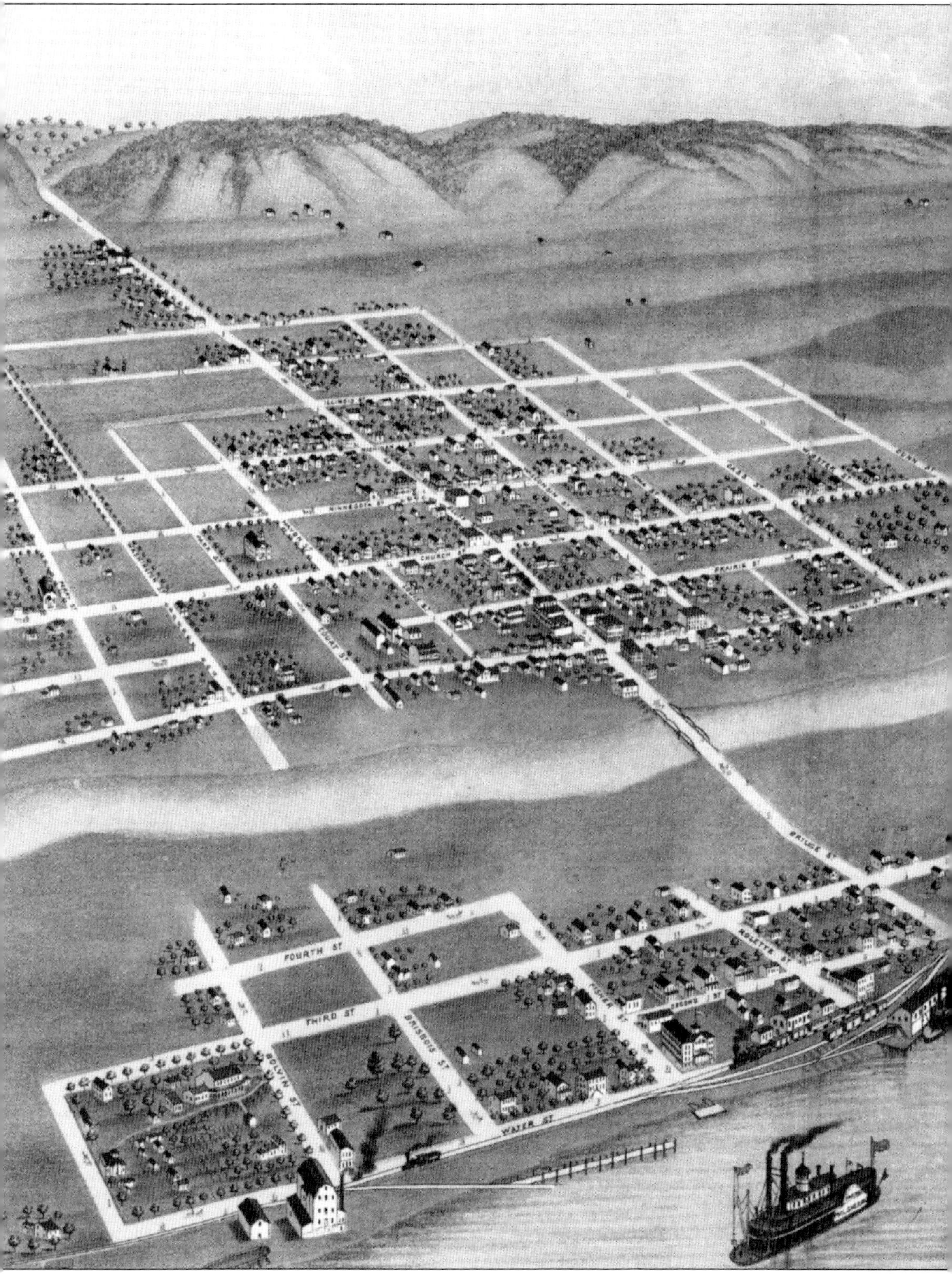
FOURTH ST
THIRD ST
BOLVIN ST
BRISBOIS ST
WATER ST
BRIDGE ST
CHURCH ST
COURT ST
PRAIRIE ST
CASS ST

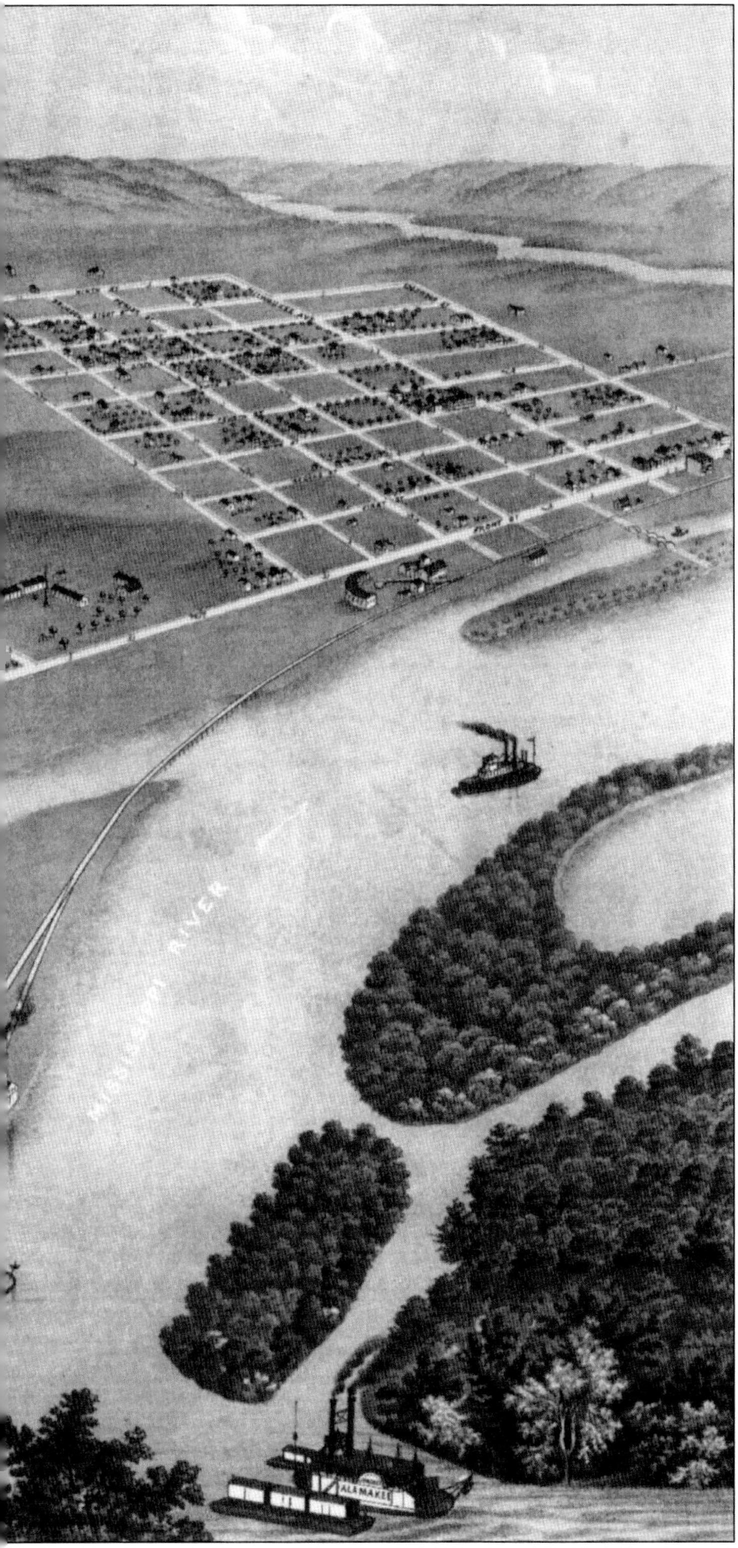

By 1870, Prairie du Chien had grown to a population of about 3,000. Loosely governed by the Prairie du Chien Town Board, the township and individual developers platted and graded streets. The old Main Village and the Village of St. Friol disappeared into Upper Town. Lower Town, below the Fort Crawford Military Tract, was the creation of individual speculators, and the street names identified who they were. All hoped prosperity would continue.

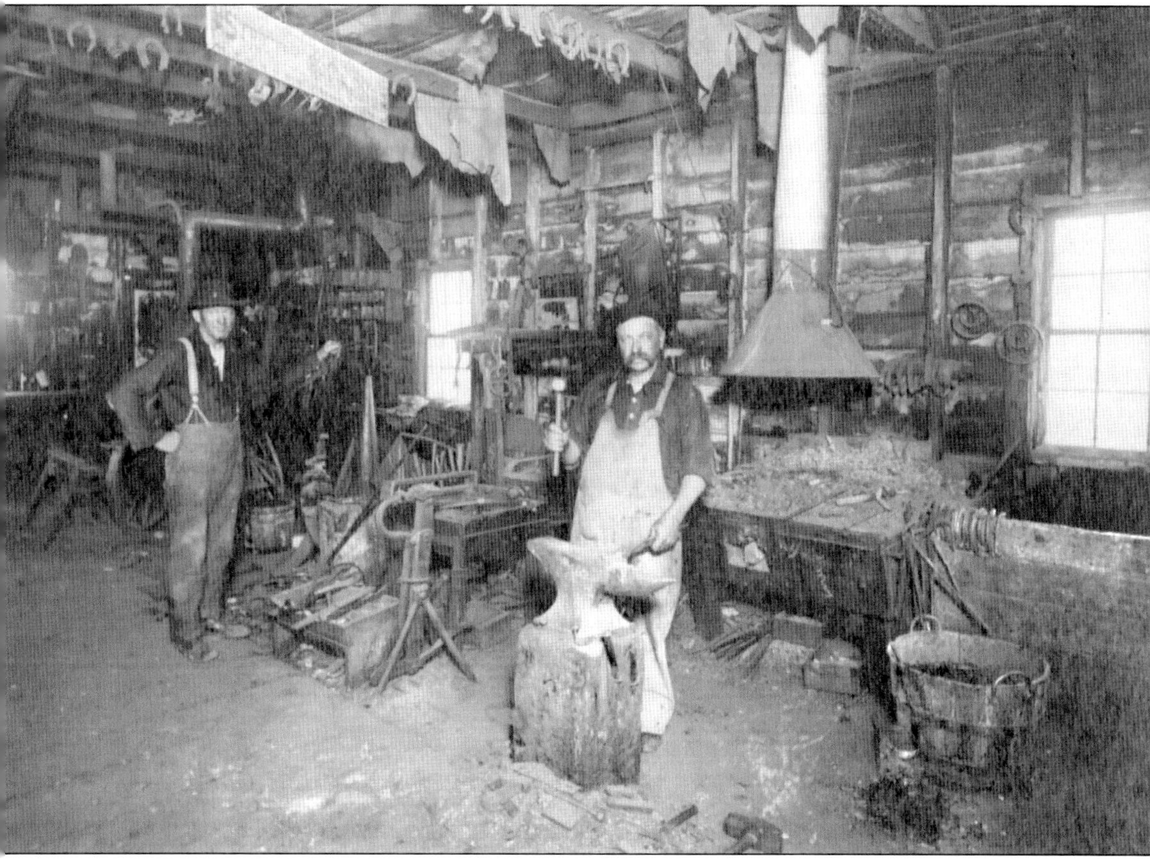

The cultural and economic shift affected the families of early French Canadian settlers. Some left Prairie du Chien; others adapted. Oliver Cherrier had come to the prairie in the early 19th century. He and his son were blacksmiths fulfilling contracts, first for fur traders, then Indian agencies. Oliver's grandson Maurice (right) adapted, shoeing horses and repairing wagon wheels. (Courtesy Prairie du Chien Historical Society.)

Three

From Villages to City

The city is substantial built in regular squares, and the wide, well-shaded streets run at right angles; the drainage is natural and perfect, and the city is free from all malarial influences, making it a very healthy place.

—S. C. Judson, 1887

By 1870, Prairie du Chien was coalescing into one community. The Village of St. Friol and much of the farmland to the east was a grid of platted streets and the site of county government, homes, and commercial structures; this was Upper Town. A bridge connected Upper Town to the island that was the location of the Milwaukee and Prairie du Chien Railroad depot in the old Main Village. Main Street joined Upper Town and Lower Town. Yet there was no form of local government.

Prairie du Chien was an area much larger than the platted and settled portion of the prairie. It was a township stretching from the Wisconsin River across the bluffs north to Sioux Coulee. Some residents of the prairie felt their community had needs different from the rest of the township and were upset over unequal tax assessment. A movement began, under the leadership of the editor of *The Courier*, to have the settlement chartered as a city. In 1872, the Wisconsin Legislature granted a city charter to Prairie du Chien.

With new optimism, the city residents responded. In 1872, several fine brick commercial buildings blossomed along Bluff Street, while established businessmen added to their structures. That same year, each ward boasted a new fire company; two schools opened, offering private education to young women and men; the Prairie du Chien School District was organized; and residents began to construct new homes reflecting the latest styles.

For the next few years, the economic boom continued with construction of a pile pontoon bridge across the Mississippi River, drilling of artesian wells, and in 1886 the arrival of a second railroad. The addition of telephone and electrical service made Prairie du Chien a desirable place to make one's home.

The beauty and amenities of the community inspired S. C. Judson to write *Views in and around Prairie du Chien, Wisconsin*, with a short history of the city. To him, the prairie and "precipitous bluffs" gave "a romantic beauty to the place and its environments." Here one could escape the high rents and cost of living found in large cities.

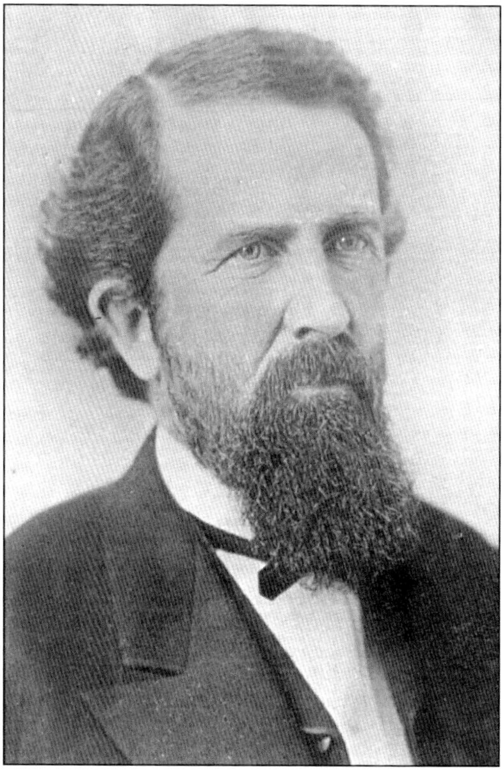

Benjamin F. Fay was elected the first mayor of Prairie du Chien in 1872. Originally from New York, Fay built a grain elevator along the Wisconsin River and was vice president of the company that operated the Bridgeport Bridge. He had headed the Citizen's Party ticket, which promised to reduce expenses and "lift the burden of outrageous taxation." (Courtesy City of Prairie du Chien.)

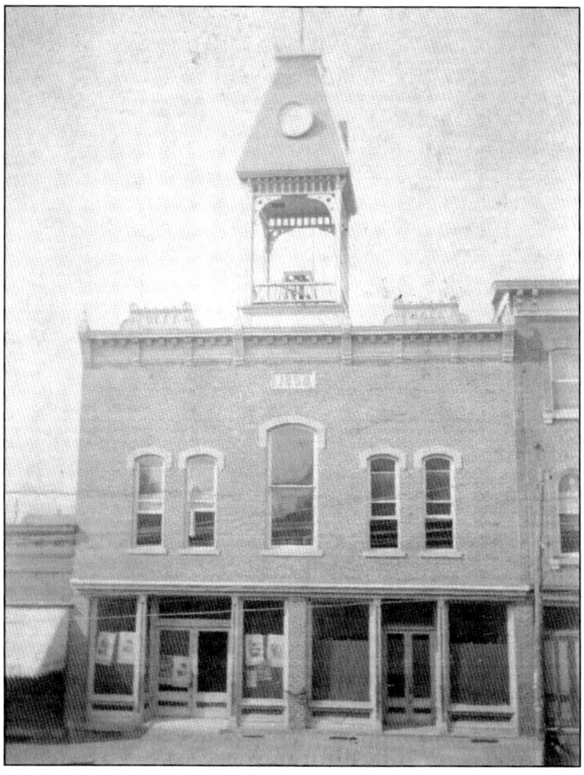

To keep expenses to a minimum, the mayor and aldermen received no salary, and the city government leased rooms for the council chambers. Not until 1894 would the government for the City of Prairie du Chien have a permanent location. The Council Room was on the first floor. On the second floor was Germania Hall, a place to hold lectures and operatic entertainment. Over the years, the structure housed the public library and the fire department. (Courtesy Martner Collection.)

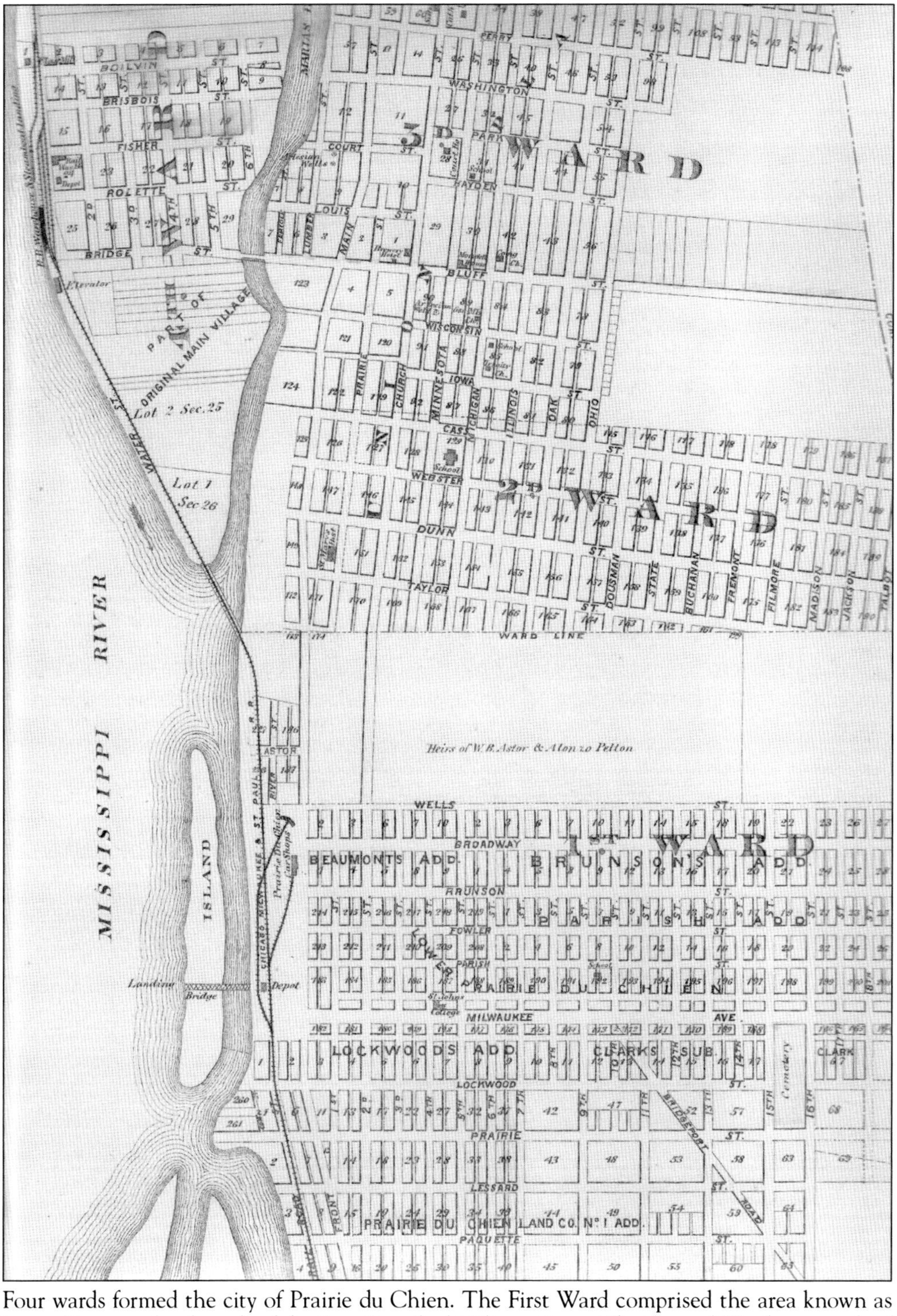

Four wards formed the city of Prairie du Chien. The First Ward comprised the area known as Lower Town on land south of the Fort Crawford Military Tract. The Second Ward was north of the tract to Bluff Street. The Third Ward was all land north of Bluff Street. The Fourth Ward was the island that had been the Main Village.

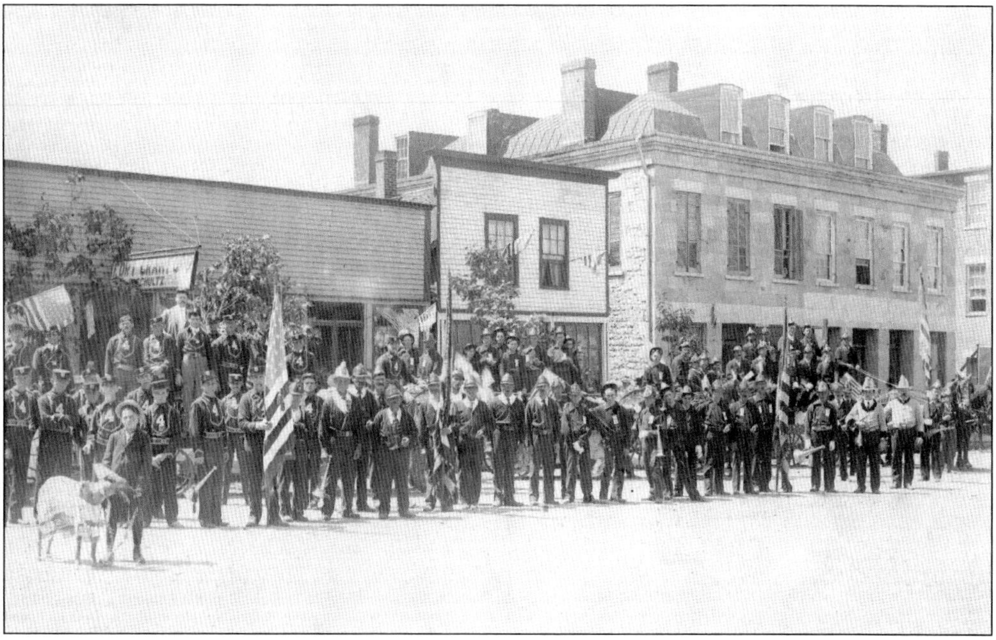

With the chartering of city government, residents organized fire protection for the community. Three volunteer companies were formed. Phoenix No. 1 was the largest, serving the Second and Third Wards. Badger Company No. 2 had its headquarters in the Fourth Ward. Aetna Company No. 3 served Lower Town, building a firehouse on First Street. In the 1890s, Cataract No. 4 organized to assist Phoenix. (Courtesy Prairie du Chien Historical Society.)

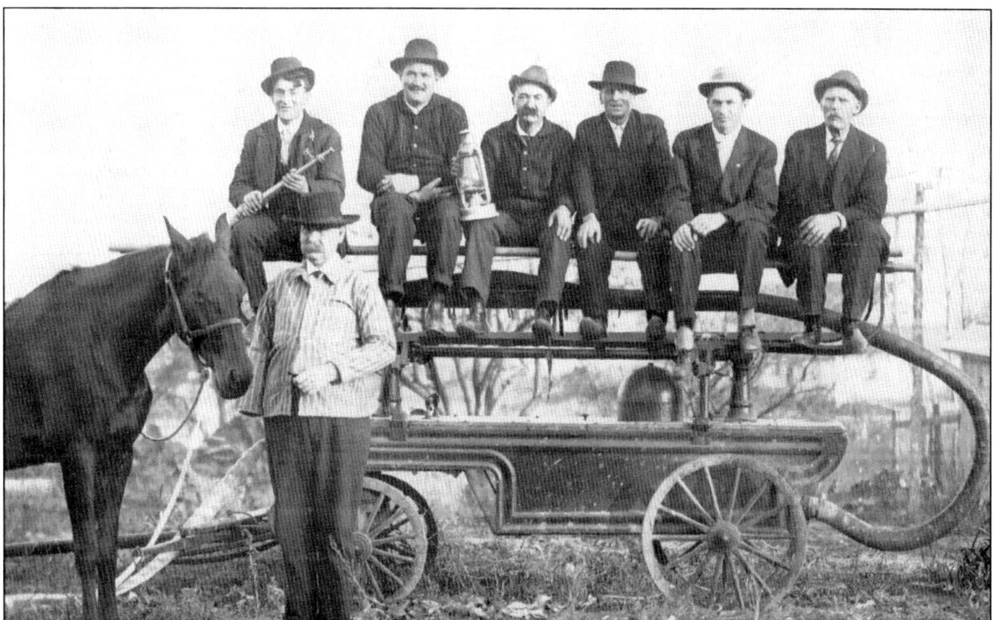

In time, each company owned a hand-pump engine and a hose cart with 3,000 feet of hose. (Courtesy Bob Ziel.)

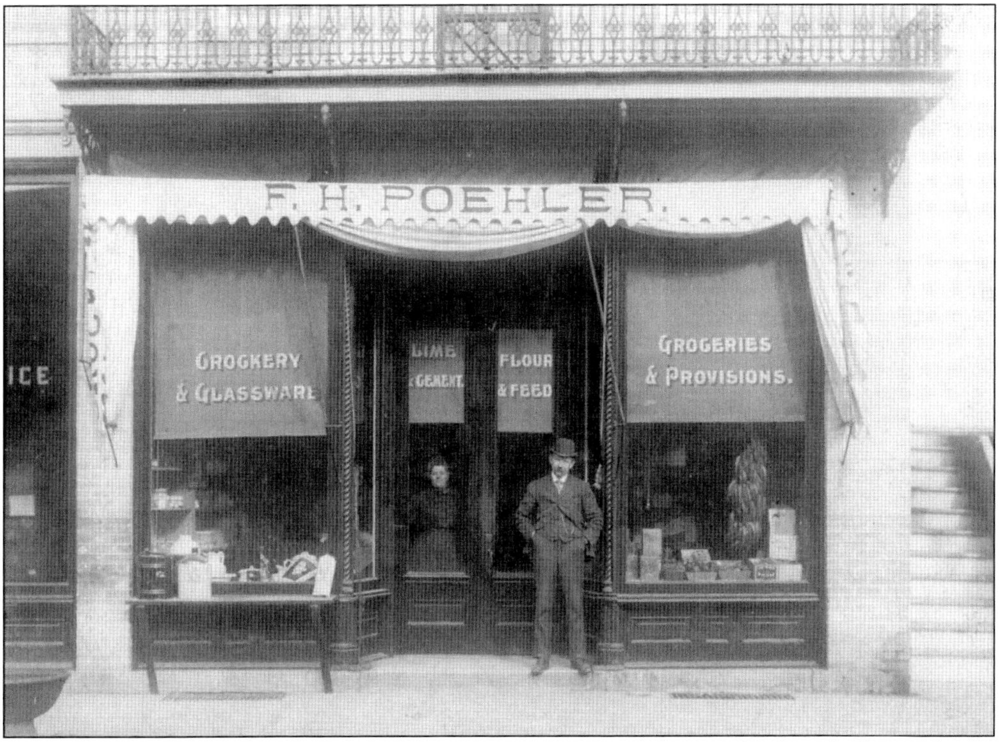

By 1870, Christian Poehler operated a retail grocery store. In 1872, he hired John Radin to construct a brick addition to his building on Bluff Street. Poehler's sons continued the business, ever expanding until they owned a three-store block, part of which they leased for other commercial activities. (Courtesy Prairie du Chien Historical Society.)

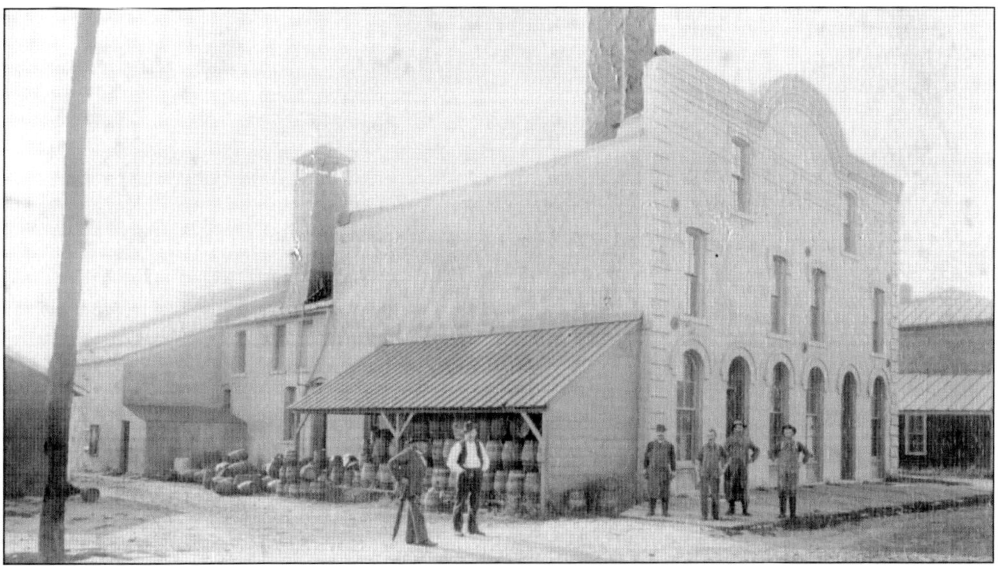

Michael Menges, who had built the new courthouse, purchased a plot of land behind the Law Block. He hired 25 to 30 men to excavate a foundation for his new brewery. At the end of 1872, the cornerstone was laid, with production of beer starting within one year. By 1884, Schumann and Menges turned out 6,000 barrels of beer annually. (Courtesy Bob Ziel.)

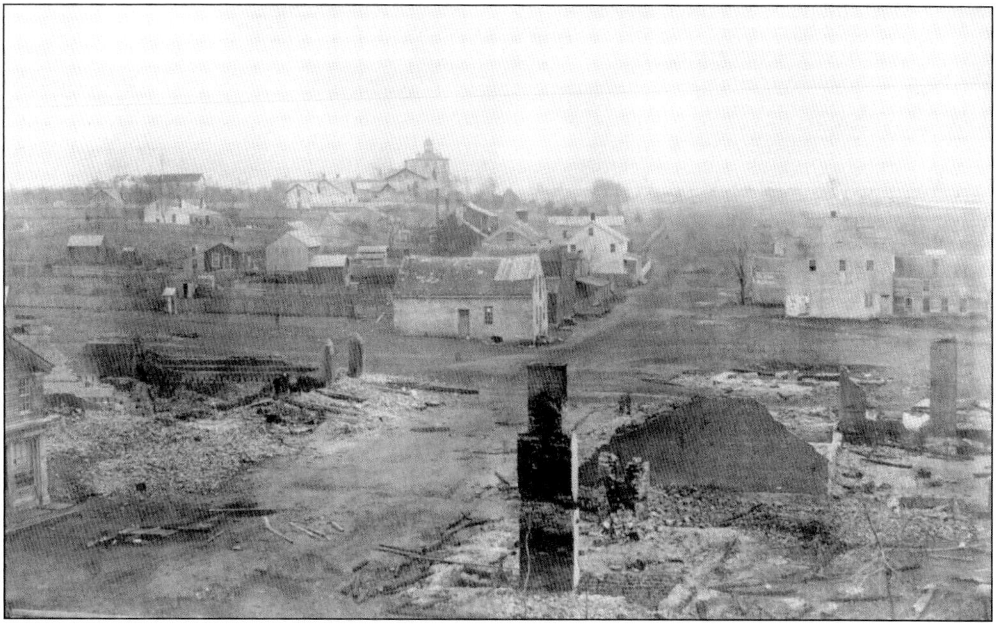

On November 7, 1872, a fire started in Antoine Boisvert's stable, spreading to the stable behind the Kane Hotel. During the night, it reignited, engulfing the hotel and jumping across Main Street to consume the Traner Carriage Works. With only buckets, the new fire companies managed to keep the fire from spreading to Bluff Street.

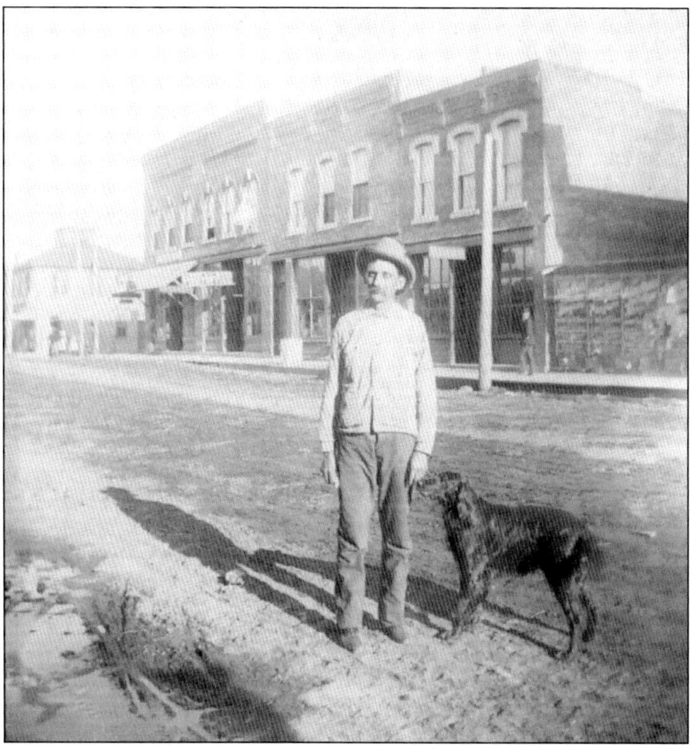

The fire on South Main Street cemented the shift of the new city's commercial district to Bluff Street. Horace Beach, who had opened a store selling agricultural implements, expanded to carry hardware and heating stoves. Behind him are the Grace Block and the double Wachuta Store. Joseph Wachuta's variety store sold groceries, confectionaries, tobacco, notions, and toys. (Courtesy Prairie du Chien Historical Society—Dyrud Collection.)

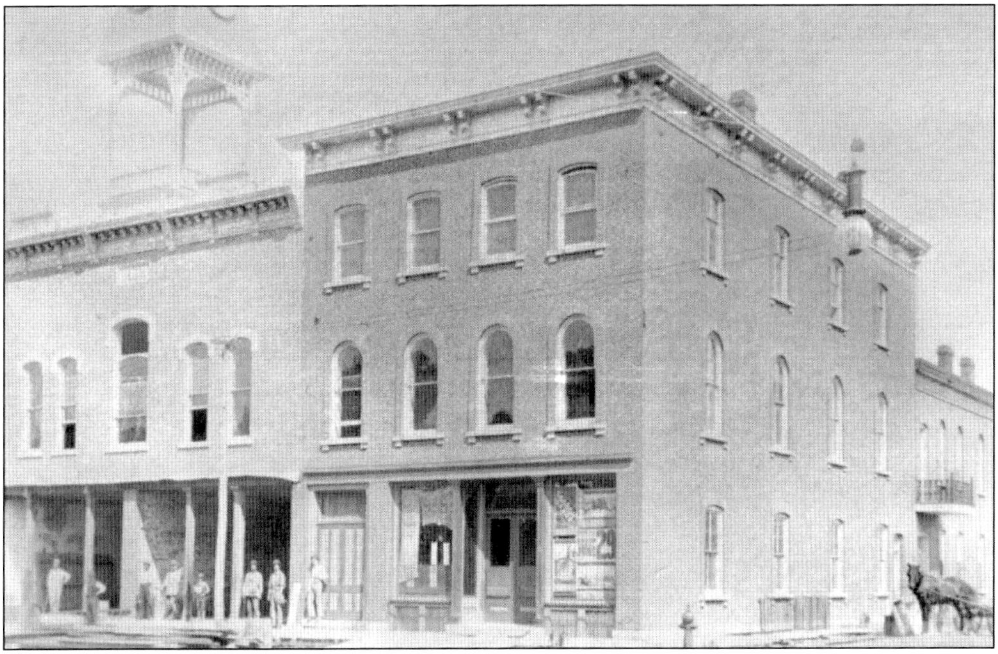

George Schweitzer opened the Commercial House in 1881. He had attempted to become the proprietor of the Kane Hotel. After the Kane burned, Schweitzer purchased the building on the corner of Prairie and Bluff Streets, remodeling it to include a billiard hall and bar. (Courtesy Bittner family.)

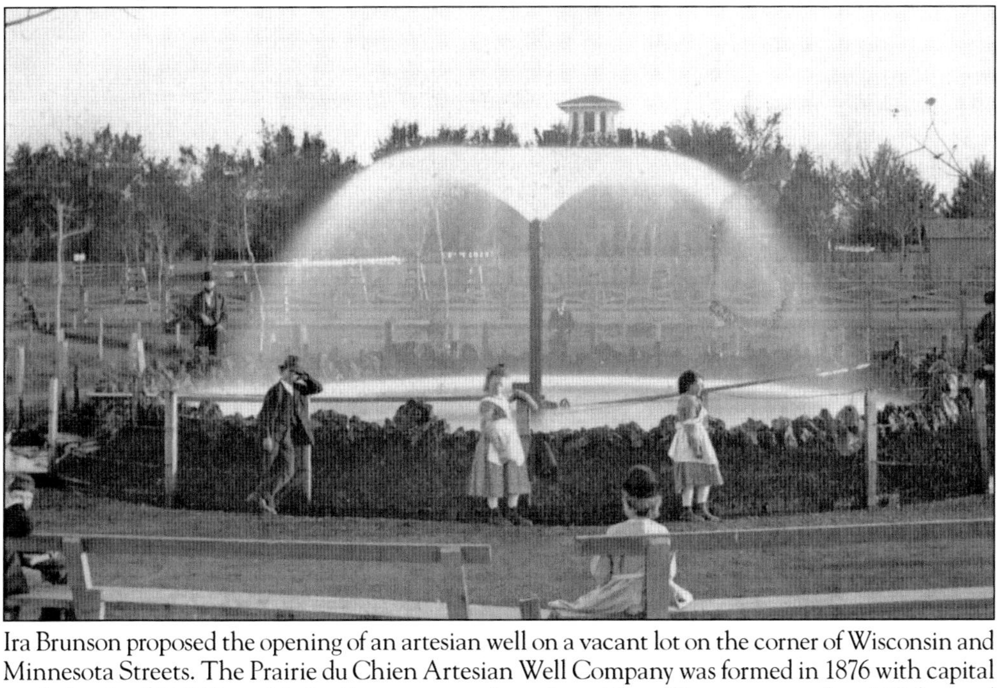

Ira Brunson proposed the opening of an artesian well on a vacant lot on the corner of Wisconsin and Minnesota Streets. The Prairie du Chien Artesian Well Company was formed in 1876 with capital stock fixed at $10,000, and Judge Brunson was elected president. Water was struck at 960 feet and gushed to a height of 70 feet. The company designed a lagoon and park around the well, planting shade and evergreen trees. A band shell graced the far corner. (Courtesy Antoine family.)

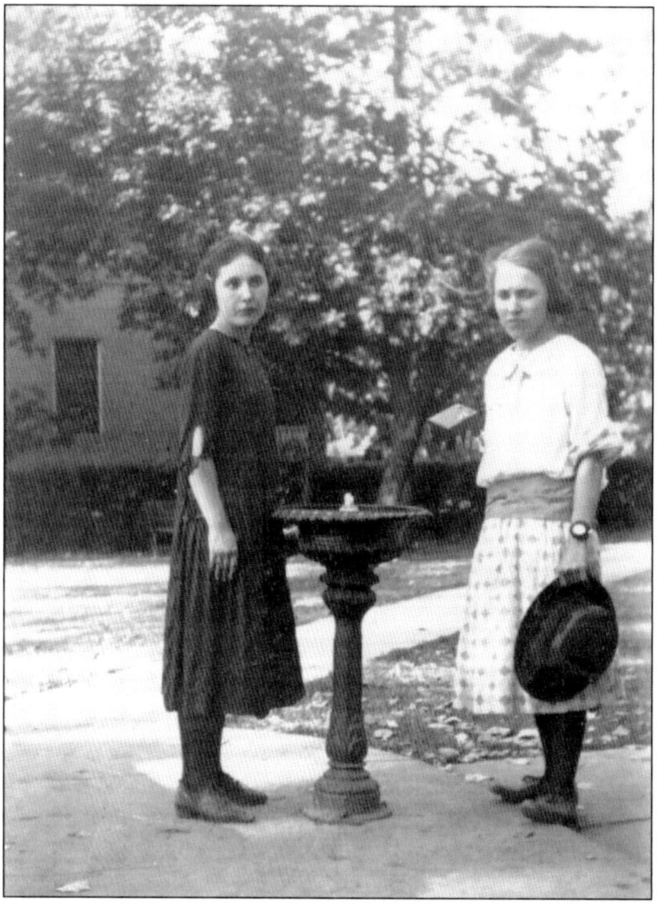

Water flowed at 20 barrels per minute. Pipes were laid to Bluff Street and mains and hydrants installed the length of the commercial district. The company also placed fountains where people refreshed themselves with a cup of water, and troughs offered a cool drink for horses. Excess water flowed down open gutters paved with stone. (Courtesy Prairie du Chien Historical Society.)

A well-drilling furor followed. Thomas L. Brower, on the board of the Artesian Well Company, lived in Lower Town, owning and operating two drug and general merchandise stores. Ira Brunson drilled an artesian well across from Brower's home. Brower designed a private park and piped water to a small fountain gracing his front yard.

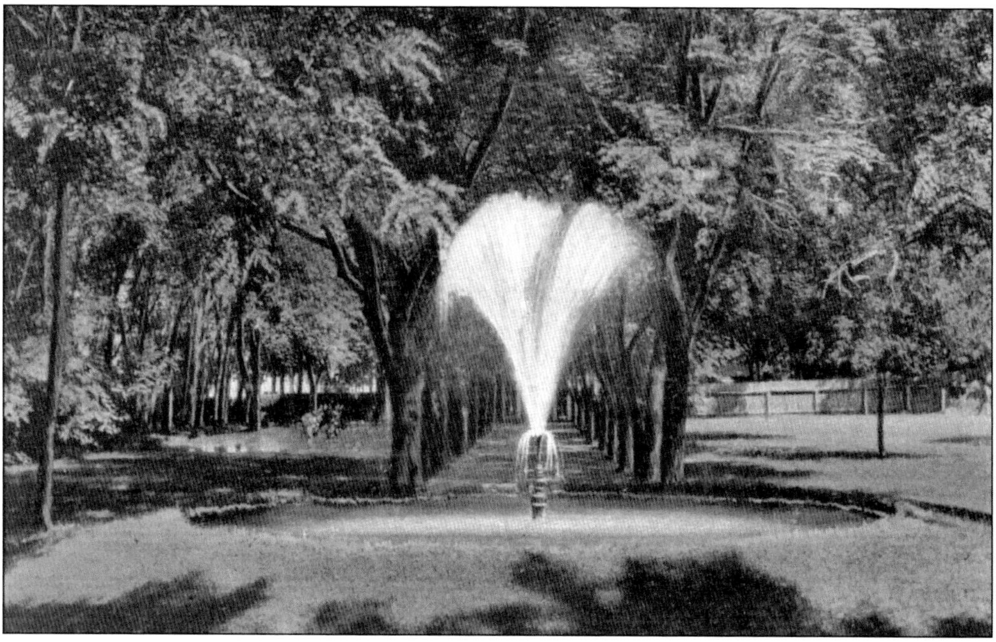

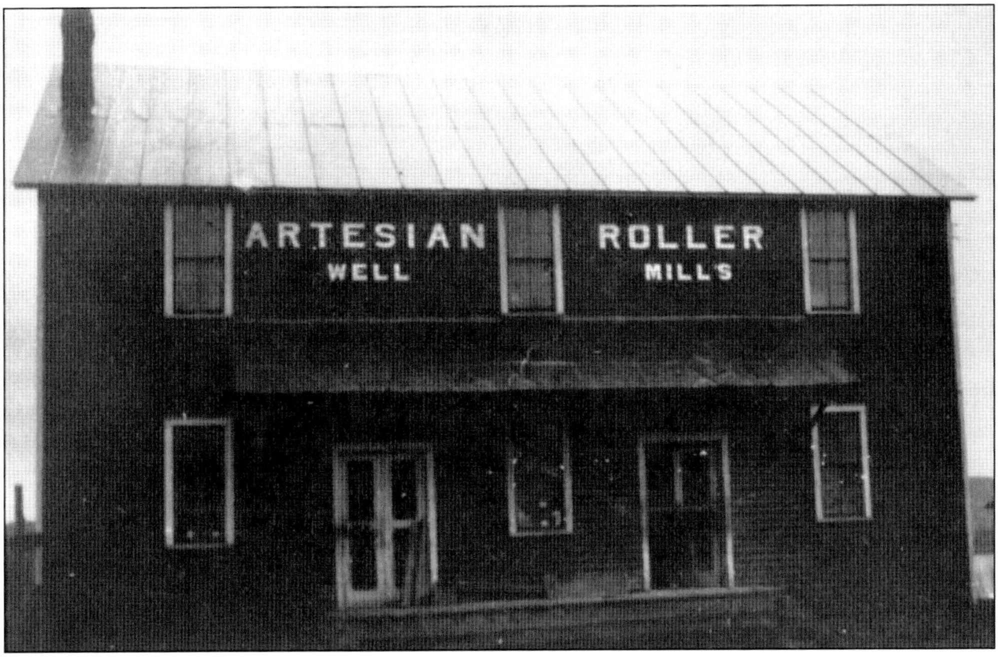

Henry Weniger experimented to see if the force of artesian water could power a flour mill. In 1878, he opened one well with an 8-inch bore and a second with a 6-inch, both 1,014 feet deep. The force of the water propelled two runs of stones able to grind 100 bushels a day. He then sank three more wells. (Courtesy Gene LaPointe.)

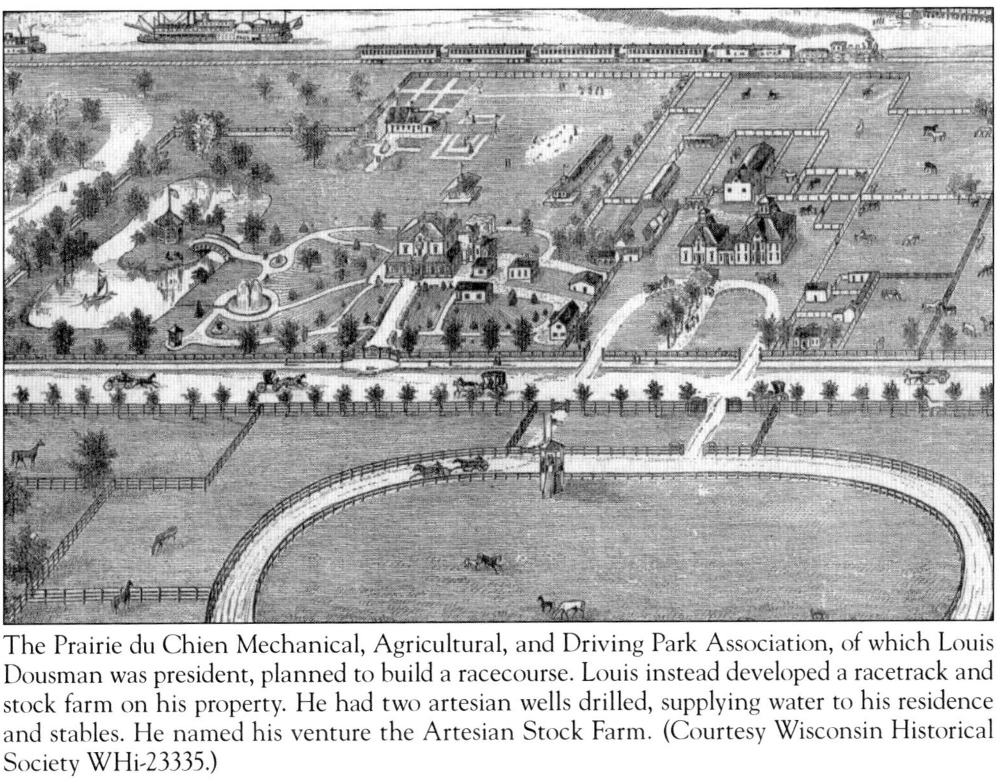

The Prairie du Chien Mechanical, Agricultural, and Driving Park Association, of which Louis Dousman was president, planned to build a racecourse. Louis instead developed a racetrack and stock farm on his property. He had two artesian wells drilled, supplying water to his residence and stables. He named his venture the Artesian Stock Farm. (Courtesy Wisconsin Historical Society WHi-23335.)

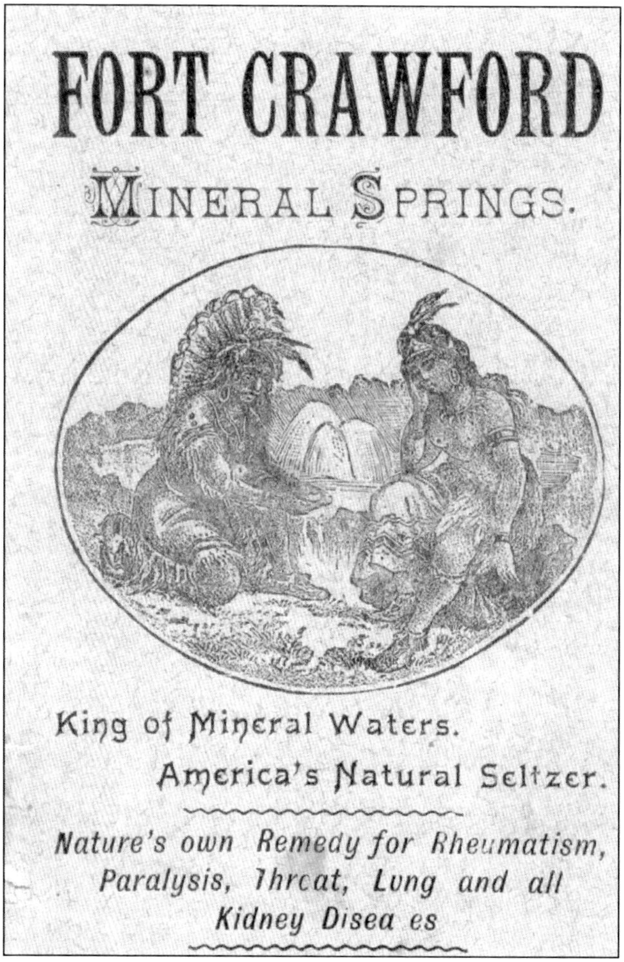

The water from the city well was analyzed and determined to be "a powerful remedial agent" to assist people with rheumatism, dyspepsia, and other ailments. In 1883, the Artesian Well Company granted Henry F. Schultz the right to bottle and sell the water. Until the 1930s, the water was bottled and sold by Schultz and his successors and the Elysian Mineral Water Company. (Courtesy Prairie du Chien Historical Society.)

Dr. John Conant, who cared for the soldiers at the Swift Hospital, saw the medical benefits of the water flowing from the Prairie du Chien well. He opened the Remedial Institute on Bluff Street to treat rheumatism and other chronic diseases. The institute successfully helped people from many states who had "failed to get relief at the Hot Springs of Arkansas."

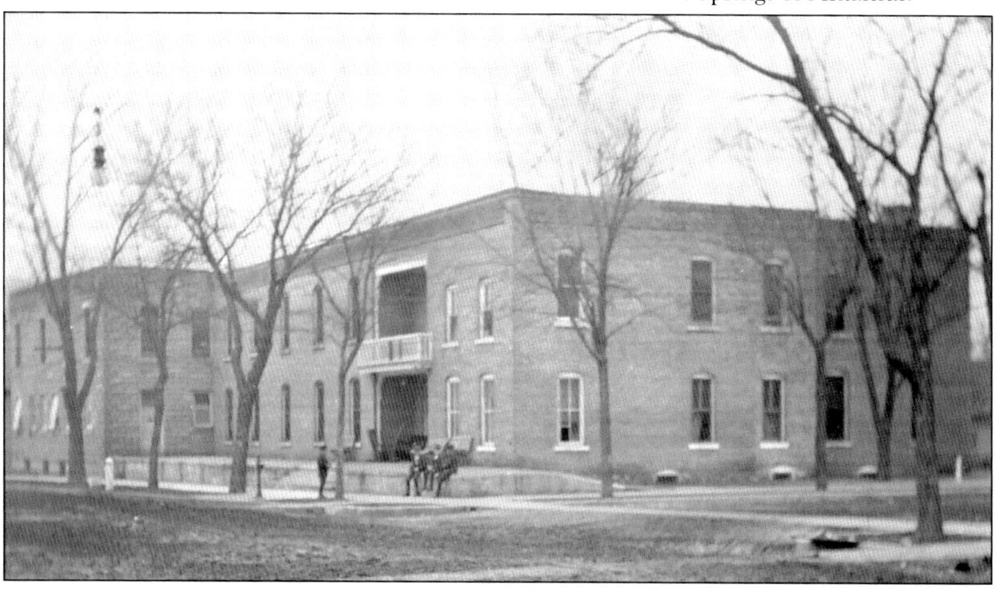

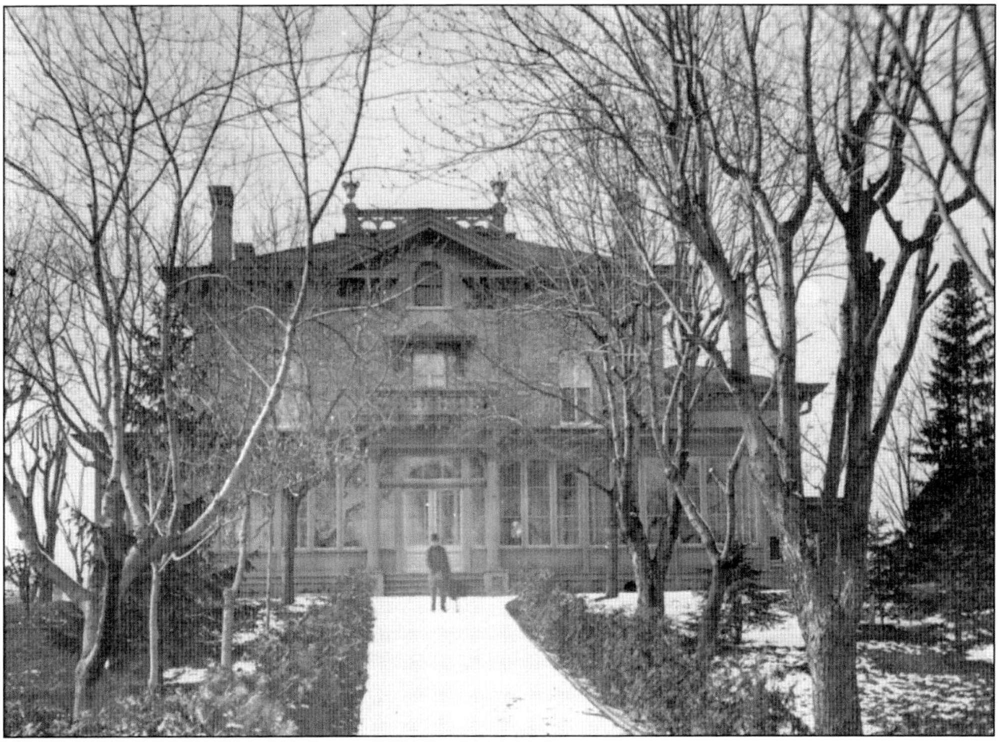

The building material of choice shifted from limestone to Milwaukee cream brick. One of the first to build a home of this brick was Louis Dousman. Louis inherited his father Hercules's vast estate. In 1872, he retained Milwaukee architect E. Townsend Mix to design a house to replace the House on the Mound. (Courtesy Martner Collection.)

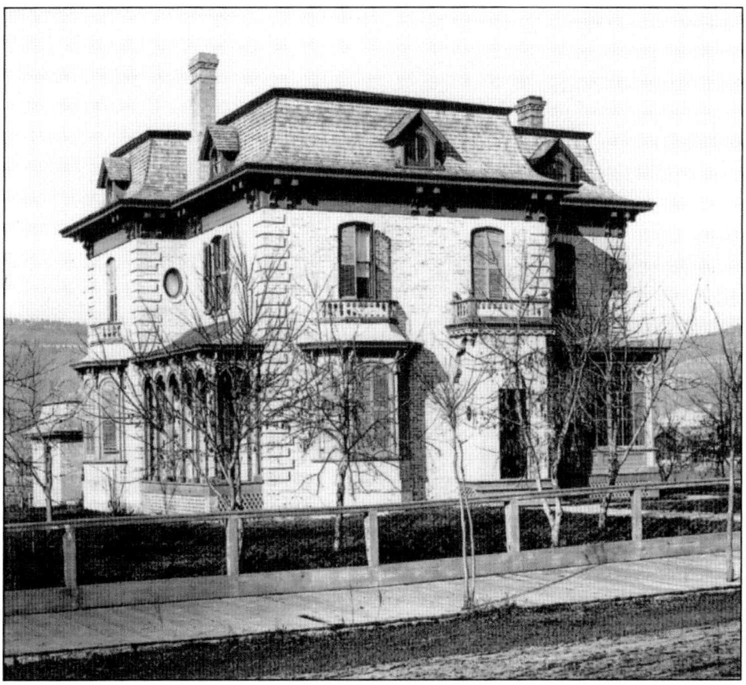

Dr. Darius Mason also constructed a new home in the building boom. He selected the cream brick and the new Second Empire style. According to *The Courier*, "The Dr. intends to make it a No. 1 residence." E. M. Wright later made this his family home. Wright inherited his father's business located on Bluff Street, selling drugs, medicines, books, stationery, and writing and art supplies. (Courtesy Martner Collection.)

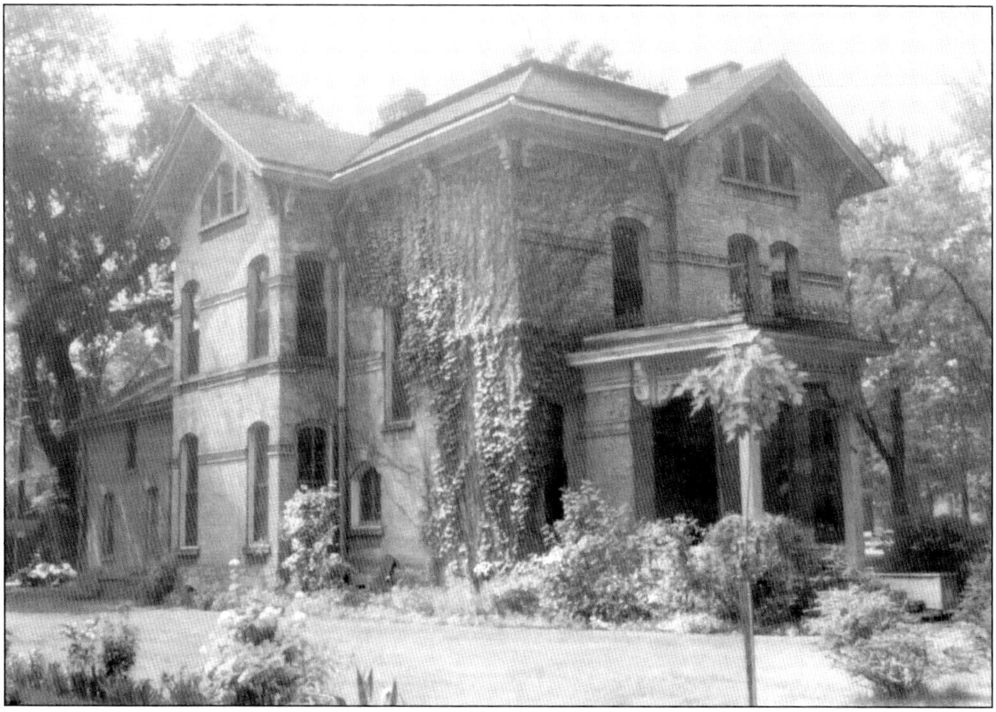

Benjamin F. Fay was also on the board of the Artesian Well Company. He found the site of the city park so pleasurable that he constructed a new home, also of cream brick, across the street. Fay had water piped under Wisconsin Street to his home and stable. The water also propelled a portable revolving fountain on his premises. (Courtesy Antoine family.)

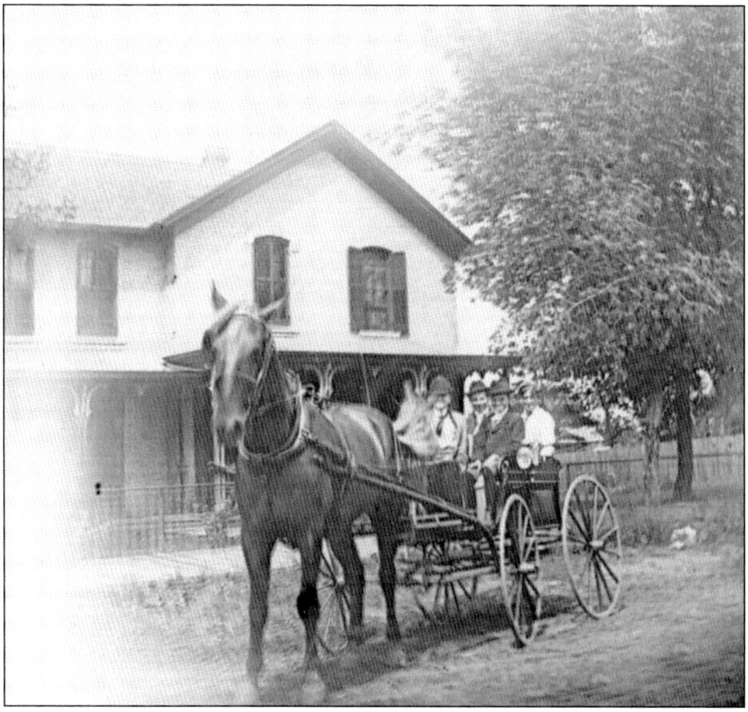

Most of the homes built at this time were less formal and less elaborate. Milwaukee cream brick was favored and chosen by the Garvey brothers. Christopher chose a lot on North Church Street for his home, while James located on South Church Street. Both were equidistant from their store on Bluff Street. (Courtesy Antoine family.)

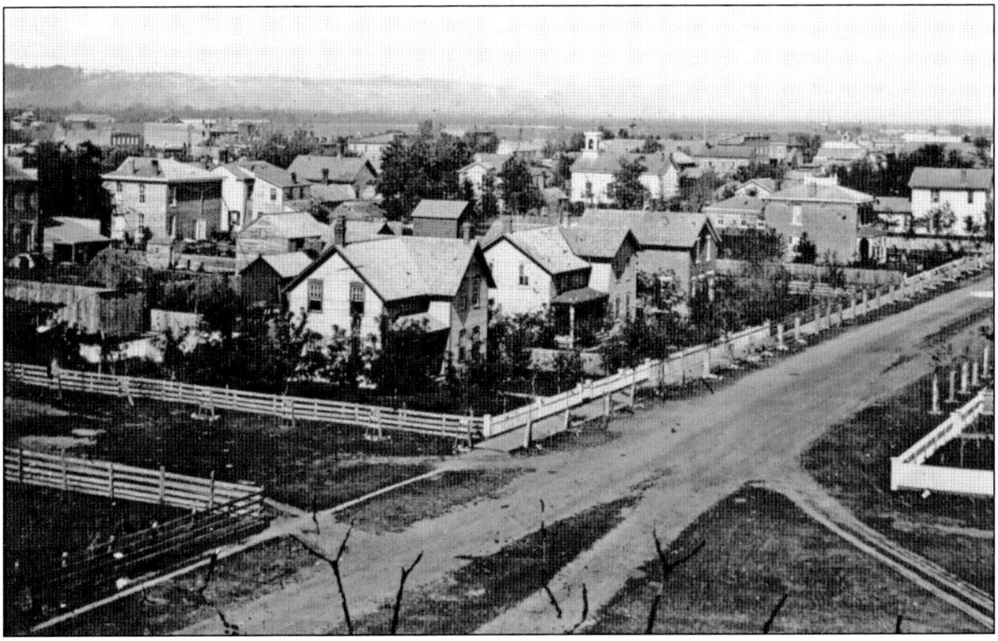

By the mid-1880s, board sidewalks fronted the homes on the major north-south thoroughfares like Minnesota Street. Striving to make Prairie du Chien more attractive, the city fathers had elm trees planted along every residential street in each of the four wards. (Courtesy Wisconsin Historical Society—Cornelius Collection WHi-[c758]5.)

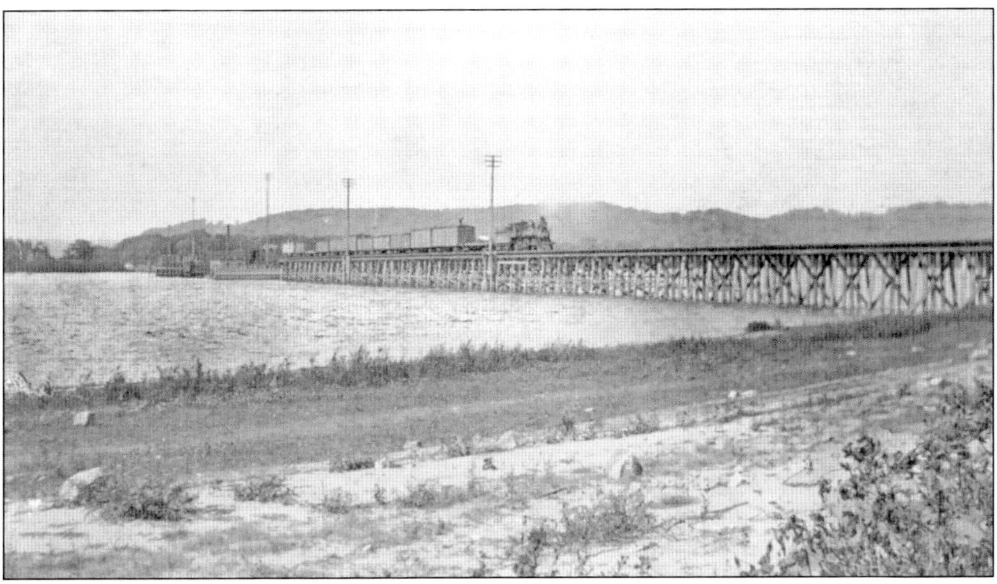

In 1872, John Lawler severed his connection with the Milwaukee and St. Paul Railway, retaining the franchise for transfer of business across the Mississippi River. He focused his attention on a better means to cross the river. The result was a Pile Pontoon Railroad Bridge that opened on April 15, 1872. (Courtesy Martner Collection.)

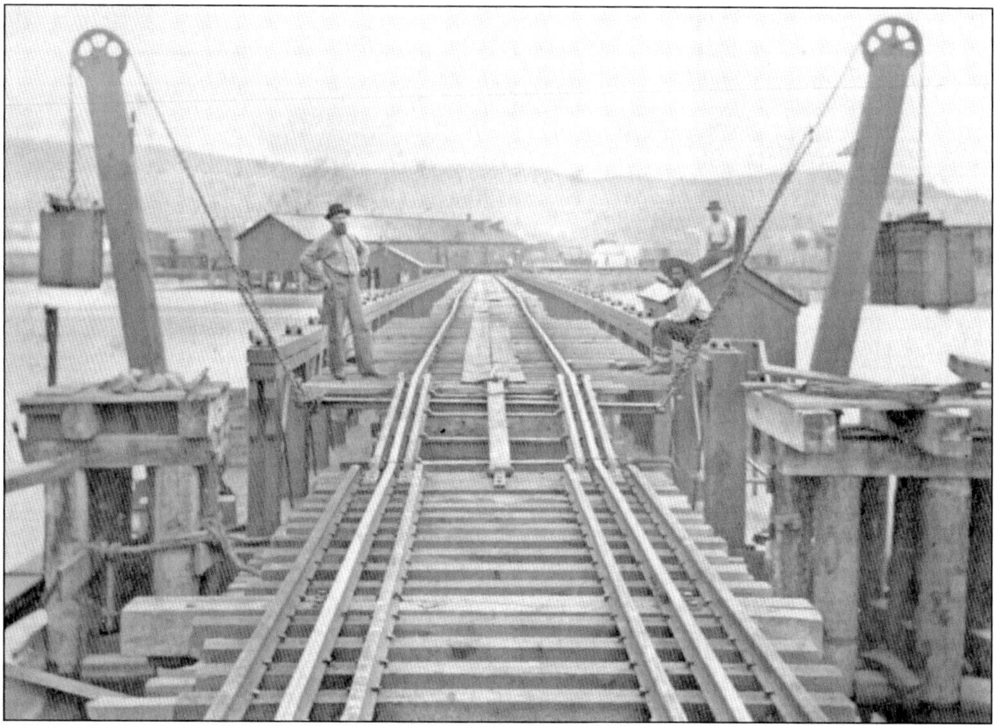

The bridge John Lawler constructed and patented was built of wood pilings, except for an expanse across each channel of the river, which was spanned by a 408-foot pontoon drawbridge. While the piles were fixed, the pontoons opened into the current to allow river traffic to pass. The track on each pontoon could be adjusted. No matter the stage of the river, the tracks on the pontoons connected with the track on the pilings. (Courtesy Martner Collection.)

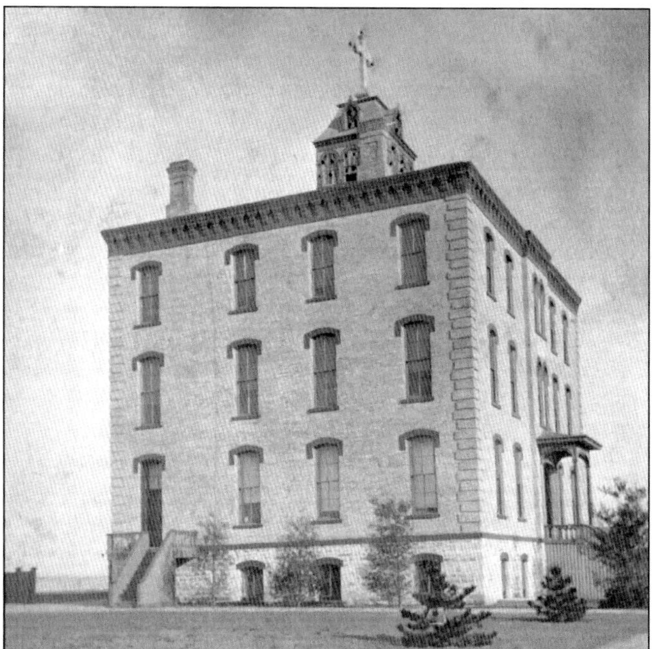

Early in 1872, Father Abbelen, pastor of St. Gabriel's Church, enlisted the aid of John Lawler to convince the School Sisters of Notre Dame to come to Prairie du Chien to teach. Lawler offered to give the sisters 7 acres of the Fort Crawford Tract and money to open a secondary school for young women. The cornerstone for the first building of St. Mary's Institute was laid on June 30, 1872.

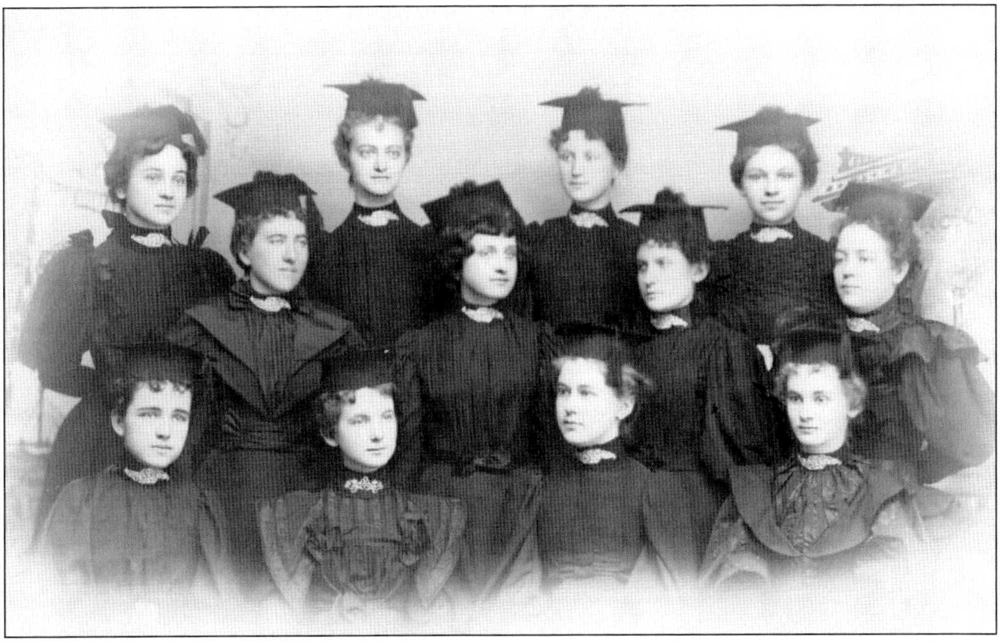

Enrollment increased, and by 1878 more classrooms were needed. John Lawler and Peter Doyle, later secretary of state for Wisconsin, paid E. Townsend Mix to design and erect a structure to the south. In 1883, a dormitory to house 100 students was built. On June 27, 1895, twelve young ladies graduated from St. Mary's Institute. The name of the school was changed to St. Mary's Academy two years later. (Courtesy Antoine family.)

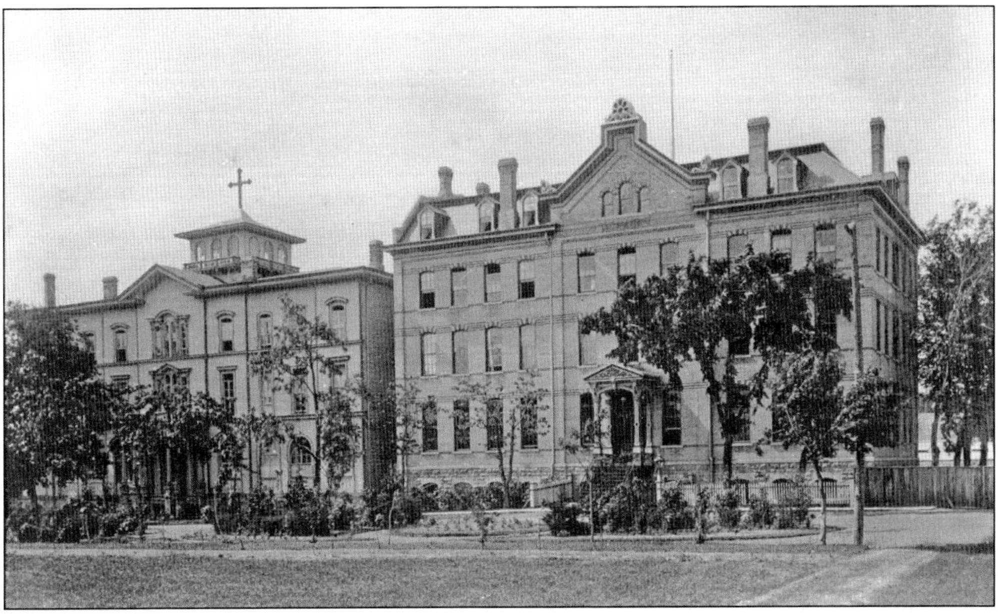

John Lawler purchased the Swift Hospital building in 1866. Lawler and local businessmen established the Prairie du Chien College. When this folded, Lawler then offered the building to the Christian Brothers. Five years later, Lawler gave the property to the Society of Jesus. The Jesuits opened the College of the Sacred Heart, and the frame structure was named Lawler Hall. Enrollment flourished, and in 1882 Koska Hall was built. (Courtesy Antoine family.)

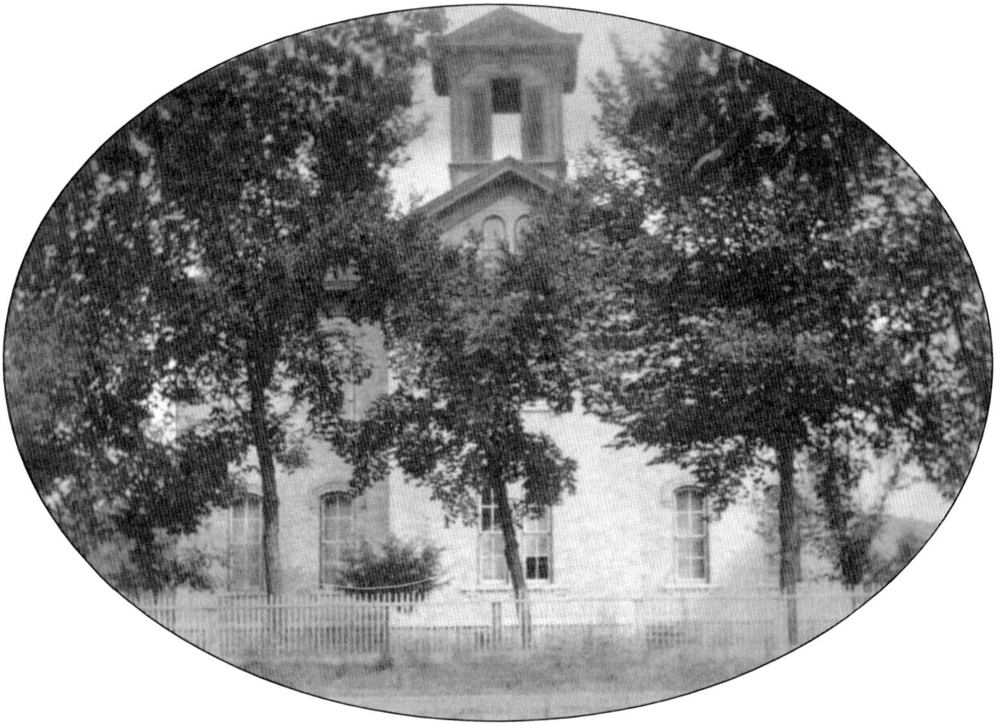

In 1872, Prairie du Chien became an independent school district. Three years later, a school board and superintendent were appointed to organize and operate the district. According to *History of Crawford and Richland Counties*, because of "his well-known zeal in promoting the cause of education," John Lawler was appointed president of the board of education, which had representatives of the four wards. They approved a graded high school. Built of cream brick, it stood until 1917.

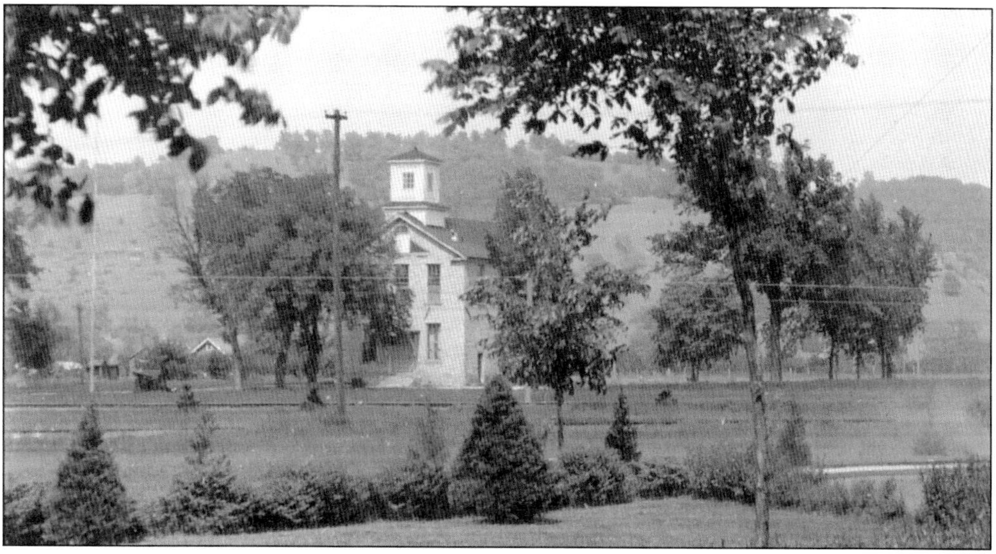

Until the organization of the school district, Catholic religious orders, the German Society, or individuals conducted formal education in Prairie du Chien. In 1842, a school organized in Lower Town and a two-story stone building was constructed in 1857. With the formation of the school district, this became the First Ward School. (Courtesy Ken and Louise White.)

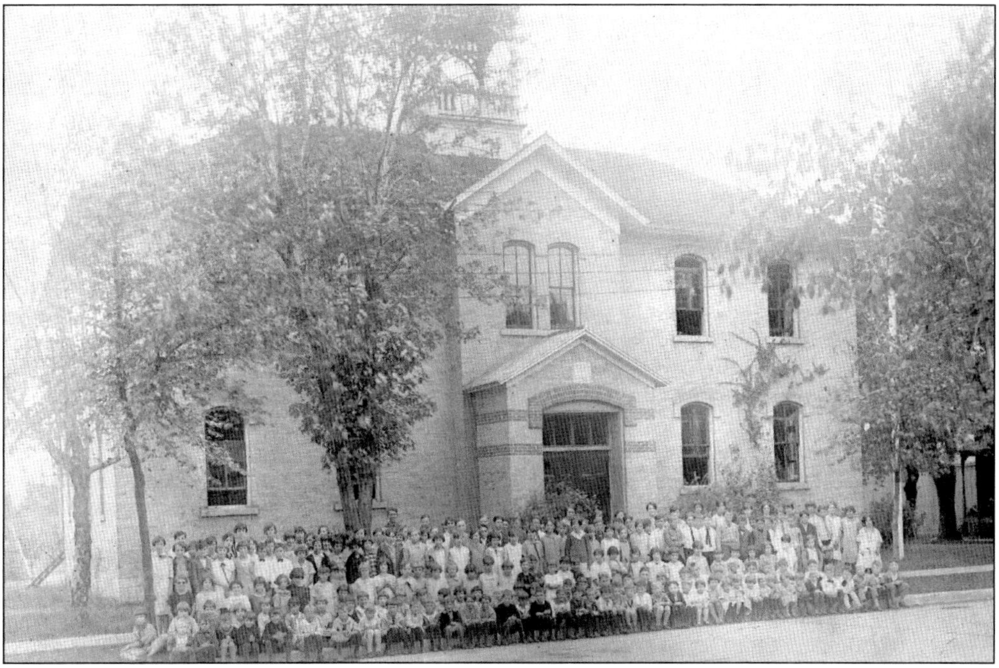

Early Catholic schools operated by sisters of various religious orders were housed in temporary spaces. In the 1860s, the classes shifted to a house built by Fr. Lucien Galtier. Beginning in 1891, a large building for primary grades and the Columbian School housed the growing number of students. This structure continued as part of St. Gabriel's School until 1961. (Courtesy Bob Ziel.)

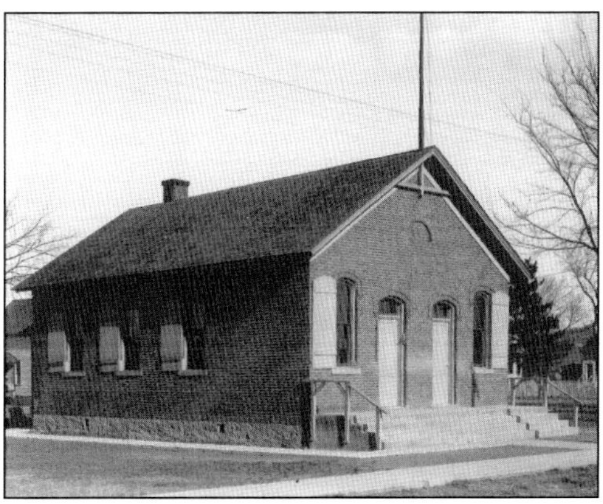

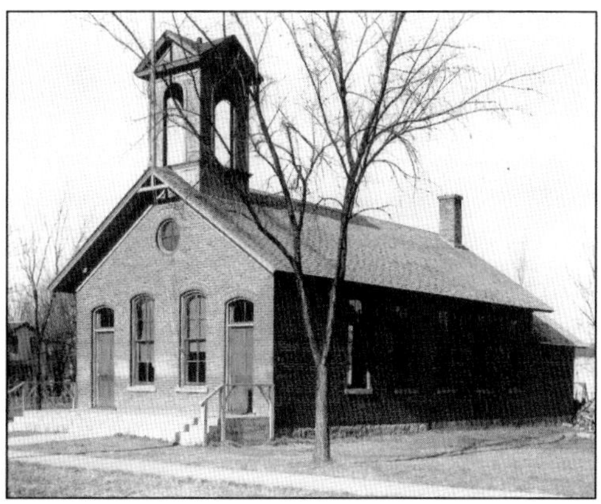

Many of the residents of the Third and Fourth Wards sent their children to St. Gabriel's School. That may be the reason the public schools in these wards were small. The Lincoln School (left) served the Fourth Ward, and the Washington School (right), called "Little Red," stood on Park Street. (Courtesy Gene La Pointe.)

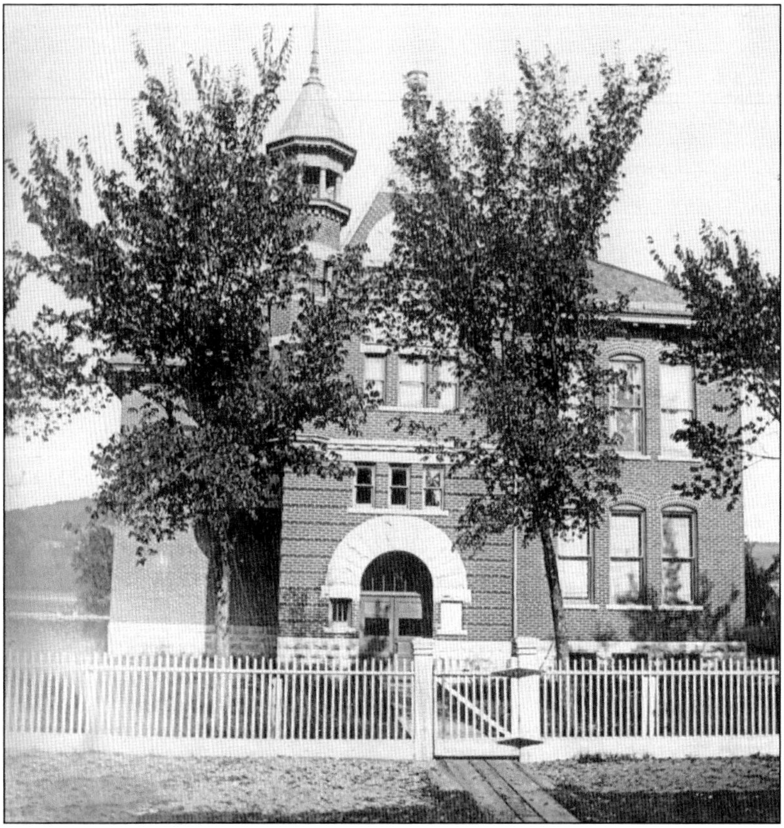

In 1897, a red stone structure was erected on Minnesota Street north of the graded high school. This new building was designated the high school, while the older building housed the primary grades. (Courtesy Antoine family.)

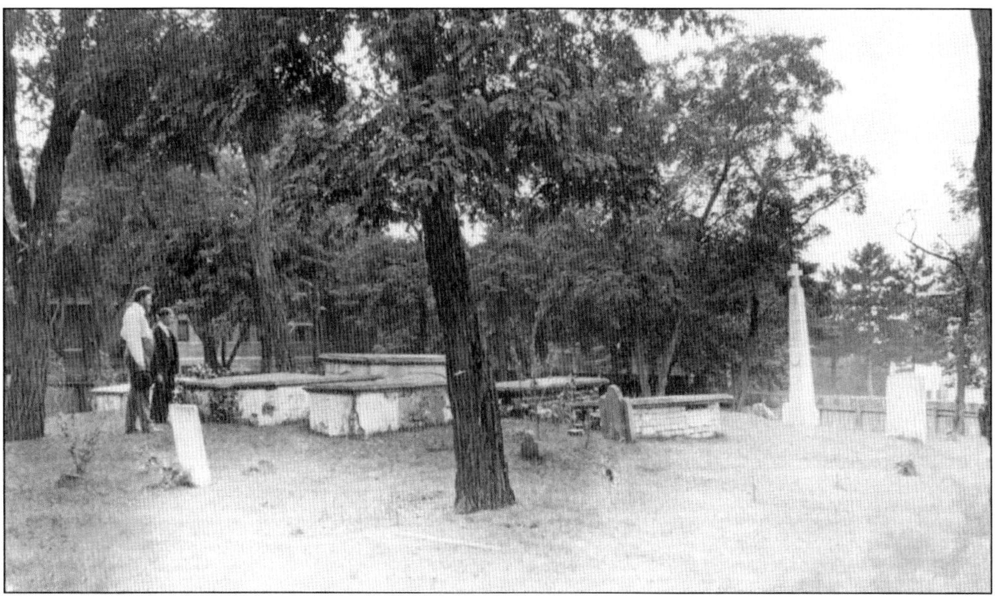

North of John Lawler's home was the old Fort Crawford Cemetery. It was the final resting place of officers and their family members who had died while stationed at Fort Crawford. Later soldiers who had died while patients at the Swift Hospital were buried there. Lawler maintained the cemetery. In 1905, Congress appropriated funds for its care. (Courtesy Martner Collection.)

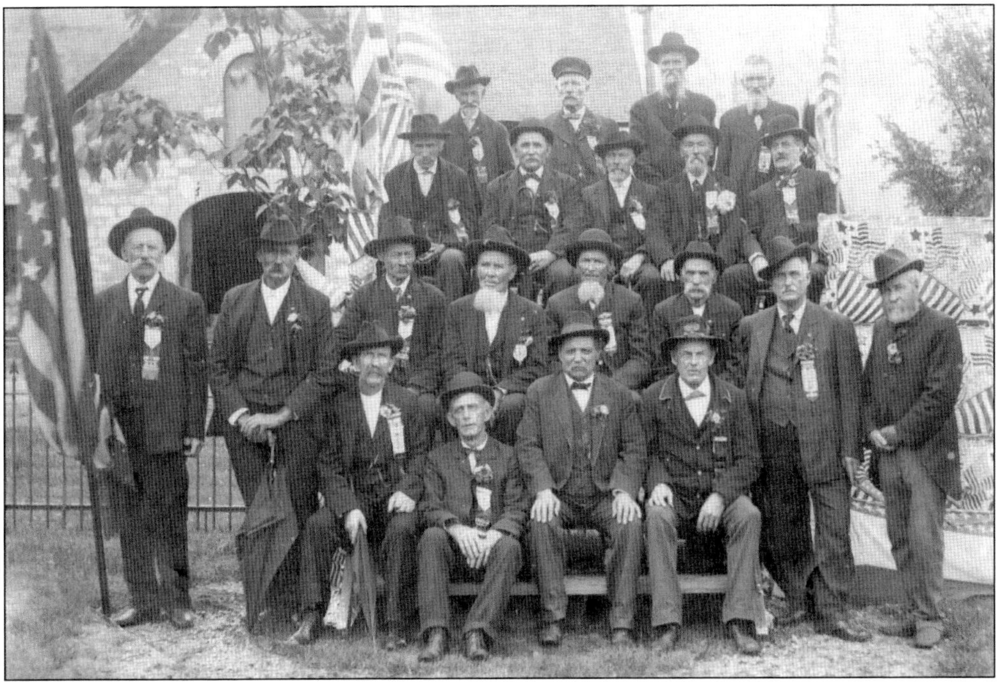

Philip W. Plummer Post 37 of the Grand Army of the Republic organized on July 18, 1882. The following year, the post conducted Memorial Day observations with a program at the Fort Crawford Cemetery. The post continued in existence until 1941 with the death of William Huard. (Courtesy Martner Collection.)

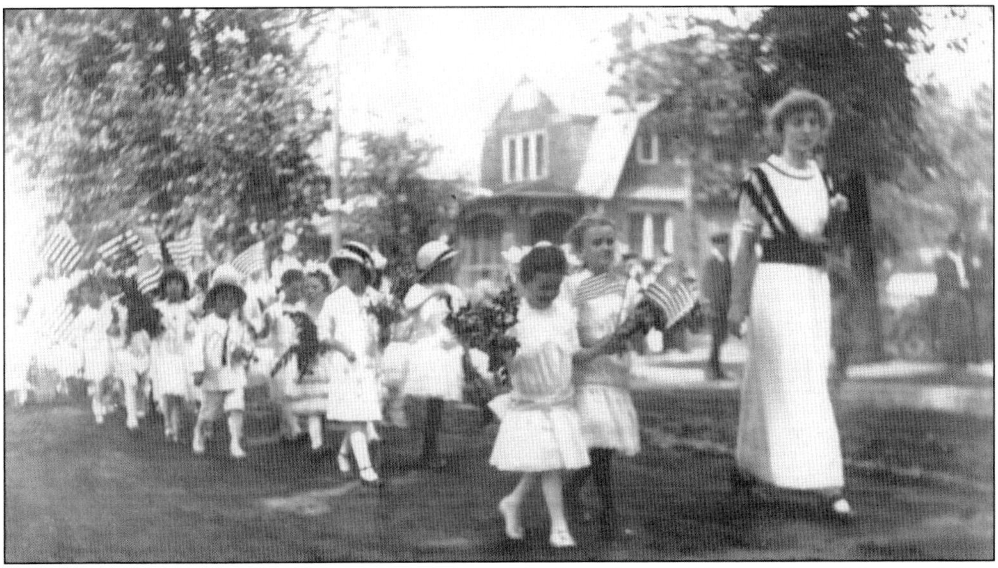

After the proclamation that a day should be set aside to honor fallen soldiers, Memorial Day ceremonies at Prairie du Chien began with a parade that marched along East Bluff Street down South Church Street to the cemetery. Included in the event were veterans, members of fire companies, and children carrying flowers. After speeches, renditions of patriotic songs, and readings, the children placed their flowers on the graves. (Courtesy Prairie du Chien Historical Society—Grelle Collection.)

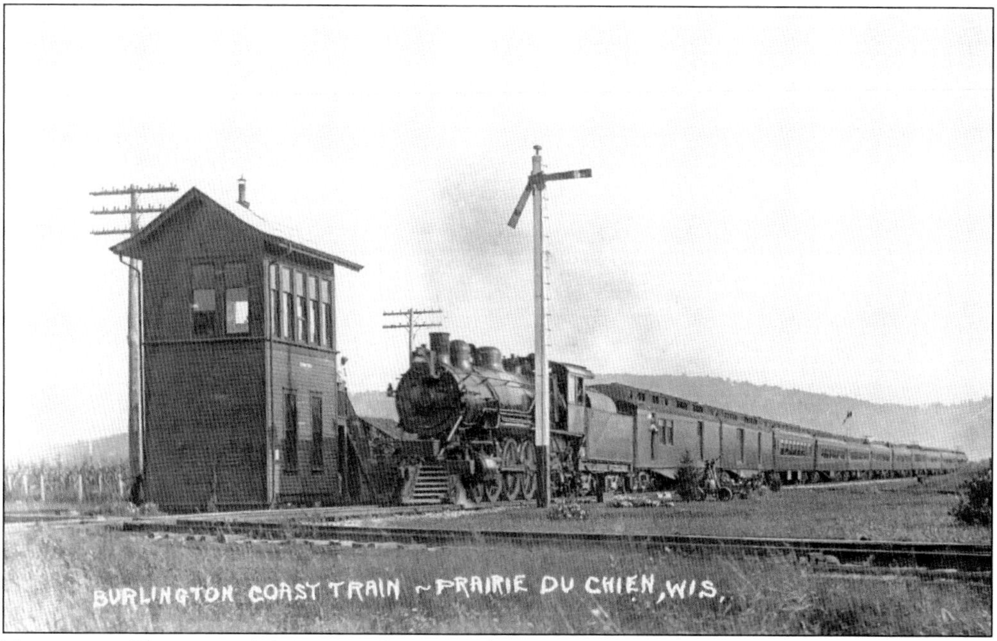

To connect Chicago with Minneapolis-St. Paul, the Chicago, Burlington, and Quincy Railroad plotted a new line along the east bank of the Mississippi River. In August 1886, the first train crossed the Wisconsin River into Prairie du Chien. Taxis waited at the station to transport visitors to the Remedial Institute or Commercial House. (Courtesy Bob Ziel.)

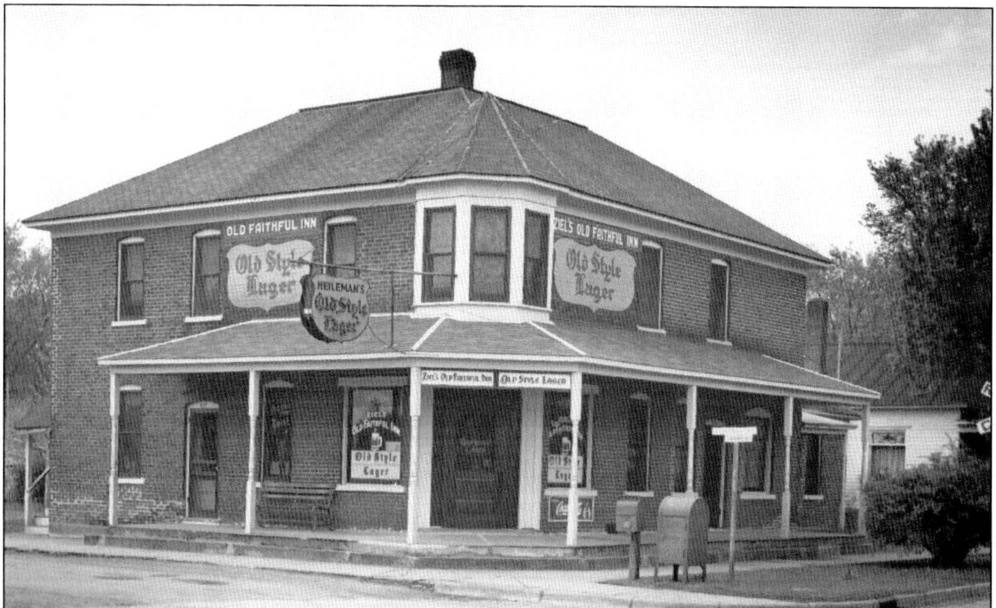

As the railroad progressed laying track, the coming of the rails spurred construction of new buildings. *The Union* newspaper reported, "W. Tesar is erecting a structure in the north west corner of Bluff and Illinois streets. . . . T. B. Norris' new building corner of Illinois and Bluff streets." These buildings, like the Old Faithful Inn, catered to the needs of trainmen and passengers. (Courtesy Prairie du Chien Historical Society—Peckham Collection.)

Immigrants from Bohemia began settling in Crawford County after the Civil War. By the mid-1880s, many families resided in Prairie du Chien. Many of them spoke and understood only Bohemian and wished to have their own parish. In January 1891, several their native language residents approached John Lawler for a donation of land on which to build a church and rectory. The cornerstone for St. John Nepomuc was laid that same year. (Courtesy Ken and Louise White.)

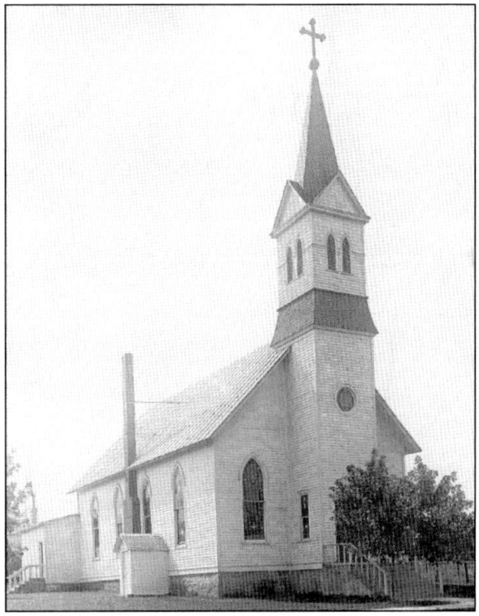

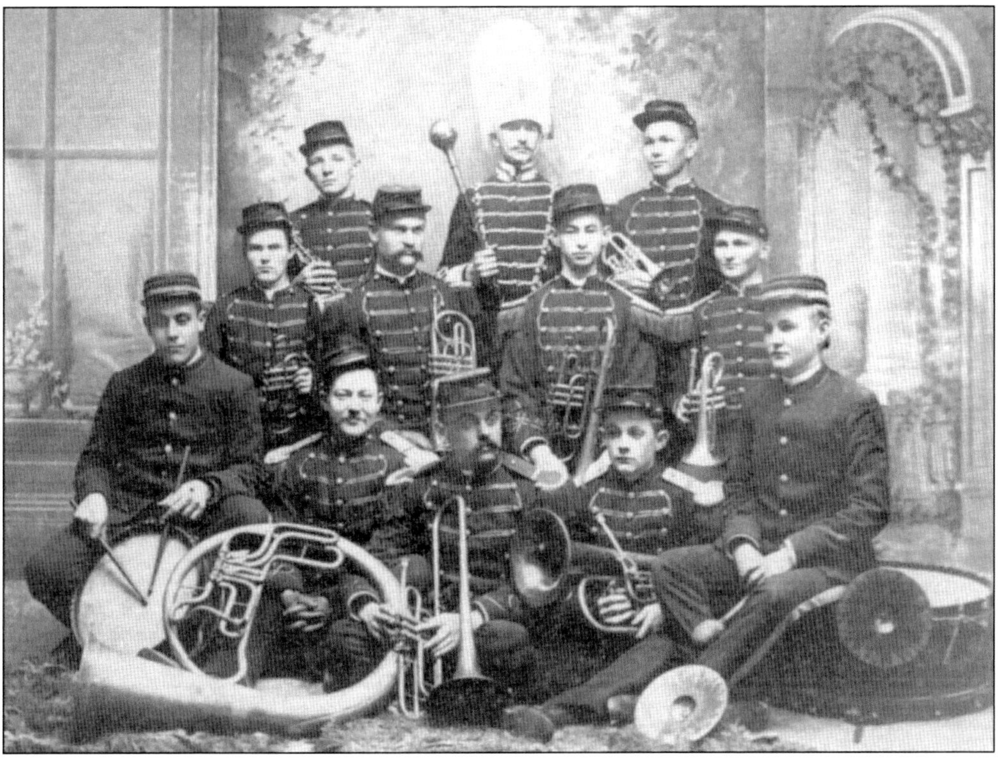

The Bohemian Band of Prairie du Chien organized in 1879 under the direction of Matthew Chapek, reorganizing with new members in 1881. The musicians were Matthew Chapek, M. Tahle, W. Tesar, Joseph Zeman, C. Zeman, Matt Hanzlicek, Fred Batchelder, Charles Pion, and Winzel Strauski. Some of these men also played in Macket's Celebrated Brass Band, which is seen here. C. Zeman is at the top left, Joseph Zeman is at the top right, and Fred Batchelder is second to the left in front. (Courtesy Antoine family.)

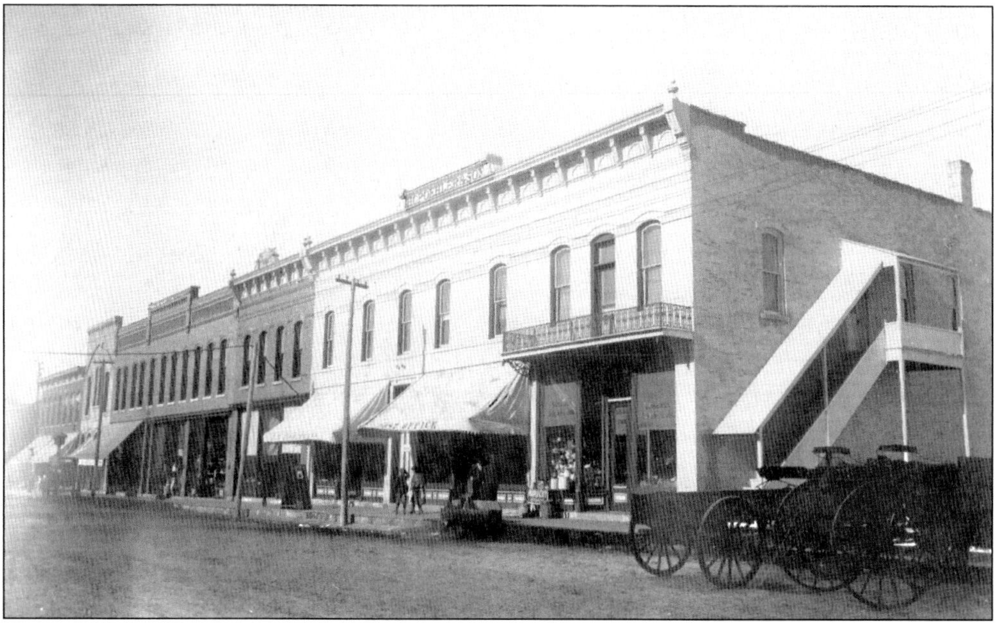

In 1894, a group of businessmen organized to equip the community with electric lights. As the 19th century neared its close, Prairie du Chien was a safe, stable community. Businesses along Bluff Street prospered, two trains provided daily passenger service, public and private schools offered education to all, and quiet residential streets spread north and south from Bluff Street. (Courtesy Prairie du Chien Historical Society—Otto Collection.)

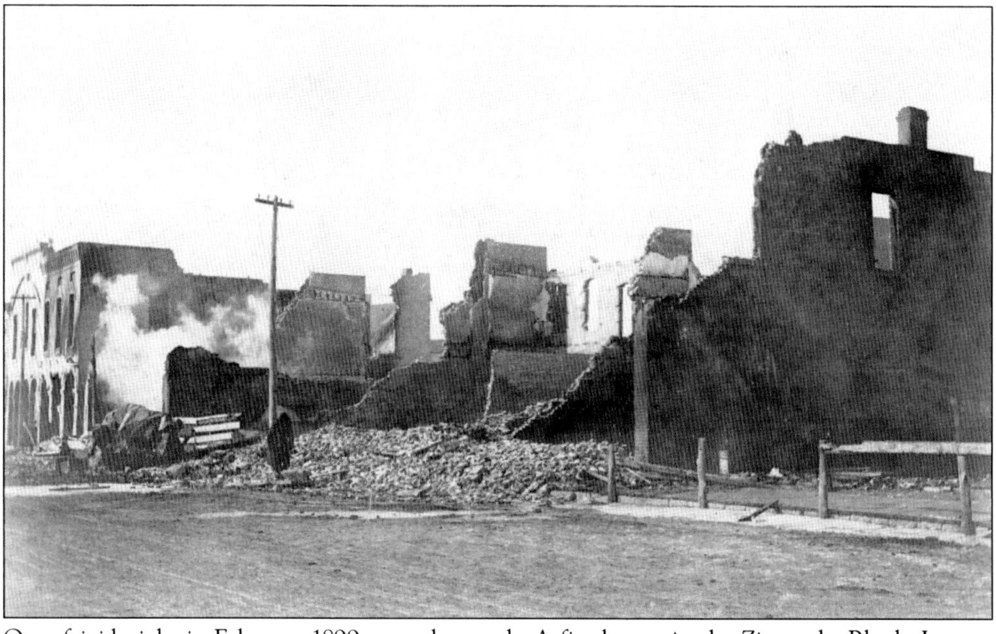

On a frigid night in February 1899, tragedy struck. A fire began in the Zieprecht Block. It soon spread to Horace Beach's hardware before moving on to P. Uher and Sons. By the time the fire had been put out, four blocks of buildings were destroyed, and the inventory of 10 businesses lay in ashes. The Poehler family lost a block of four stores, their business, and their living quarters. (Courtesy Jim Trentin.)

Four

A Comfortable Community

I know this little town lives unproclaimed
On the banks of a rushing river….
In the quiet of this town
There is something living gently—

—Laura Sherry, 1931

The merchants of Bluff Street reconstructed their buildings that had been destroyed by fire on that long day in February 1899. They restocked their shelves and business continued, but downtown had grown as much as it ever would. Several smaller fires would change the configuration of Bluff Street but not enlarge the commercial district. Bluff Street, though, became the gathering place of Prairie du Chien. Fraternal and business organizations held their meetings and social gatherings in Bluff Street buildings. For special occasions, the street could be transformed into a fairground. Any parade marched the length of the street, and everyone gathered to marvel at the floats and applaud the precise marching.

Horses and wagons gave way to gasoline-powered vehicles, so there no longer was a need for water to flow along the curbs, but the water fountains still bubbled. When a bridge was finally built to span the Mississippi River, the entrance/exit opened onto Bridge Street joined to Bluff Street.

Here was the heart of the community, where a person could walk up and down the sidewalks and purchase food, clothing, hardware, notions, toys, or whatever was needed. He or she could then visit a bank, stop for lunch, ice cream or a cold draft, and even inspect the latest model of car. Local and national events were played out on Bluff Street.

Beyond Bluff Street, arching elms created a cool canopy for a pleasant stroll along residential streets. Large stylish houses were being constructed on South Church Street, and these needed to be inspected as they progressed from basement to roof trim. Beyond them, the Steiner and Polodna families were busy building houses on the ends of town.

As the century turned, some of the men who were building new homes also invested in small manufactories that offered employment to men and women.

Prairie du Chien had not become the economic center Alfred Brunson had touted and promoted. Rather, it was the retreat Judson had envisioned.

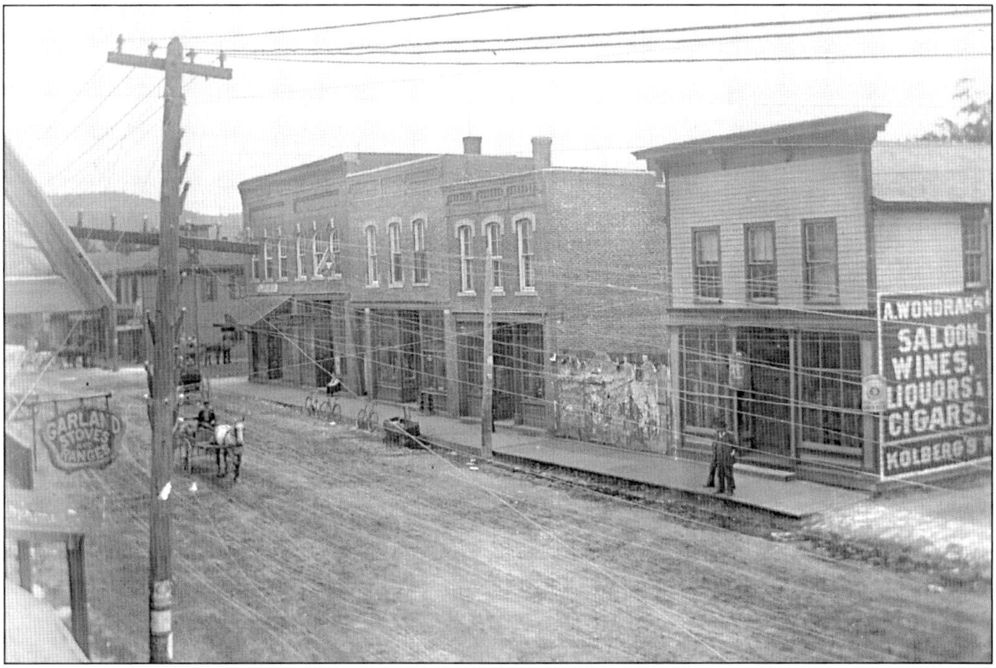

In the great fire of 1899, the buildings on the other side of Bluff Street had been threatened. Burning debris blew on the roof of the Wandrak Building. *The Union* speculated that had the building burned, the Wachuta Block would have caught on fire, stating it would be "hard to say where it could have stopped." But fire companies from as far away as LaCrosse helped save the city from complete disaster. (Courtesy Antoine family.)

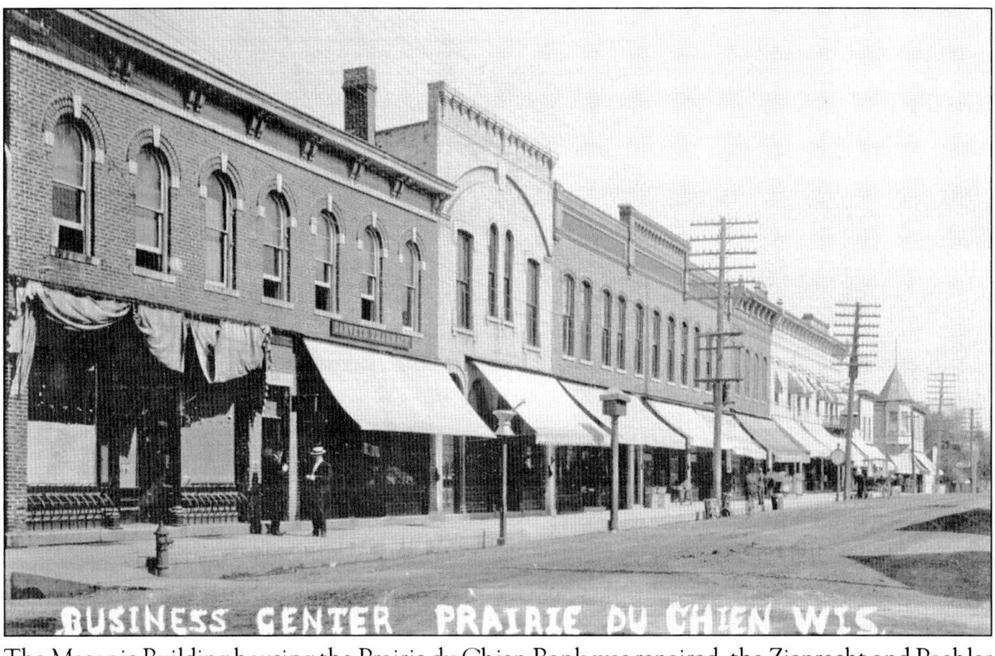

The Masonic Building housing the Prairie du Chien Bank was repaired, the Zieprecht and Poehler Blocks to the east were reconstructed, and telephone and electric lines were restrung. The business center was now intact. (Courtesy Antoine family.)

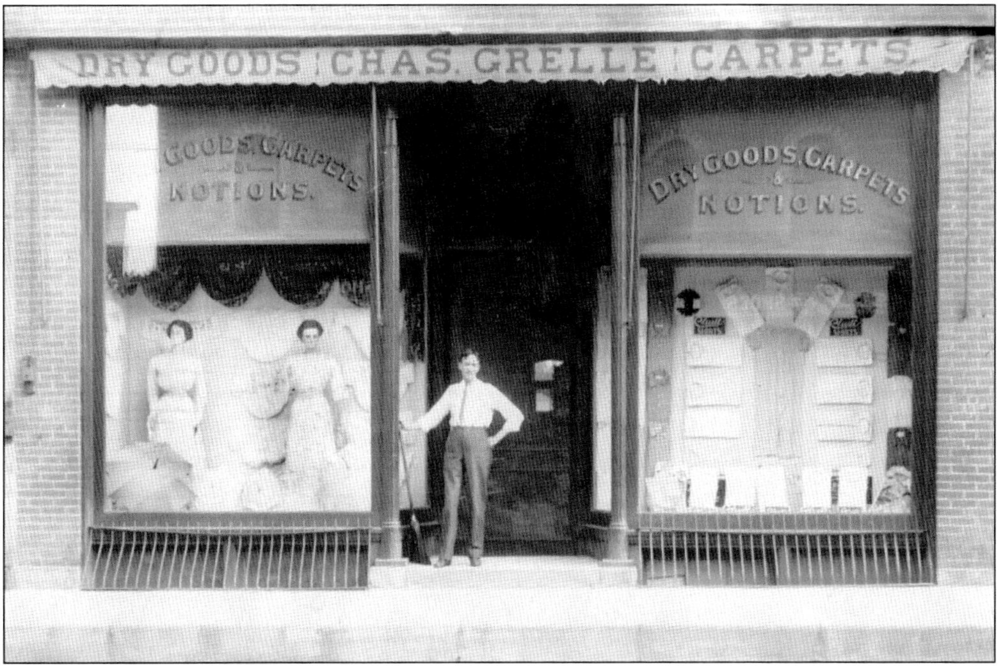

The dry goods business of Charles Grelle Jr. was severely damaged in the 1899 fire; only the west and front walls remained standing. He managed to remove only a small portion of his inventory but continued to operate out of the Case Building until his store was rebuilt. (Courtesy Bob Ziel.)

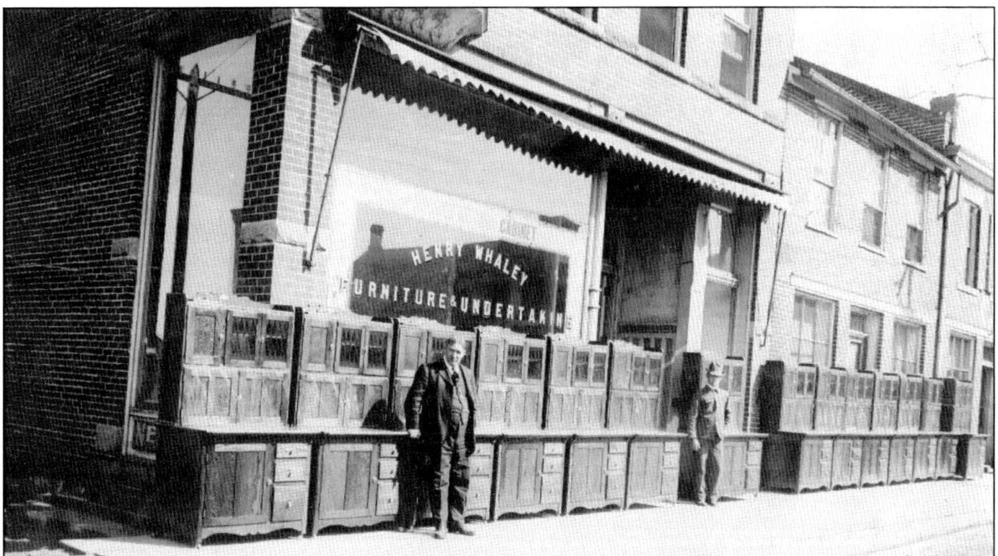

Christopher Grelle, Charles's grandfather, was one of the German immigrants to make Prairie du Chien his home. He was a cabinetmaker and undertaker. On the site of his business, his grandson built a store in 1900. Henry Whaley continued in the same occupation in the Grelle Block, offering the latest styles in home furnishings and undertaking services. (Courtesy Ken and Louise White.)

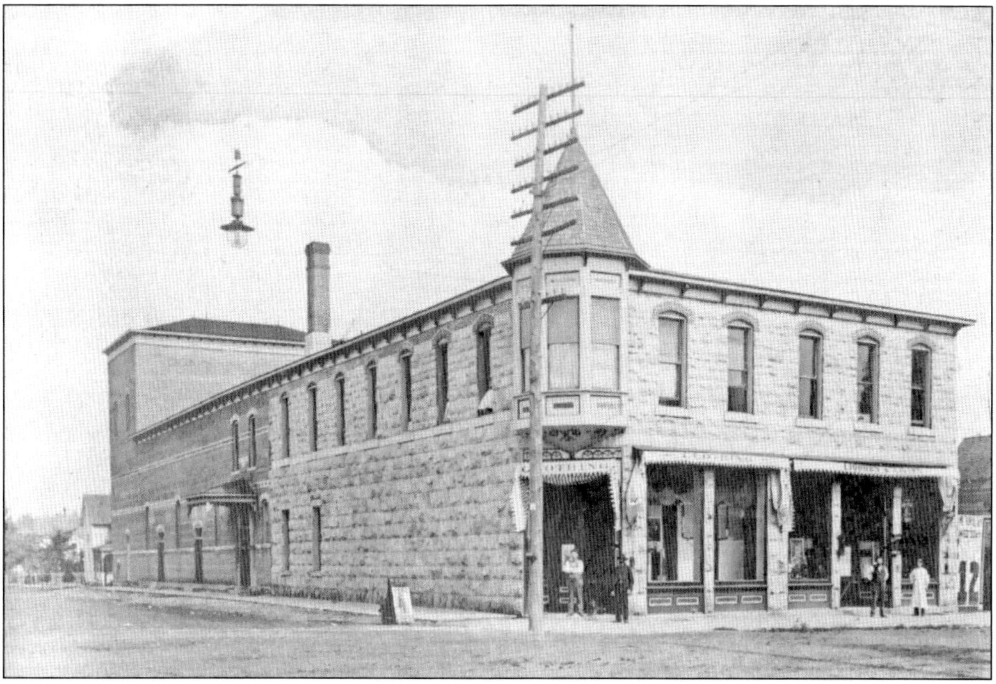

In 1823, Judge James Duane Doty applied to the Post Office Department for the establishment of a post office at Prairie du Chien. When the application was granted, Doty became postmaster. The post office was housed in a variety of structures, changing location with changes in postmasters. In 1915, it relocated to the Metropolitan Block. (Courtesy Bob Ziel.)

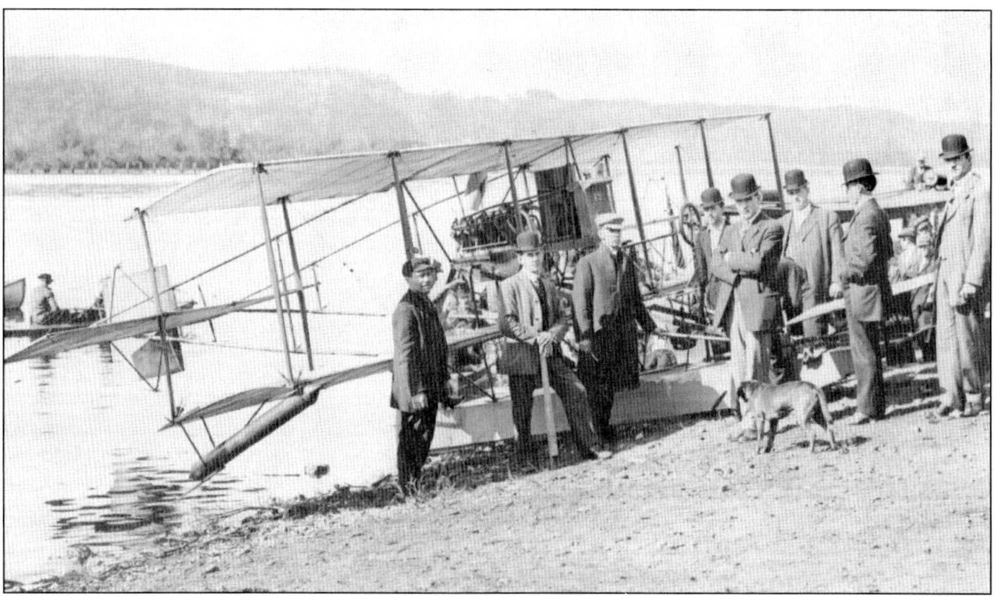

On October 11, 1911, Hugh A. Robinson landed his Curtiss hydro-aeroplane at Prairie du Chien. He brought the first mail for residents of the city by air, including a personal note for Patricia Garvey. Upon Robinson's arrival, Mayor McCloskey and many people, on foot and by water, greeted him. Robinson's flight was the first transportation of mail by an aquaplane. (Courtesy Ken and Louise White.)

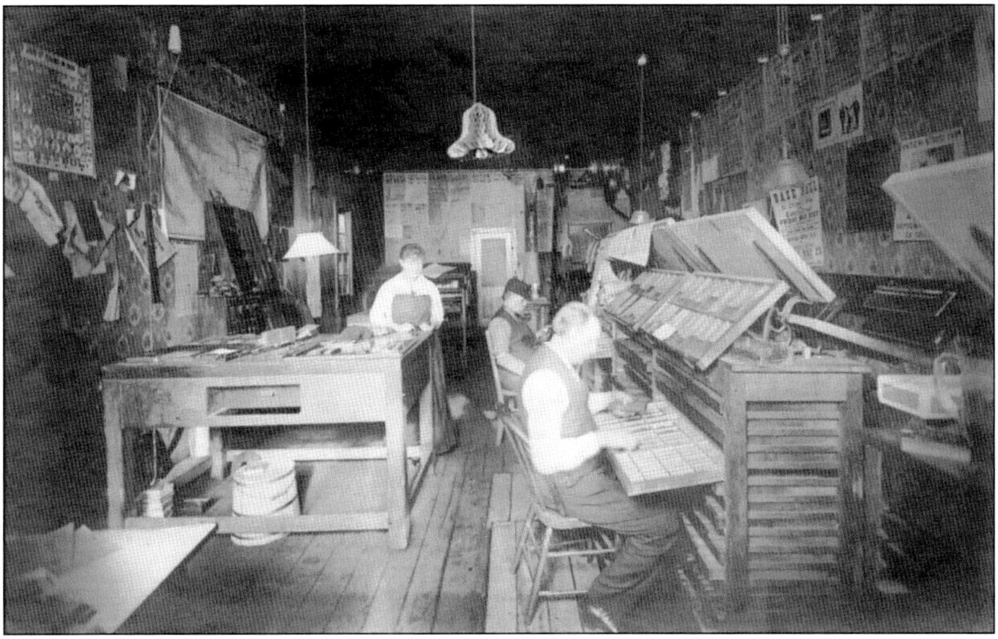

Wallace W. Martner established *The Crawford County Press* in 1904. It joined *The Courier* and *The Union* in publishing weekly newspapers. Martner also maintained an office on Bluff Street. *The Union* ceased operations in 1911. That same year, Henry E. Howe purchased *The Courier*, which continues to be published by the Howe family. (Courtesy Martner Collection.)

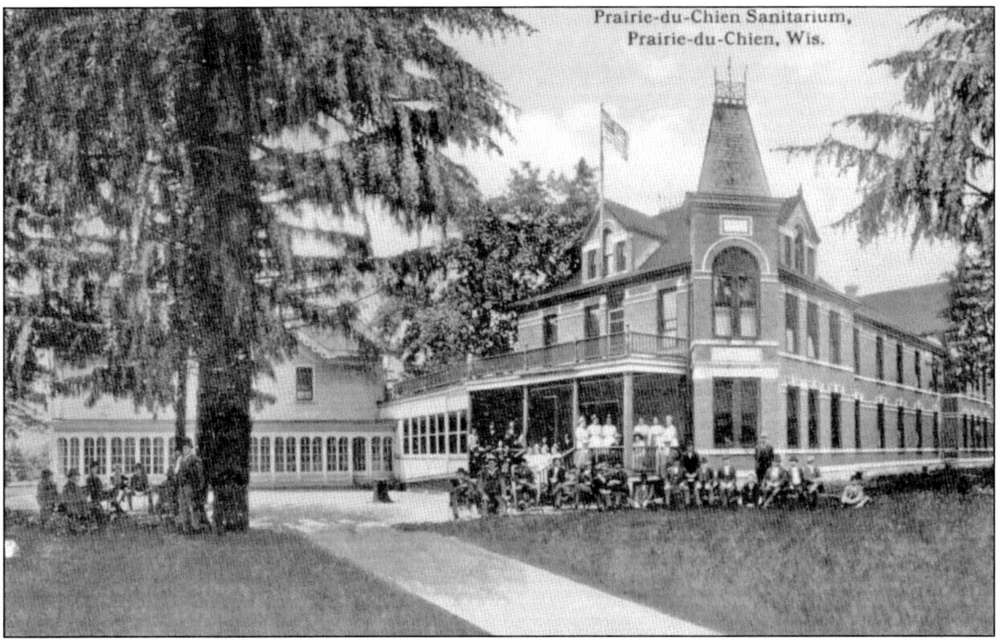

F. W. Bayless of Elkader, Iowa, purchased the Lawler family property in 1902. He, too, wished to offer treatment using artesian water for inflammatory rheumatism, arthritis, sciatica, neuritis, and "other ailments." Over a 996-foot-deep well, he constructed a long two-story, redbrick building, naming it the Prairie du Chien Sanitarium. Baths were located in the basement, and rooms were on the upper two floors. (Courtesy Virginia Antoine.)

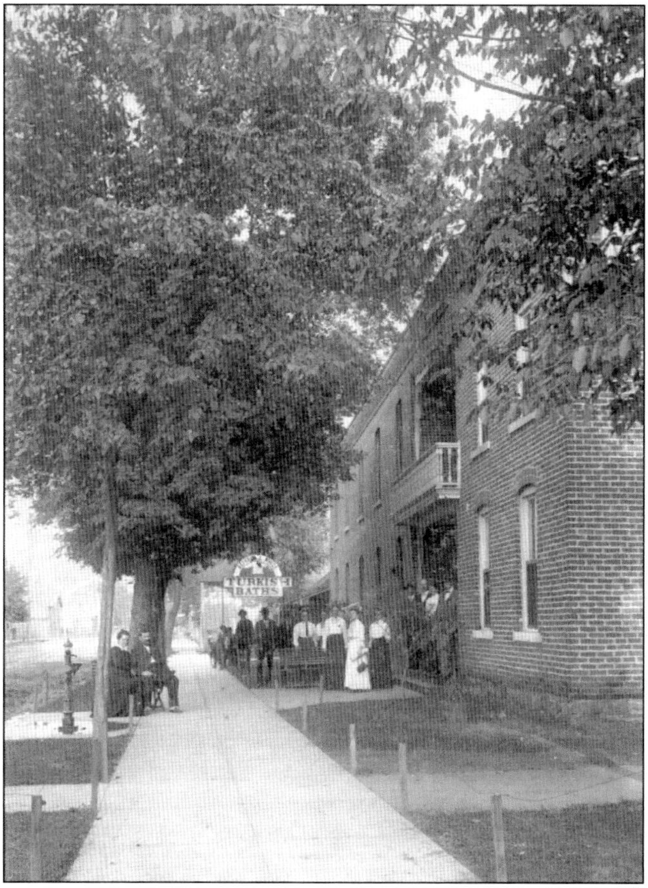

The Remedial Institute on Bluff Street was acquired by Dr. J. W. Rathbun and operated as Rathbun and Rosecrans Sanitarium. It offered the same cures using artesian water as did the Prairie du Chien Sanitarium. Known as "The Old San," Rathbun's facility slowly changed to a hotel with the amenities of Turkish and Russian baths. The hotel was destroyed by fire in 1964. (Courtesy Martner Collection.)

In 1891, Robert D. Paris purchased the Brillion and Famechon hotel properties and offered stock in the Prairie du Chien Woolen Mills. In the adapted buildings, the employees spun, dyed, and wove wool into yard goods and blankets. By 1930, the company produced 500,000 yards per year. (Courtesy Bittner family.)

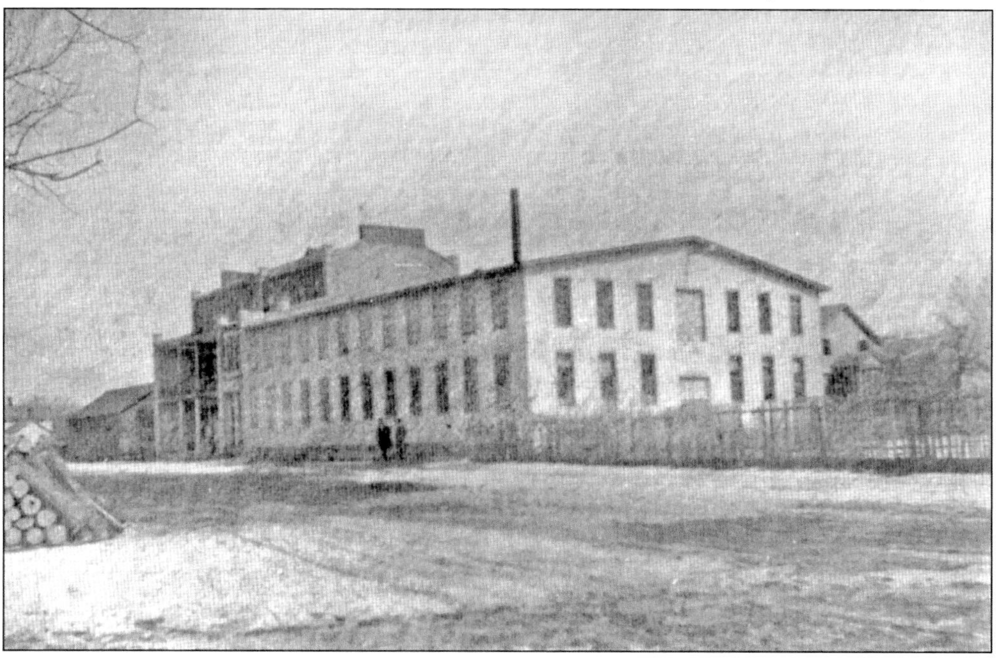

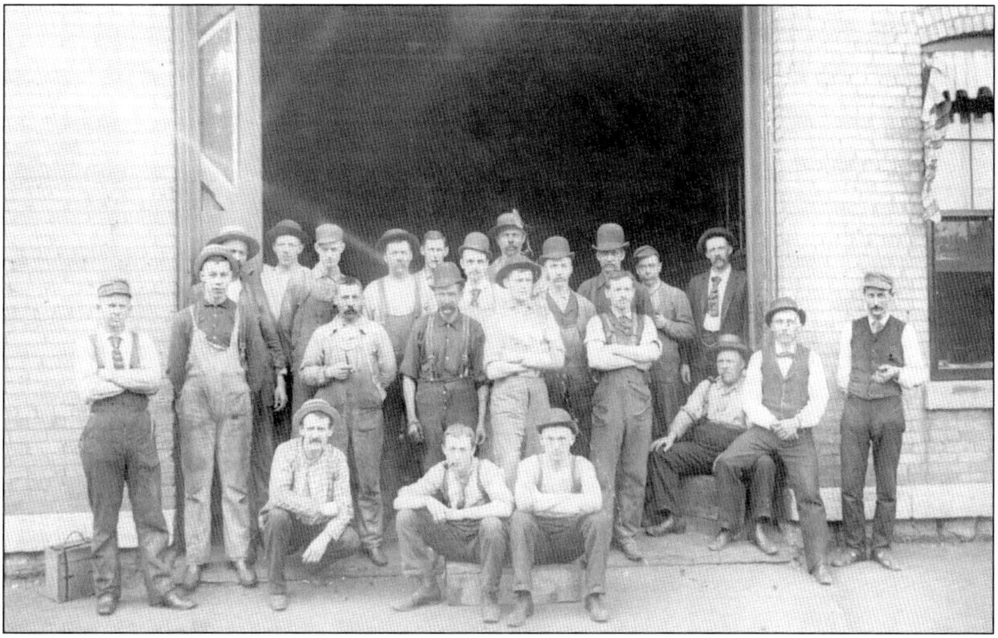

Enlarged several times, the mills employed 135 people at the business's peak. In 1935, Burgess Cellulose purchased the facility, retooling to fabricate insulation and sponges. To the residents, it was known as "the sponge factory," smelling like rotten eggs. In 1965, the 3M Company took over the plant and made synthetic sponges until 2001. (Courtesy Prairie du Chien Historical Society—Dyrud Collection.)

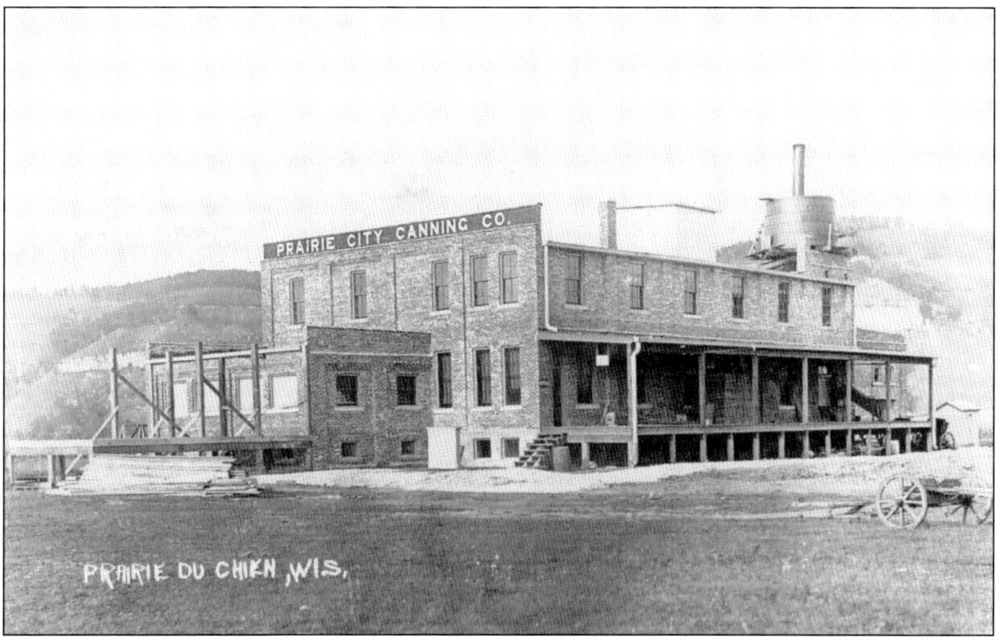

The Prairie du Chien Canning Company organized in 1912. Owners purchased the Nugent and Smircna farms nestled next to the bluffs and constructed a two-story factory. On 250 acres, employees planted and harvested tomatoes and cabbages. Area truck farms also produced vegetables for the company. (Courtesy Martner Collection.)

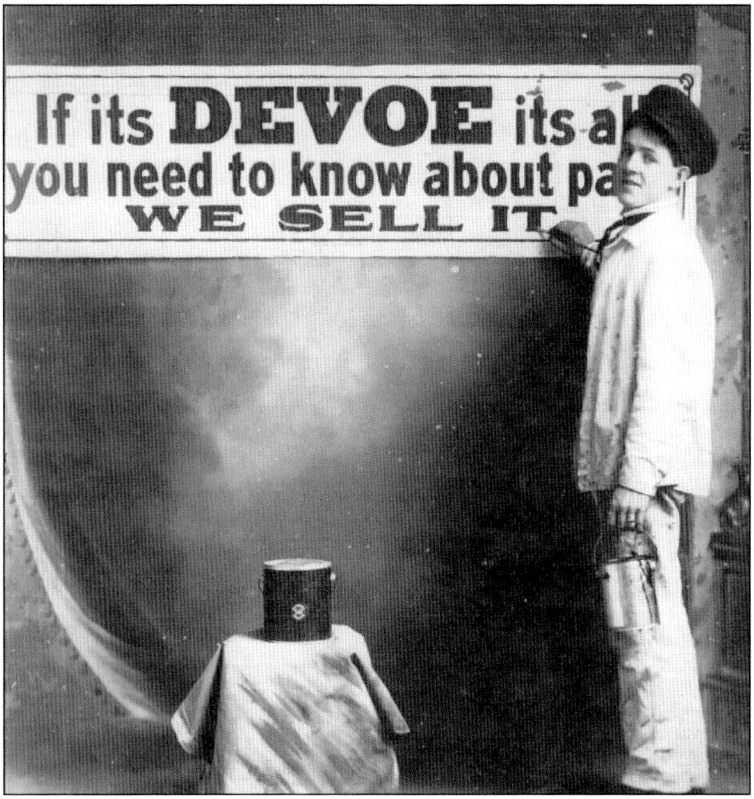

Small entrepreneurs operated amidst the factories and stores. Peter Gokey was a sign painter, decorating floats and creating marquees for many people, including Arthur Brower. The Brower family patent medicine manufactory had shifted, and by 1900 they sold paints. (Courtesy Martner Collection.)

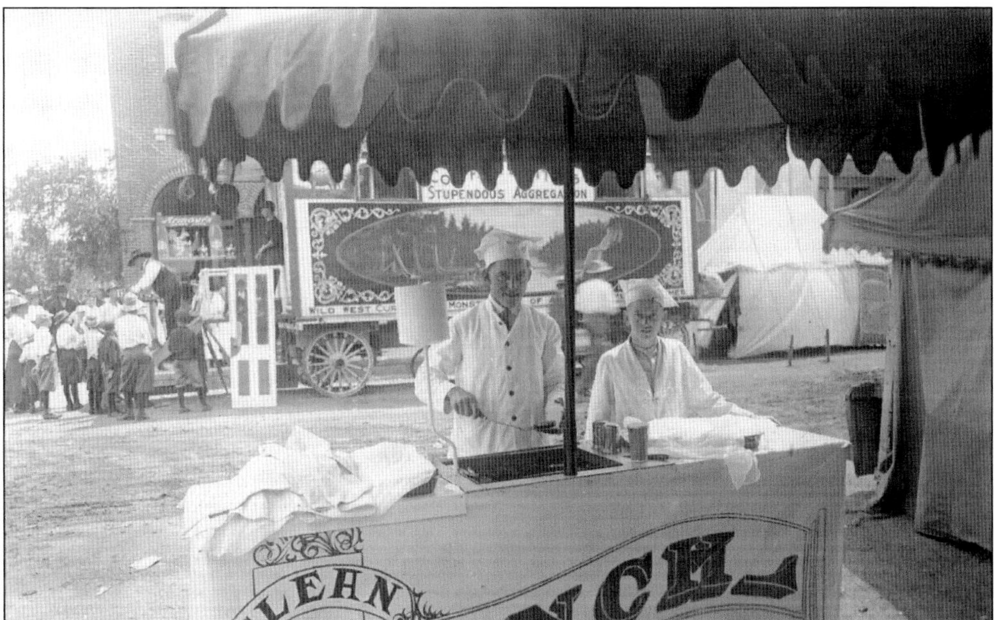

In 1909, Pete Gokey built and set up his Clean Lunch Stand. The stand was a portable facility sheltered by an awning or umbrella. Pete offered freshly cooked hamburgers and always asked, "With or without onions." (Courtesy Bob Ziel.)

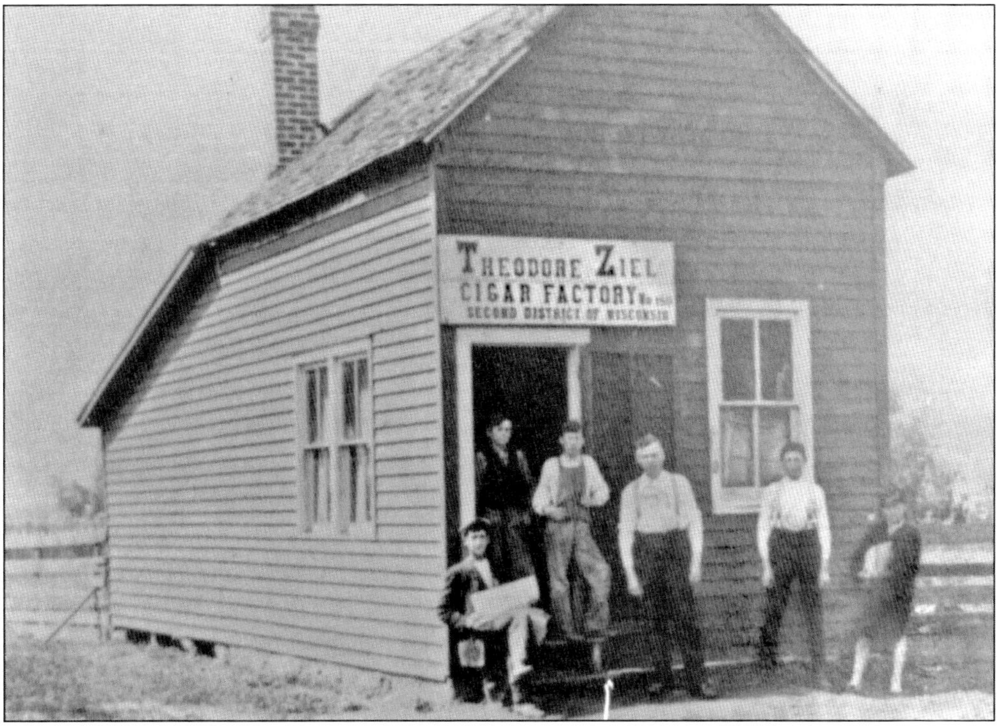

Theodore Ziel opened a small factory on South Church Street, where he manufactured Avia and Little Buck Cigars. The Evert Cigar Factory was also a family-owned business and was located on North Main Street. (Courtesy Gene La Pointe.)

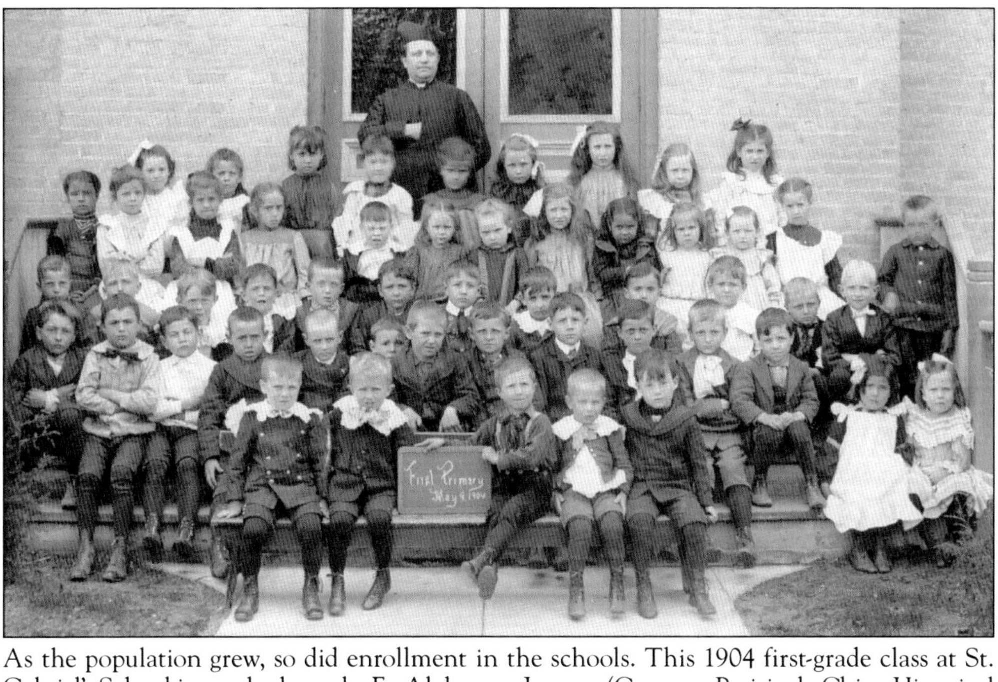

As the population grew, so did enrollment in the schools. This 1904 first-grade class at St. Gabriel's School is watched over by Fr. Alphonsus Joerres. (Courtesy Prairie du Chien Historical Society—Grelle Collection.)

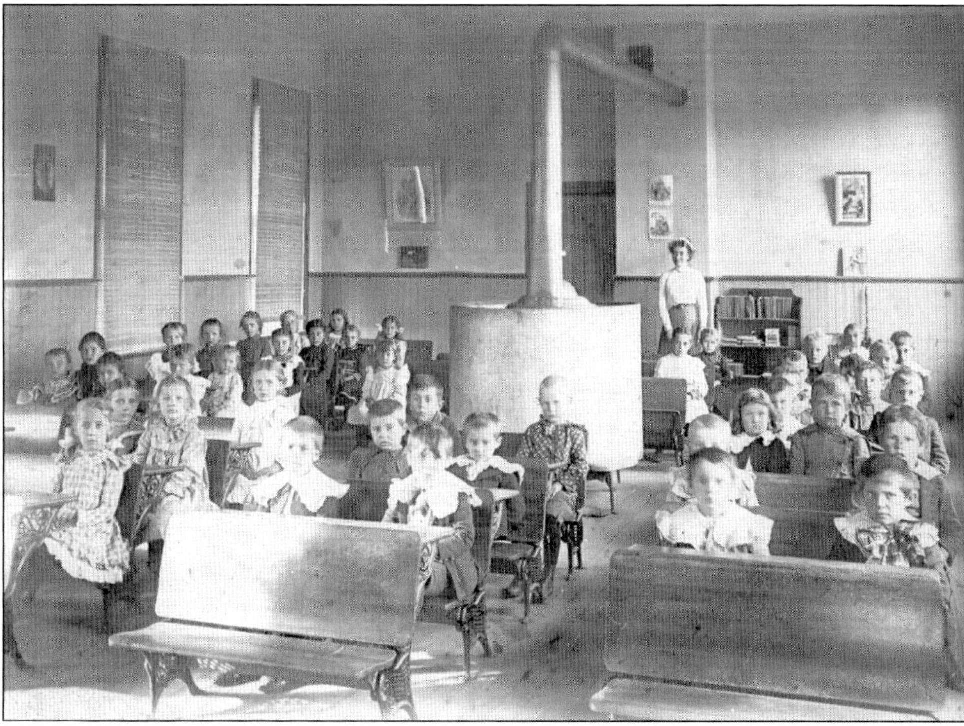

At the other end of town, female teachers instructed pupils in "the old rock school." At the end of the day, they carried wood into the building for the large stove that stood in the center of each classroom. (Courtesy Bob Ziel.)

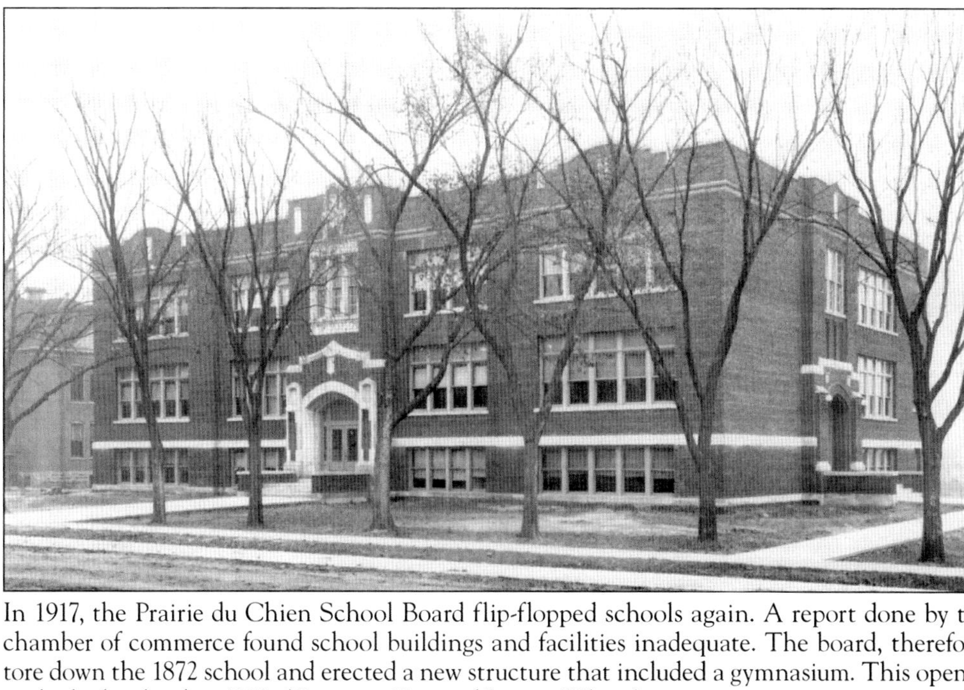

In 1917, the Prairie du Chien School Board flip-flopped schools again. A report done by the chamber of commerce found school buildings and facilities inadequate. The board, therefore, tore down the 1872 school and erected a new structure that included a gymnasium. This opened as the high school in 1918. (Courtesy Ken and Louise White.)

Following the national interest, the administration introduced sports to the school year. The Prairie du Chien High School baseball team played on a diamond laid out on a field that had been part of the Fort Crawford Military Tract. William Utendorfer coached a team for many years. The community fielded club teams, including the Prairie Pirates. (Courtesy Prairie du Chien Historical Society—Otto Collection.)

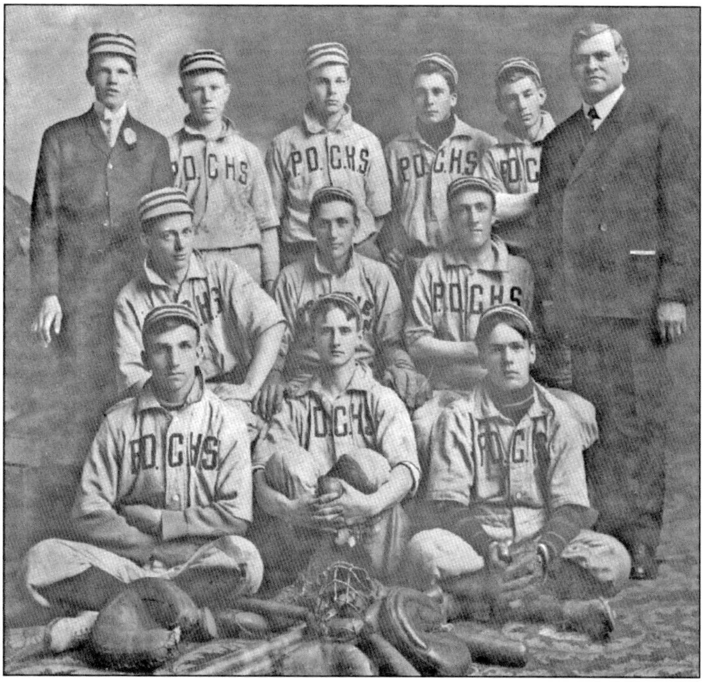

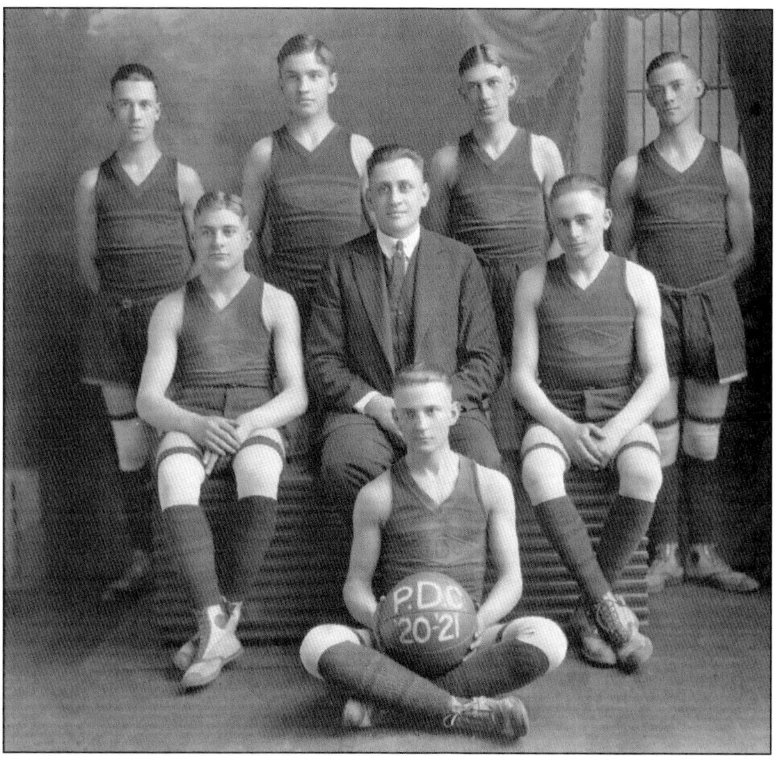

The gymnasium in the new high school meant that the school district could have a basketball team. During the 1920–1921 school year, William Schubert was the coach. Russ Gordon is seated to the left of the coach, and Bill Schubert is to the right of the coach. (Courtesy Jim Trentin.)

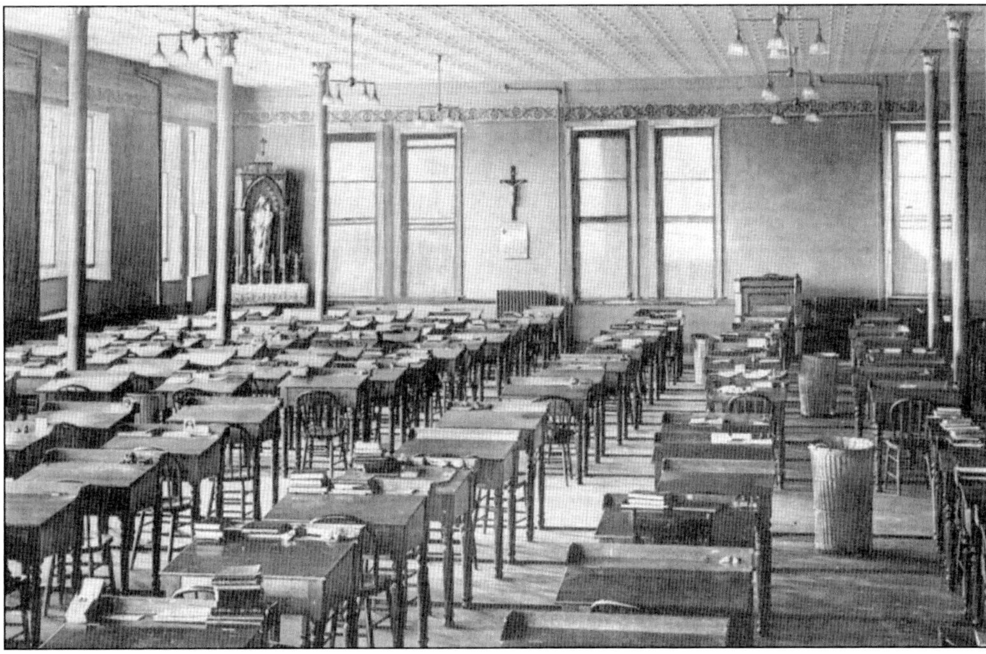

Open to day students and boarders, the College of the Sacred Heart erected Campion Hall in 1909–1910. The building contained classrooms and living quarters, with one dormitory holding 96 students. With the opening of the hall, the Jesuits changed the name of the school to Campion College.

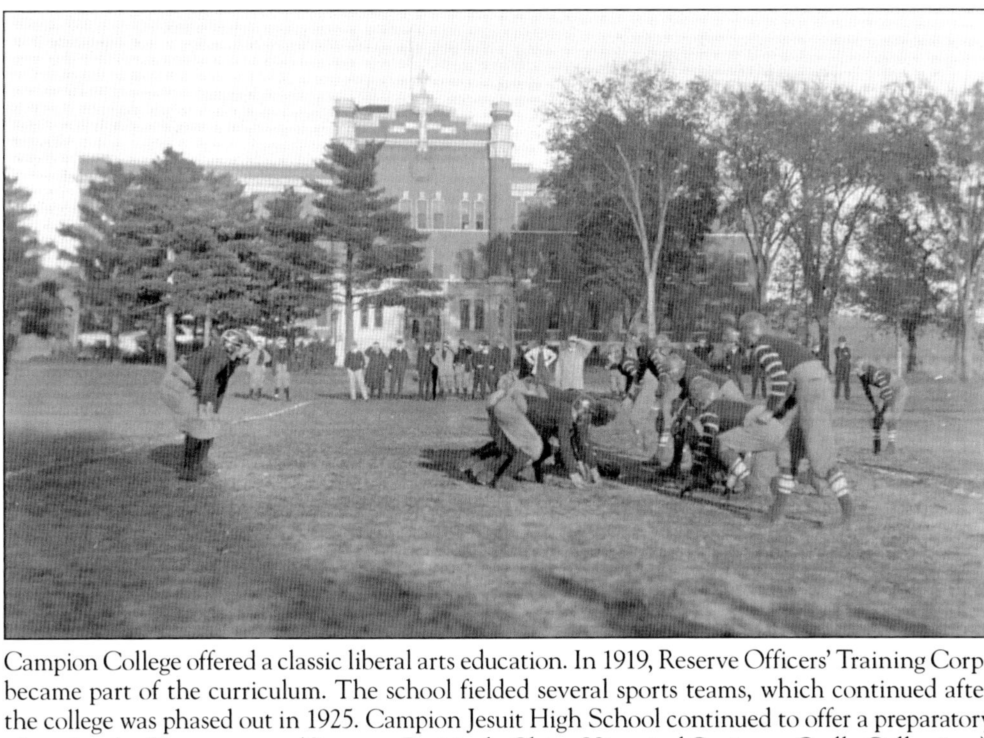

Campion College offered a classic liberal arts education. In 1919, Reserve Officers' Training Corps became part of the curriculum. The school fielded several sports teams, which continued after the college was phased out in 1925. Campion Jesuit High School continued to offer a preparatory education for 50 more years. (Courtesy Prairie du Chien Historical Society—Grelle Collection.)

Fr. James Daly, S. J. (right), was professor of English literature at Campion and a poet. He began a correspondence with American literary Joyce Kilmer (left), and Kilmer became deeply attached to Campion. Though in the U.S. Army, Kilmer obtained leave and delivered the 1917 commencement address before his deployment to France. (Courtesy Antoine family.)

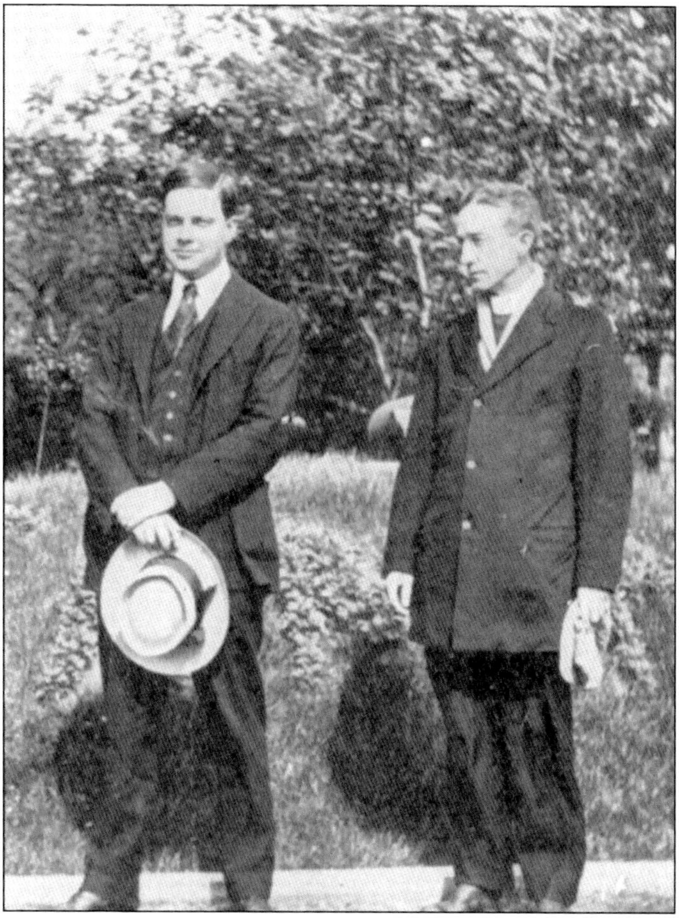

Shortly after Joyce Kilmer's death in July 1918, Fr. Claude Perrin, S. J., a Campion professor, offered family funds to erect a library at Campion in memory of Kilmer. The Joyce Kilmer Memorial Library was dedicated October 31, 1937. (Courtesy Virginia Antoine.)

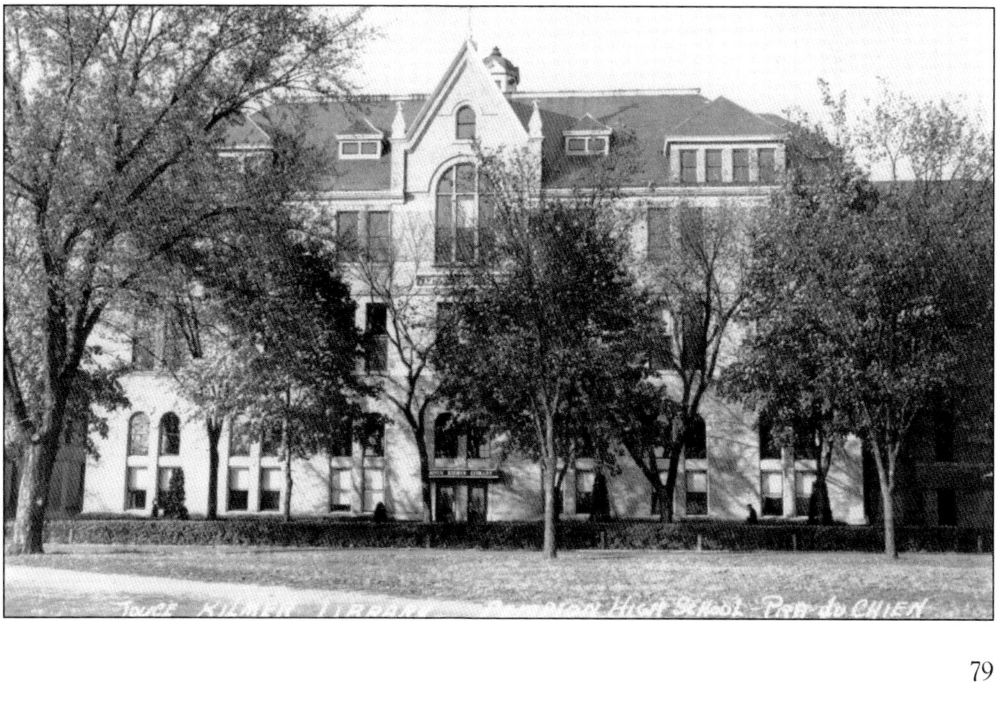

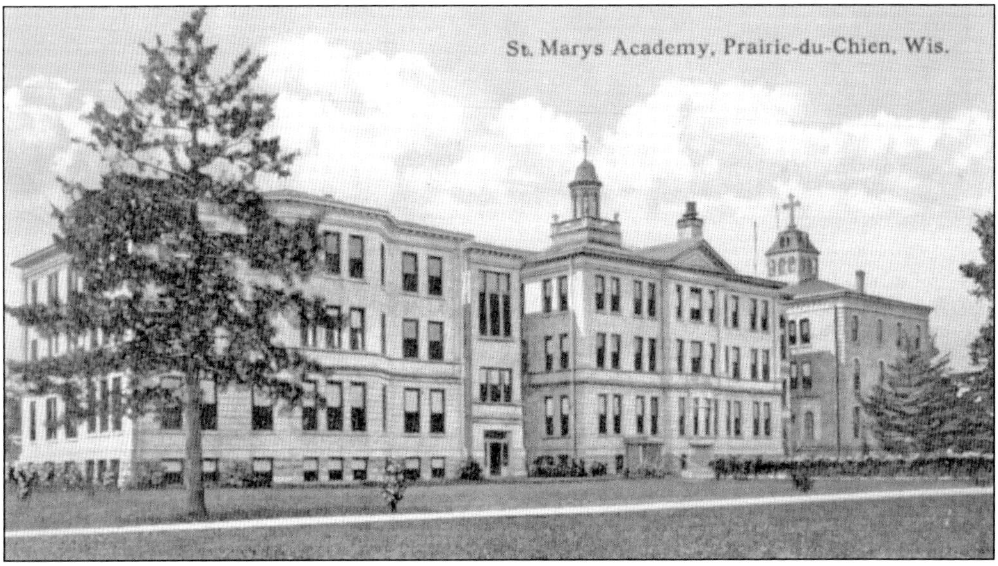

Enrollment at St. Mary's Academy also continued to grow. In 1910, the Sisters retained Dubuque architect Fridolin J. Heer to design another addition to the school. To focus on the new building, Heer relocated the school entrance to the north side of the property, designing a circular drive. (Courtesy Virginia Antoine.)

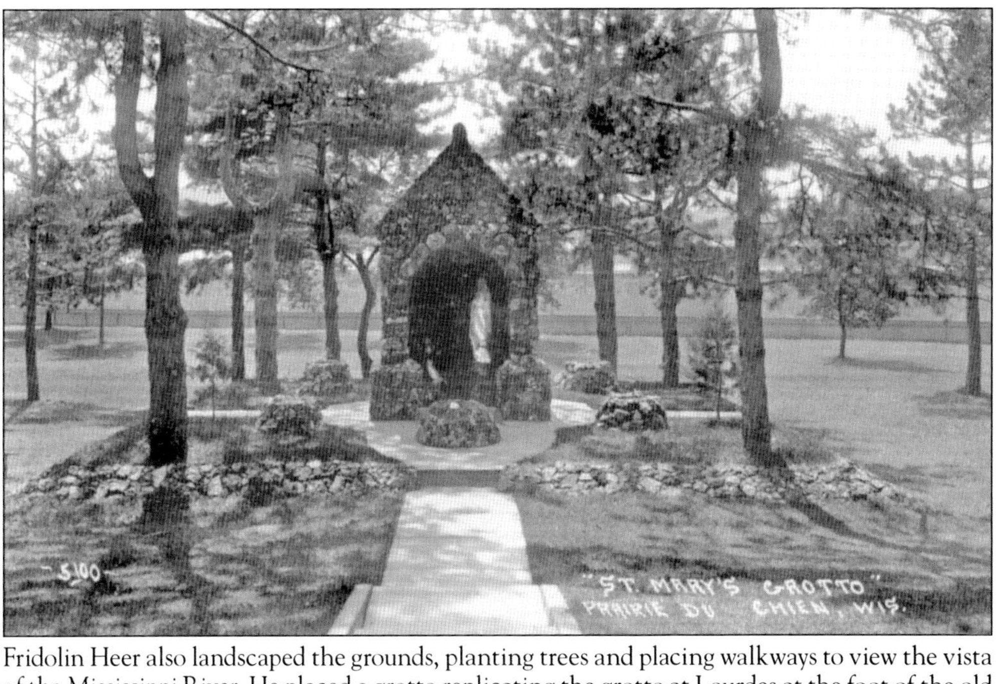

Fridolin Heer also landscaped the grounds, planting trees and placing walkways to view the vista of the Mississippi River. He placed a grotto replicating the grotto at Lourdes at the foot of the old entrance. (Courtesy Antoine family.)

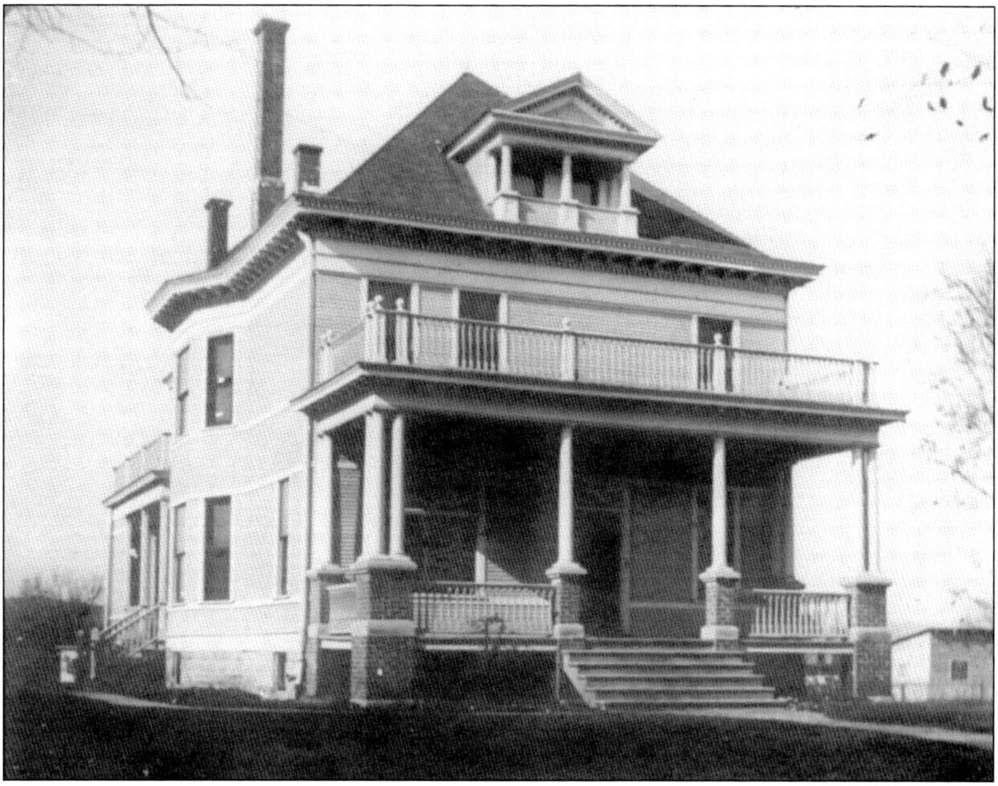

In 1920, the brothers Charles, Edward, and Frederick Grelle each had an architect design a new home for them. Built in the American Foursquare style, their residences fronted on South Church Street near their parents' home. (Courtesy Prairie du Chien Historical Society—Grelle Collection.)

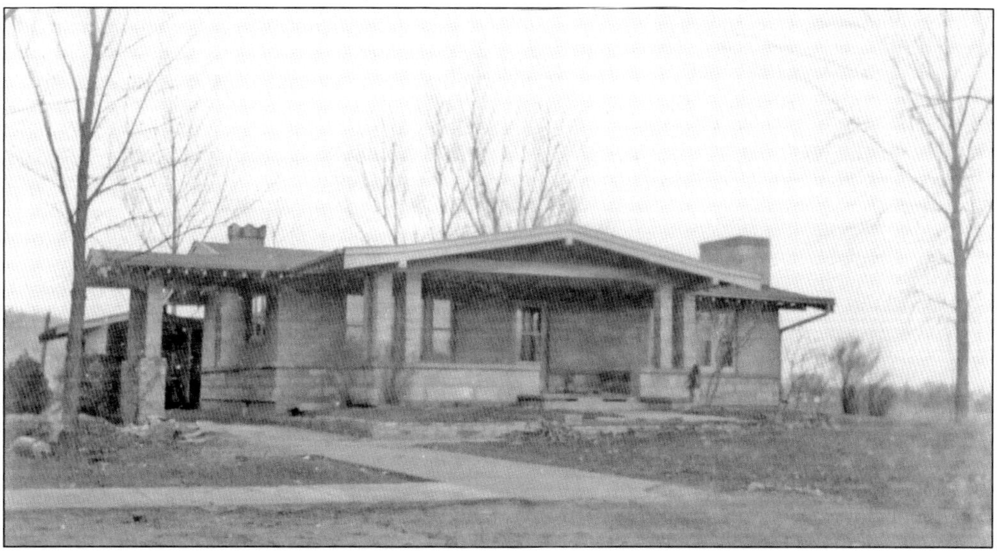

Dressed limestone blocks fashioned the front and portico of Dr. Pinkerton's Prairie style house. The house was built on South Church Street across from the ruins of Fort Crawford, and the limestone was probably recycled from the barracks or hospital buildings. (Courtesy Prairie du Chien Historical Society—Peckham Collection.)

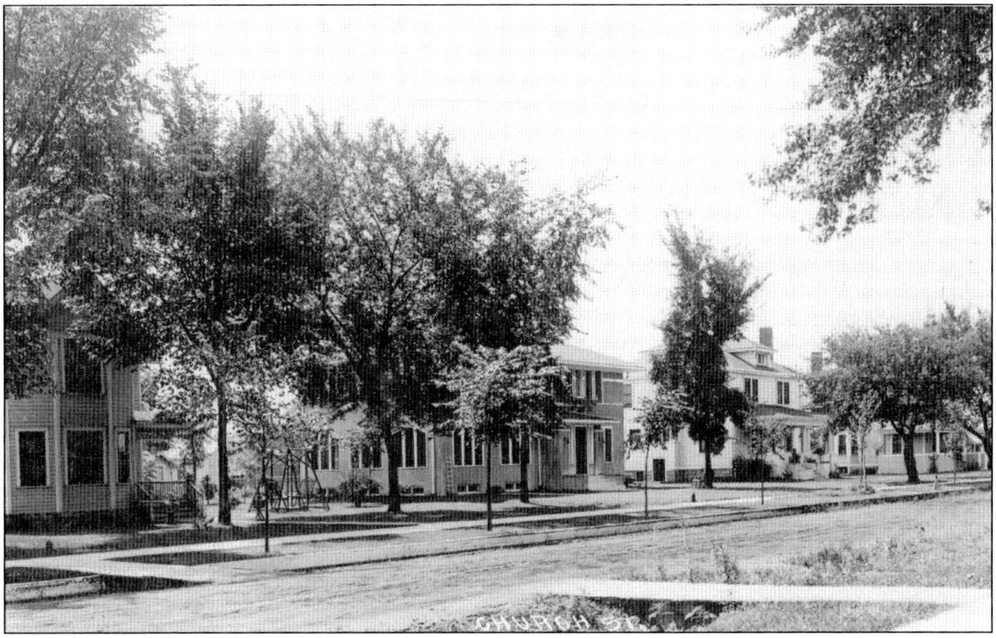

As more fashionable homes were built along South Church Street by the Satter, Paris, and Billings families, the street became known as "silk stocking row." (Courtesy Virginia Antoine.)

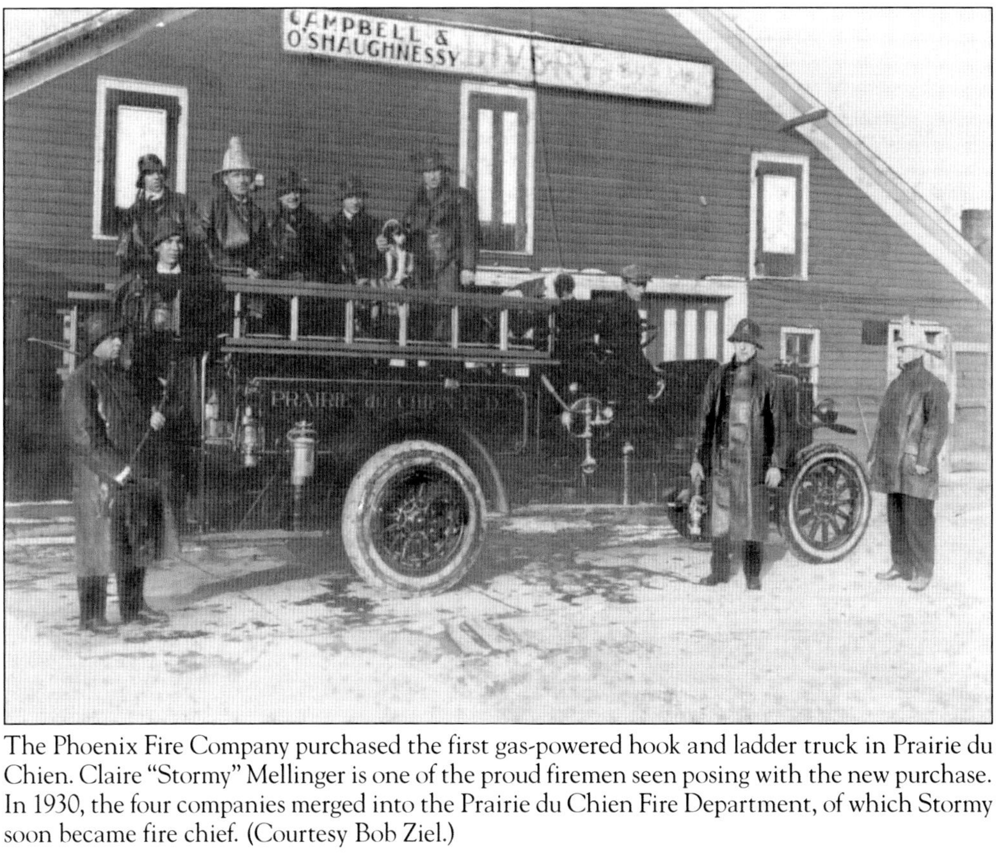

The Phoenix Fire Company purchased the first gas-powered hook and ladder truck in Prairie du Chien. Claire "Stormy" Mellinger is one of the proud firemen seen posing with the new purchase. In 1930, the four companies merged into the Prairie du Chien Fire Department, of which Stormy soon became fire chief. (Courtesy Bob Ziel.)

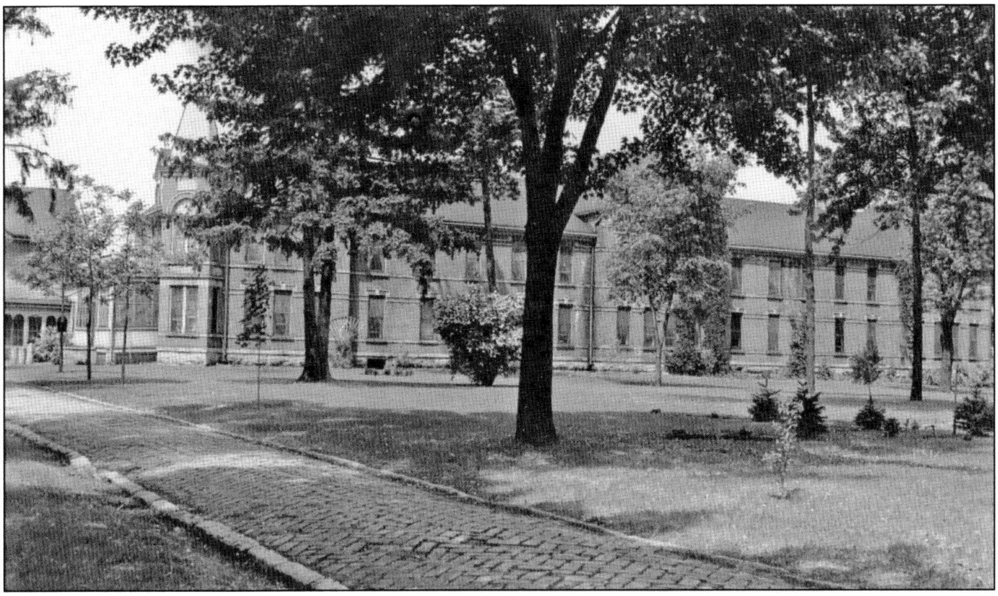

By 1930, Drs. John Kane and O. E. Satter owned the controlling stock in the Prairie du Chien Sanitarium. A physician and a surgeon, they changed the emphasis of the facility to a clinic and hospital. (Courtesy Ken and Louise White.)

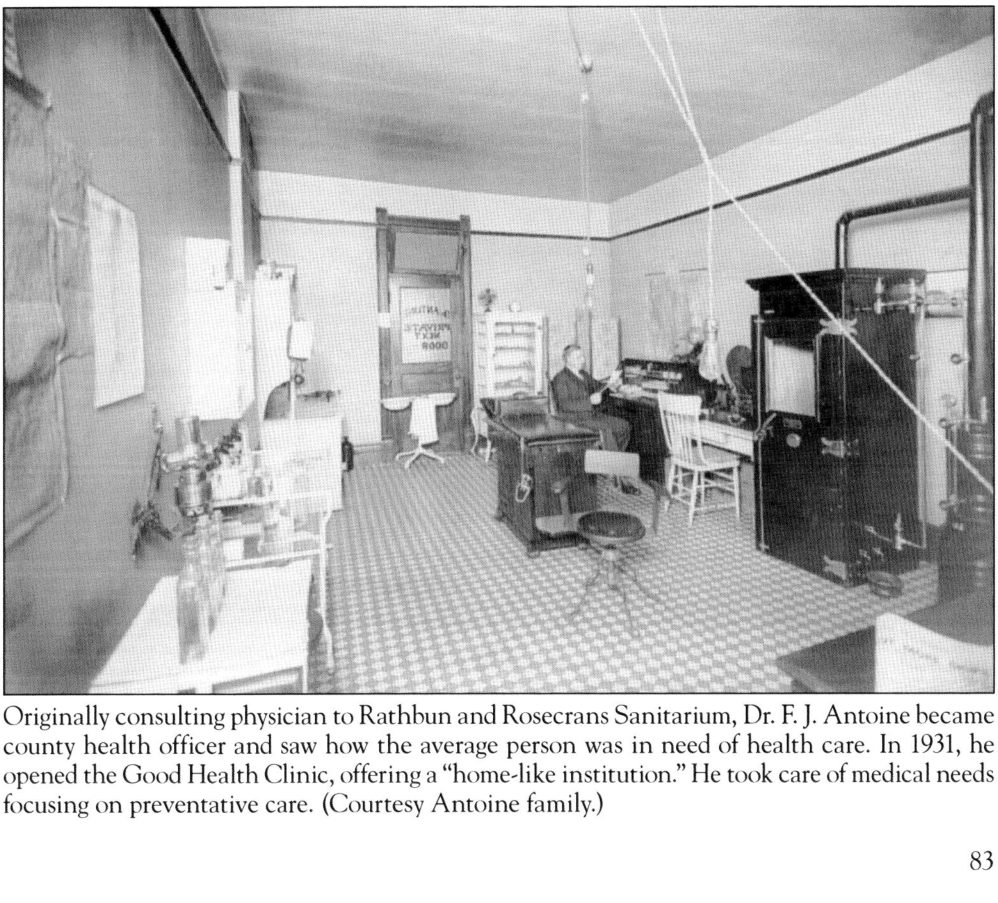

Originally consulting physician to Rathbun and Rosecrans Sanitarium, Dr. F. J. Antoine became county health officer and saw how the average person was in need of health care. In 1931, he opened the Good Health Clinic, offering a "home-like institution." He took care of medical needs focusing on preventative care. (Courtesy Antoine family.)

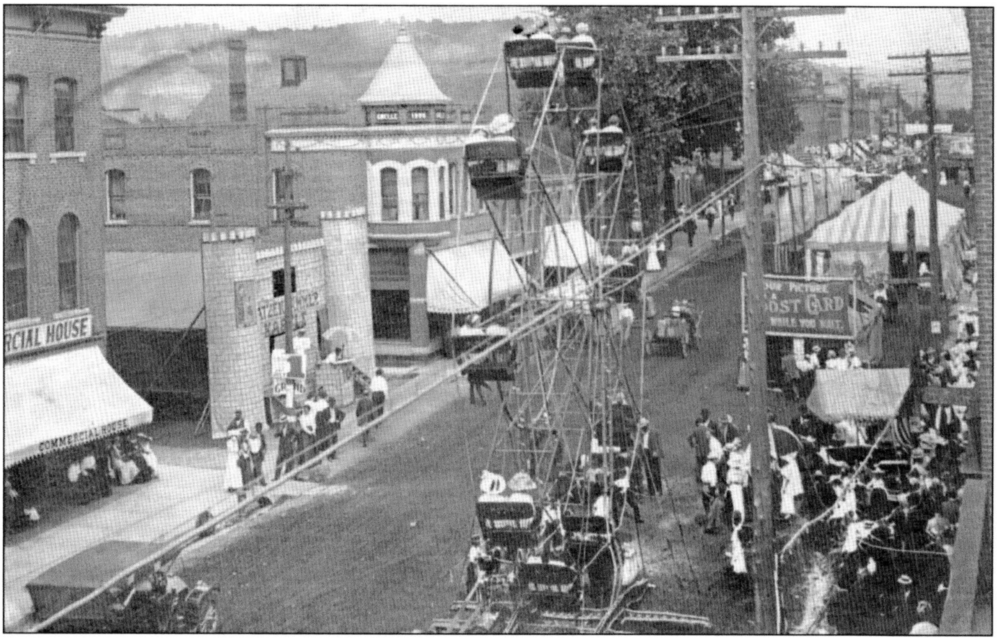

With education, employment, and health care stable, there was time for fun and social gatherings. Buffalo Bill and his Wild West Show had a shoot-out in 1895, and for several years prior to World War I a visiting carnival and fair filled Bluff Street each summer. (Courtesy Bob Ziel.)

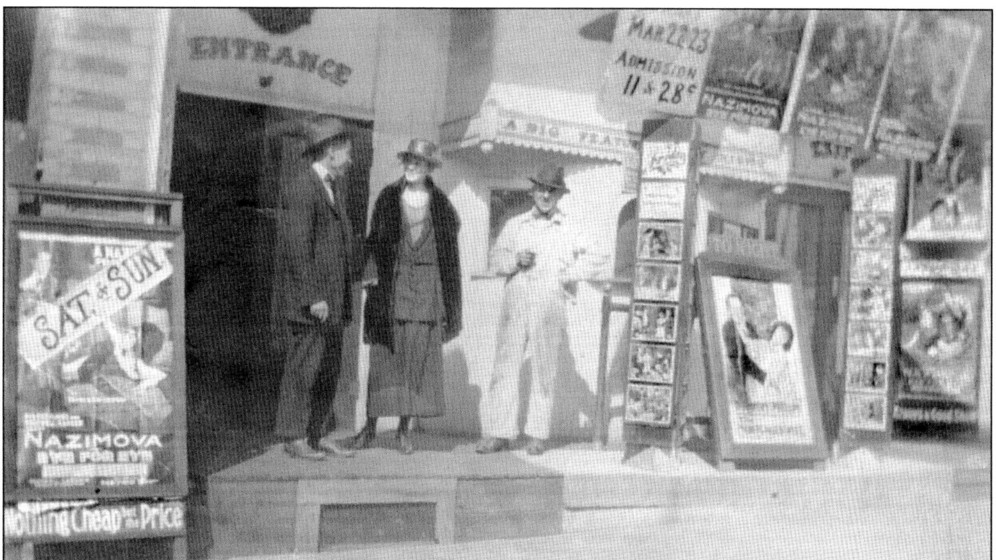

Vaudeville acts like the LaGrande Sisters offered "a show that is different from all others" on the stage at the Metropolitan Theater. Further down Bluff Street, the latest silent moves played at the Regent Theater. (Courtesy Bob Ziel.)

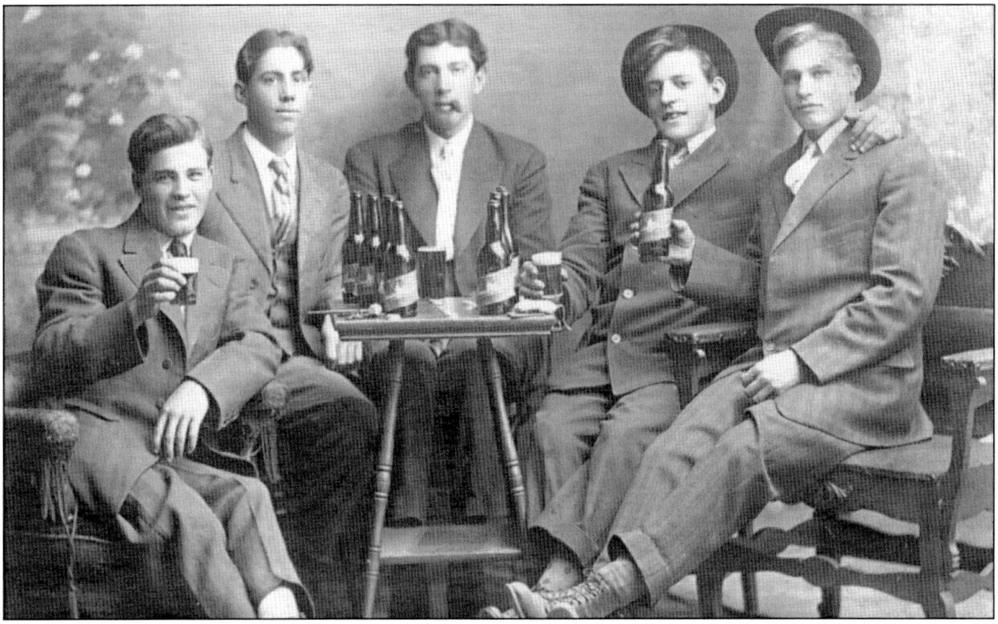

After a theater performance, young men could retire to a bar in one of the hotels or a tavern. Pictured from left to right, Joe DuChesne, Ernie Favre, Paul Lariviere, Jack St. Jacques, and Billie Bitterlee celebrate. (Courtesy Bob Ziel.)

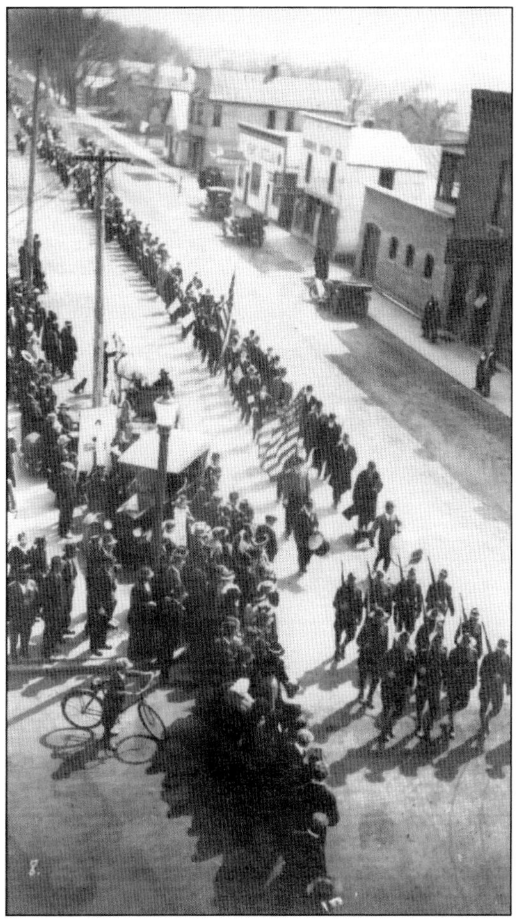

When war was declared, over 3,500 people turned out to march in and watch the Liberty Parade held April 14, 1917. Led by the Grand Army of the Republic, the parade included military organizations, the Red Cross, members of the National Guard, Campion College Band, and a long line of citizens. Beginning and ending at the courthouse square, the parade finished with ringing speeches. (Courtesy Prairie du Chien Historical Society—Grelle Collection.)

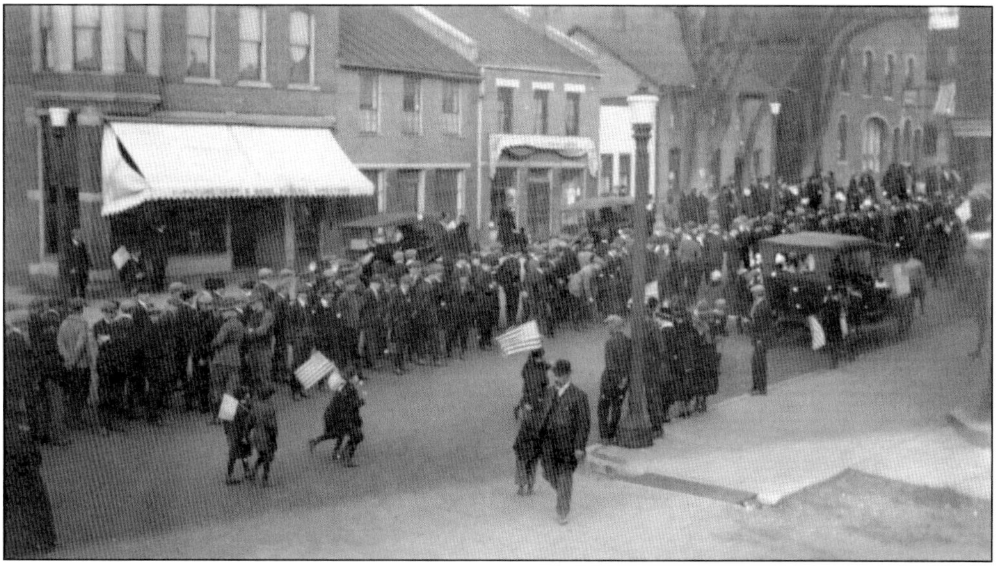

The end of the Great War was celebrated, according to *The Courier*, with the "everlasting blowing of the whistles of the electric light plant, button factory, woolen mills, pickle factory and the ringing of the fire bell and various church bells." At 2:00 p.m., a parade of students from all the schools and hundreds of residents marched in a three-quarter-mile-long line. (Courtesy Martner Collection.)

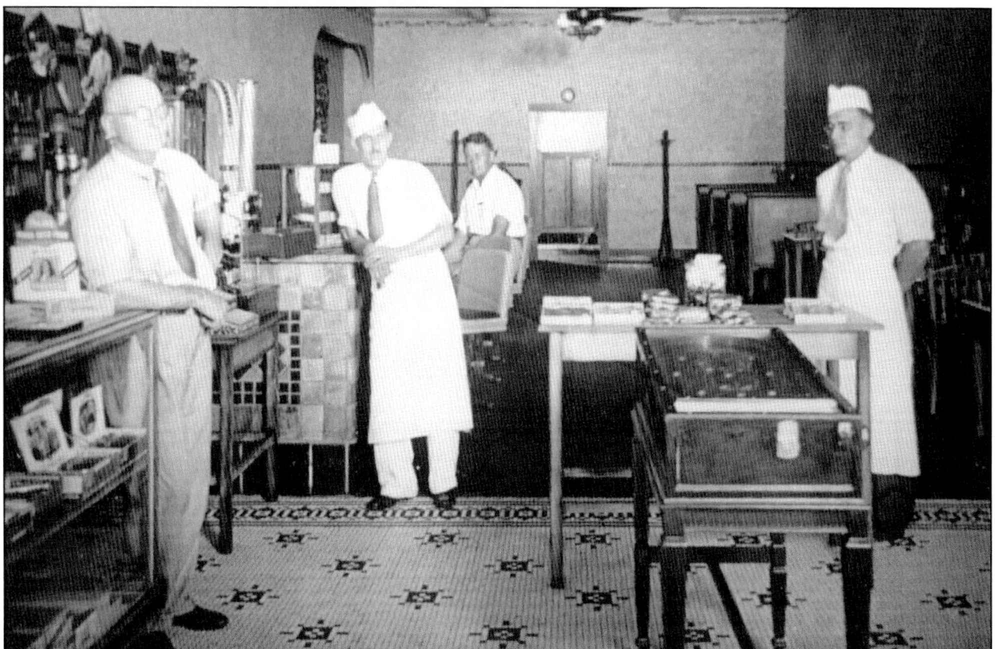

With peace, life returned to the cares and enjoyments of daily life. The Kaber family offered home-cooked meals in the building they had renovated from a laundry to a restaurant. One can still enjoy their deep-fried catfish on Friday nights. (Courtesy Kathleen Novey.)

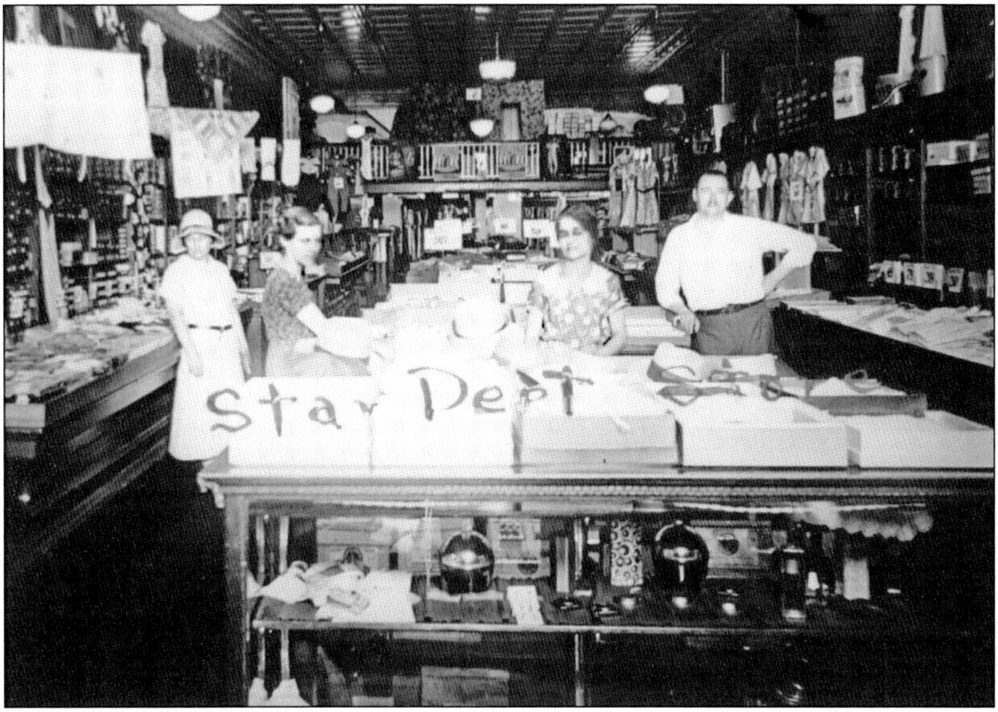

The Garvey sisters offered the latest fashions at the Star Department Store. (Courtesy Kathleen Novey.)

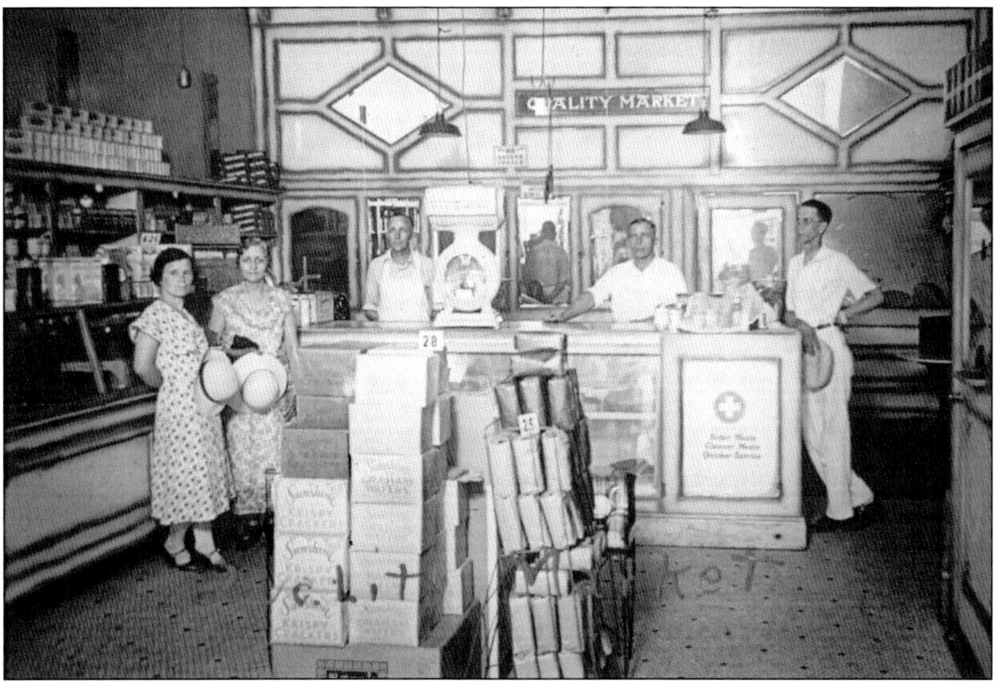

The shelves of various markets and grocery stores were stocked with packaged and canned goods, and meat markets offered fresh cuts of beef and pork. (Courtesy Kathleen Novey.)

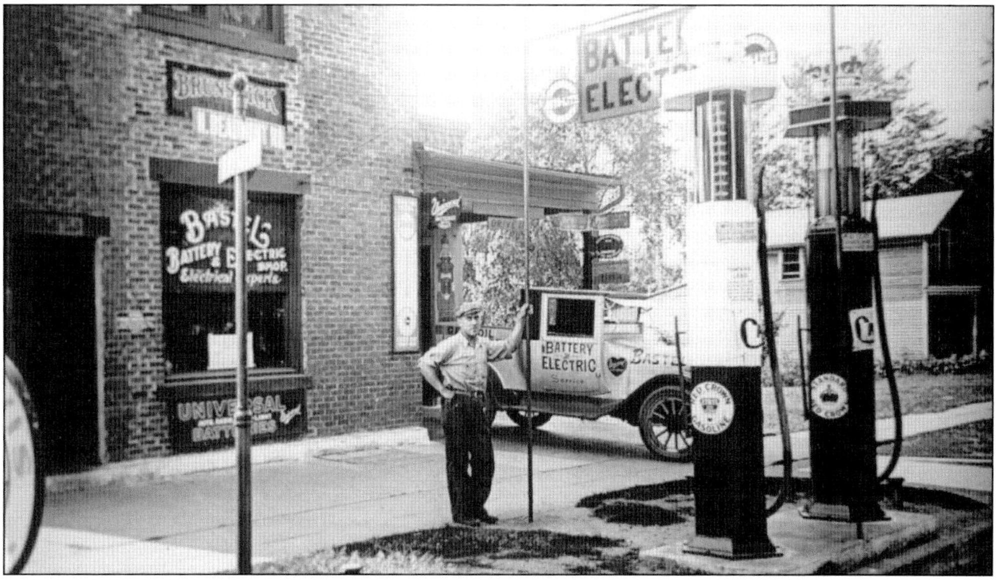

Keeping up with the demand for gas-powered cars and trucks, Ed Bastel converted the old electric power plant on North Church Street into a garage. (Courtesy Kathleen Novey.)

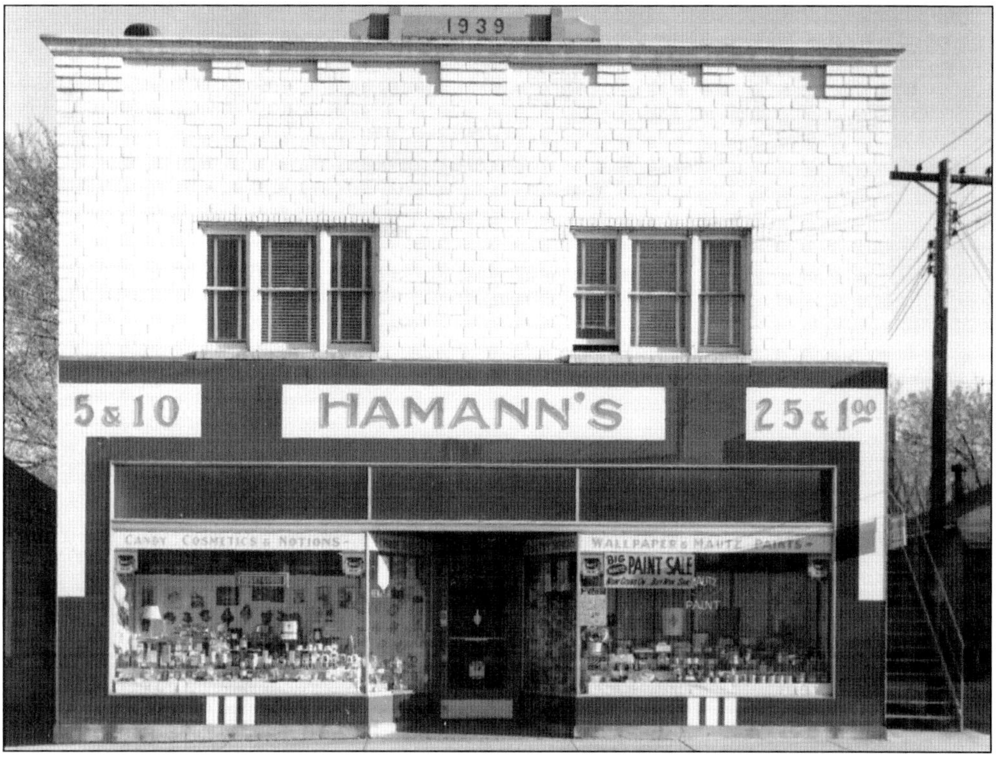

One of the last commercial structures on Bluff Street opened in 1939. The Hamann family introduced a new shopping concept to the community, the five-and-dime store. Every child's treat was to walk to Hamann's, see what new toys were in the basement, and return with a white bag filled with licorice bears or sour cherries. (Courtesy Prairie du Chien Historical Society—Peckham Collection.)

Five

Mississippi River Bounty and Challenge

Along the Upper Mississippi every hour brings something new. There are crowds of odd islands, bluffs, prairies, hills, woods, and villages – everything one could desire to amuse the children. . . . the finest part of the Mississippi.

—Mark Twain, 1886

For centuries, the Mississippi River was a highway. Native people, French explorers, fur traders, and voyageurs traveled its length. The Mississippi River brought American soldiers to forts and settlers from afar to new homes. To connect with the river, the first railroad was built across Wisconsin, and men developed means to cross the river's expanse. After Prairie du Chien settled into a quiet existence, the Mississippi River continued to play a role in the lives of its residents.

To some, the waterway provided a backdrop to daily life. A person could spend a Sunday leisurely rowing from slough to slough, picnic on an island, or take an excursion on a steamboat. The bluffs beckoned all to hike and view the expanse of prairie and river below. And in winter, the frozen Mississippi offered a smooth surface to glide across the backwaters.

For others, their livelihoods depended upon the Mississippi. The commerce of the river provided many jobs, from work on a packet boat or ferry to guiding rafts of logs to cutting ice to repairing the bridges and pontoons. The natural bounty of the Mississippi offered fish to catch and fowl to hunt. With railroad connections, men who had fished and hunted for their families could now send their catches to large cities. When John Boepple introduced the method for making buttons from freshwater clamshells, a person could have employment summer and winter.

While the Mississippi River offered beauty and a means of income, every so often it let the residents of Prairie du Chien feel its power. Many springs the waters rose, covering streets, filling basements, and sometimes entering living spaces. The floods created a bond among the people affected, and the Fourth Ward had a neighborhood unity like no other. But in the end, the Mississippi caused the relocation of houses, families, and a neighborhood, changing the configuration of Prairie du Chien.

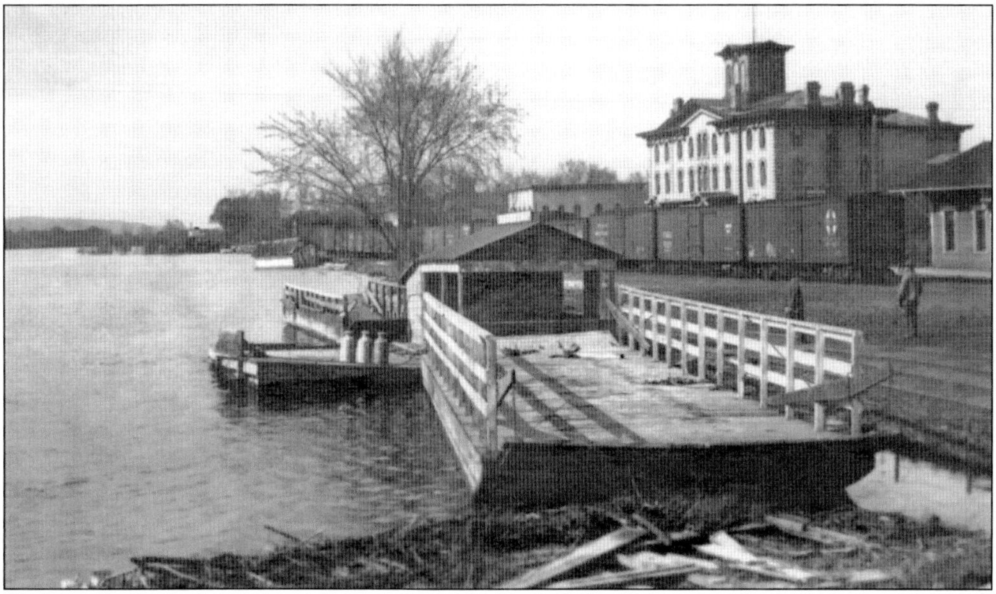

The waterfront along the Fourth Ward was the hub for traffic on the Mississippi River. Steamboats, launches, and ferries tied up to floating docks. Grain, lumber, ice, and other products could be loaded onto freight cars of the Chicago, Milwaukee and St. Paul Railway. (Courtesy Martner Collection.)

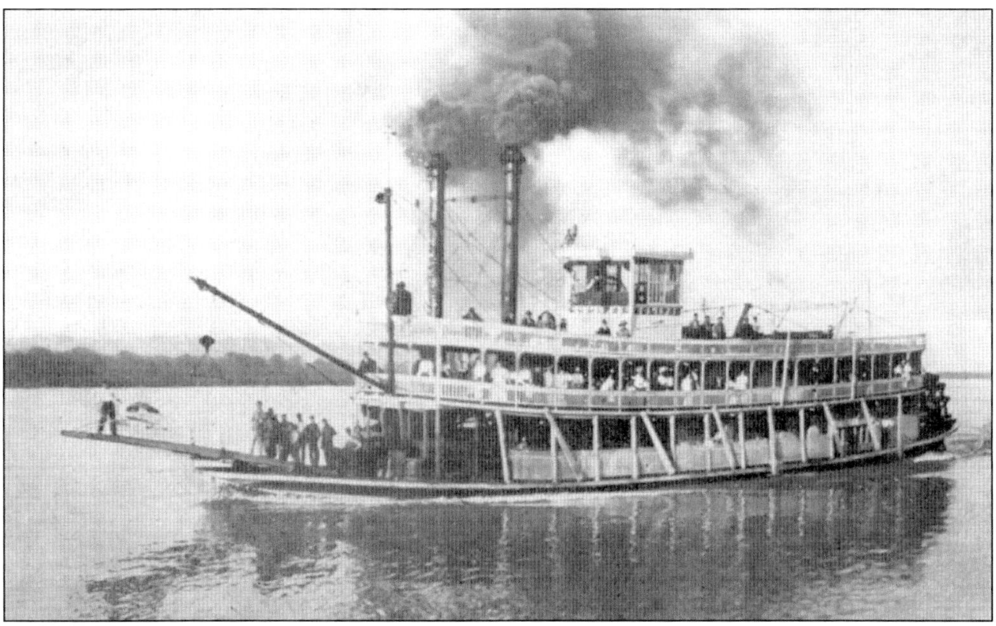

Even with the railroads, packet boats provided the easiest means to travel to the smaller communities along the Mississippi River. The *Eclipse*, a sternwheeler, ran the Dubuque–Prairie du Chien trade from 1882 to 1912 carrying passengers and goods. (Courtesy Ken and Louise White.)

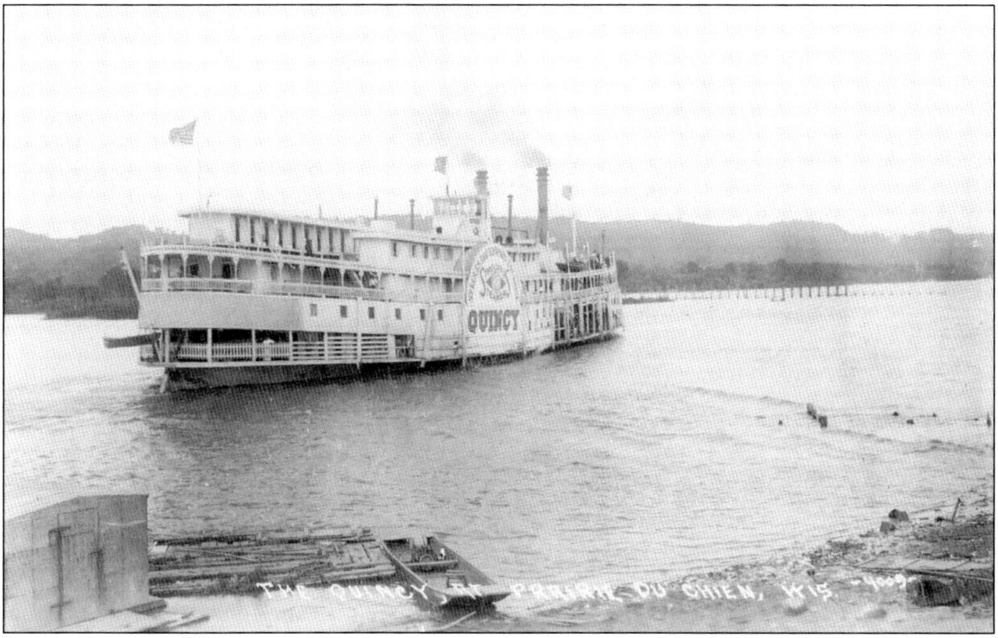

For those people wishing to travel with more amenities, the Diamond Jo Line out of Dubuque operated larger sternwheelers. The *Quincy* ran the St. Louis-St. Paul trade from 1896 to 1906 and was considered the largest floating palace on the upper Mississippi. In the background of this image of the *Quincy* are the remains of the first attempt by the Milwaukee and Prairie du Chien Railroad to construct a bridge across the Mississippi River. (Courtesy Martner Collection.)

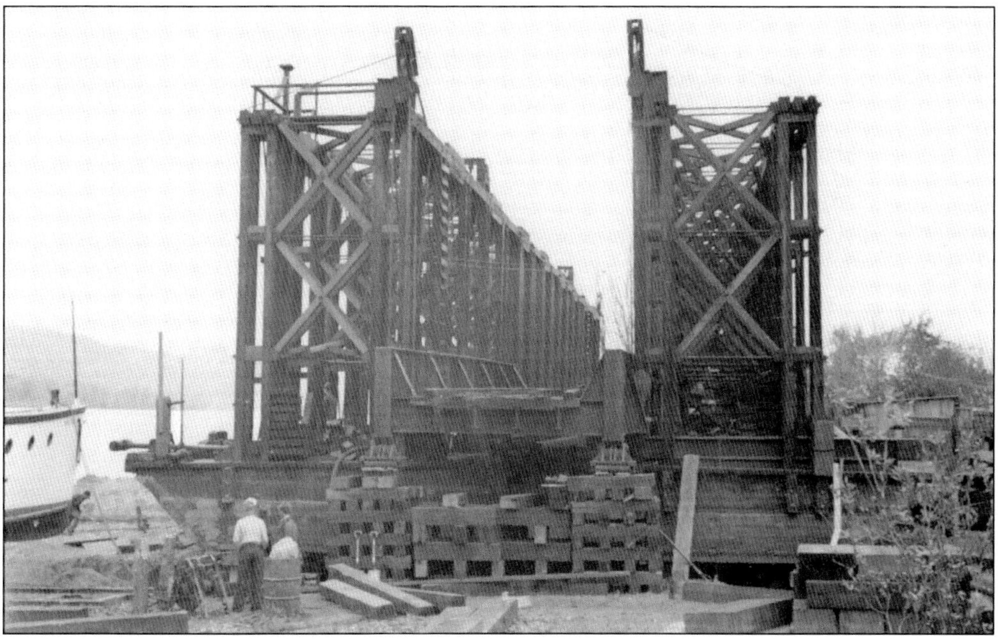

The pile pontoon bridge continued to be the only permanent connection between Wisconsin and Iowa. Originally constructed of Norway pine, the pontoons needed to be rebuilt about every 15 years. With the close of the navigation season, the pontoons were floated to Prairie du Chien for refurbishing. (Courtesy Martner Collection.)

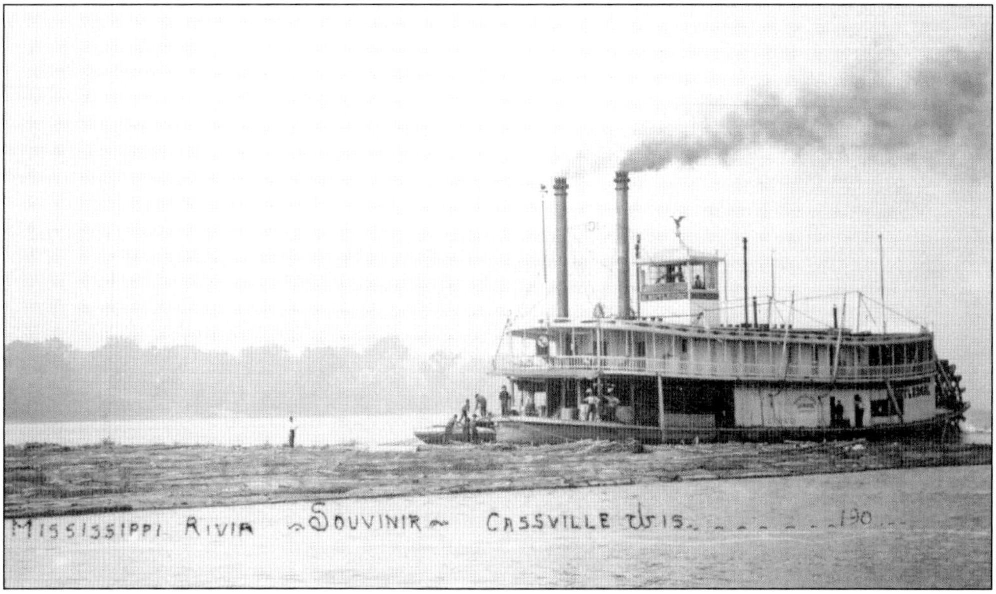

Since the opening of the Wisconsin pineries in the 1840s, lumber companies had been using the Mississippi River to float log rafts downstream. Special steamboats called rafters guided the logs. On one trip, the *E. Rutledge* passed Prairie du Chien on its way to Rock Island with a raft 1,430 feet long and 285 feet wide. (Courtesy Prairie du Chien Historical Society—Peckham Collection.)

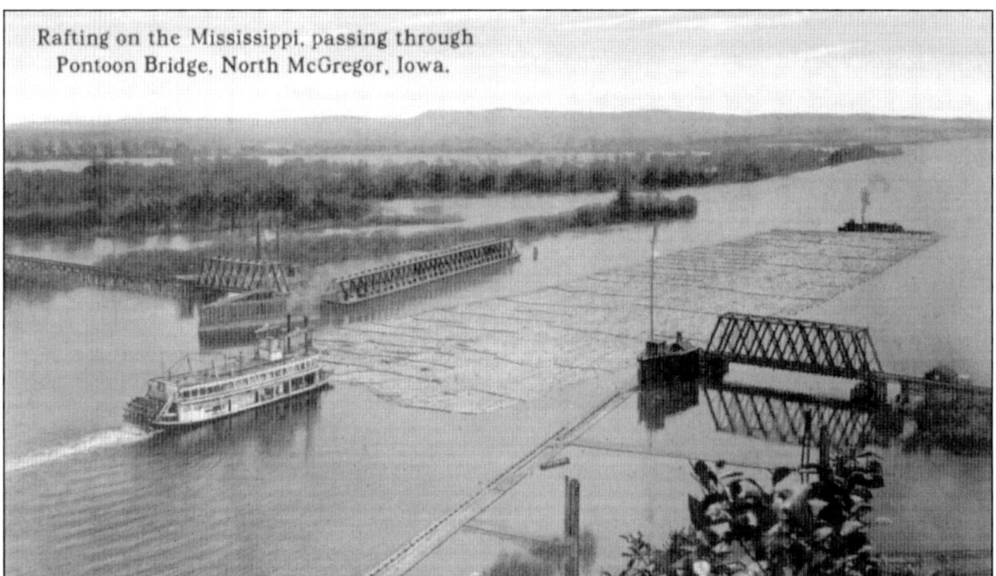

The 405-foot-wide west pontoon often opened to allow a log raft through. A sternwheeler pushed the raft, while at the bow another sternwheeler steered the raft by pulling. By this means, the log vessel stayed in the channel. (Courtesy Virginia Antoine.)

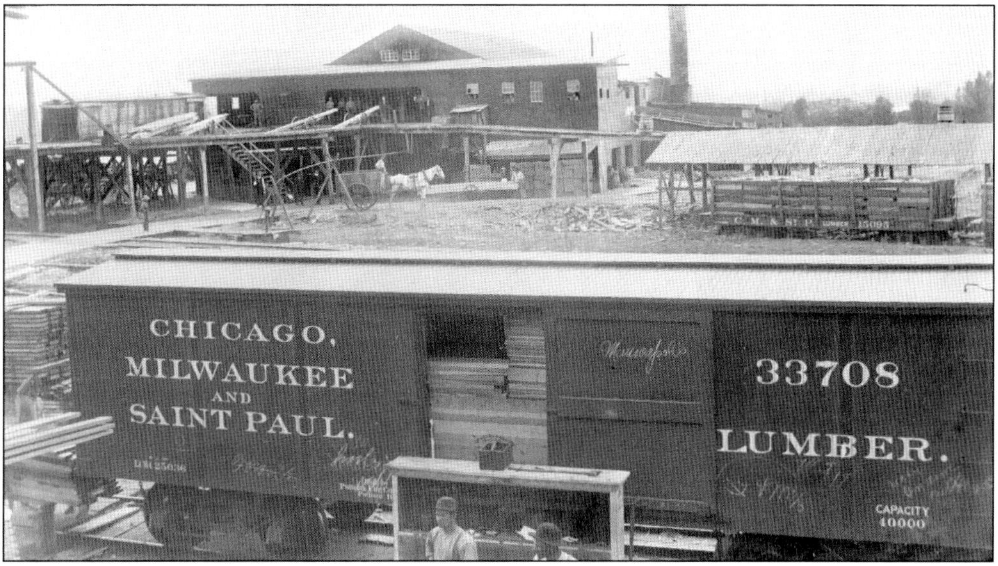

Often, the rafters guided the logs to Prairie du Chien using the east channel. They stopped and cut away one of the sections of logs that composed the raft. This was floated to Stauer and Daubenberger's sawmill located on Sawmill Slough in the Fourth Ward. The mill produced some boards and shingles for the residents and shipped the majority of the lumber to Milwaukee and Chicago. (Courtesy Prairie du Chien Historical Society.)

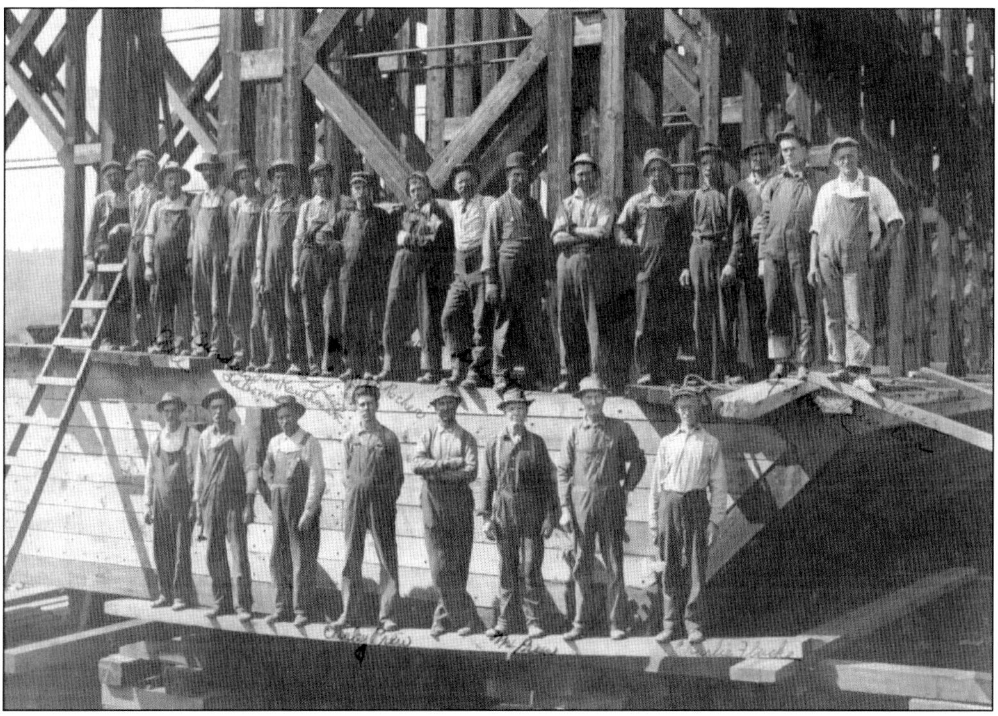

In 1914, the pontoon across the east channel was reduced in size to 209 feet, as log rafts no longer used that watercourse. A steel truss bridge spanned the space between the west piers and the pontoon. In 1932, both pontoons were rebuilt at Prairie du Chien, with the west/main channel pontoon reduced to 276 feet. (Courtesy Prairie du Chien Historical Society.)

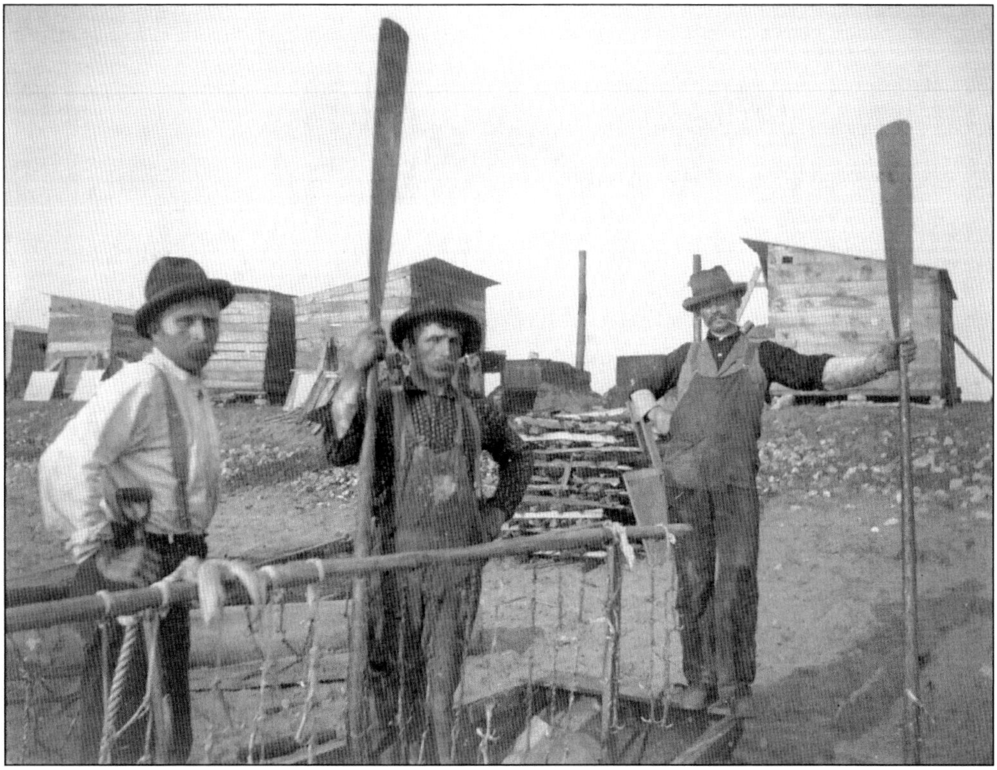

Once spring arrived and waters receded, clam fishermen, and sometimes their families, moved into shanties along the banks and on the islands of the Mississippi River. Pictured from left to right, Frank Hess, John Pelock, and Mike Pelock ready their clamming scow. (Courtesy Prairie du Chien Historical Society.)

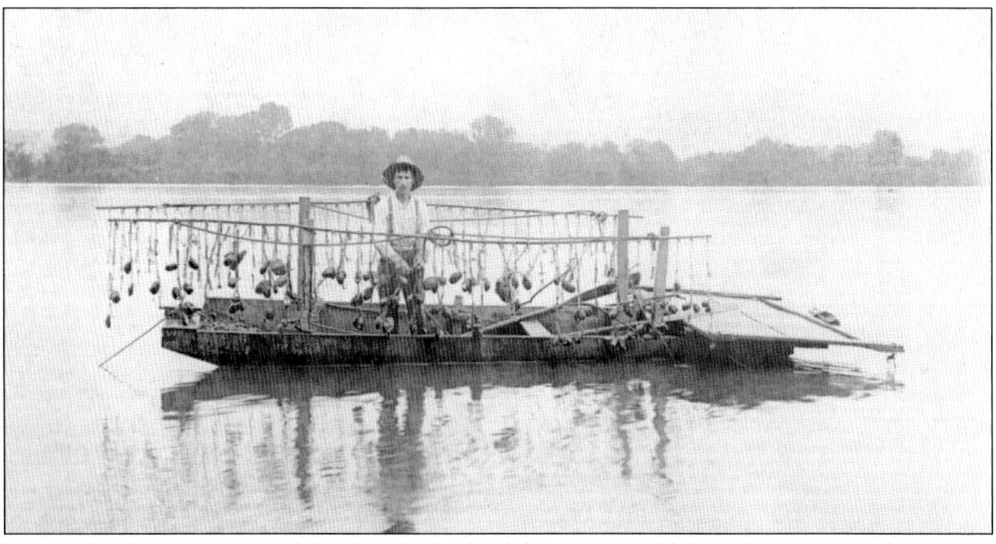

Rowing his boat upstream of the clam beds, the fisherman would drop the canvas mule into the water. Slowly drifting downstream, he would then lower one brail bar dangling with hooks over the side of the boat. When the clams clamped onto the hooks, the fisherman then raised the bar, lowered a second one, and stripped the clams off the hooks. (Courtesy Martner Collection.)

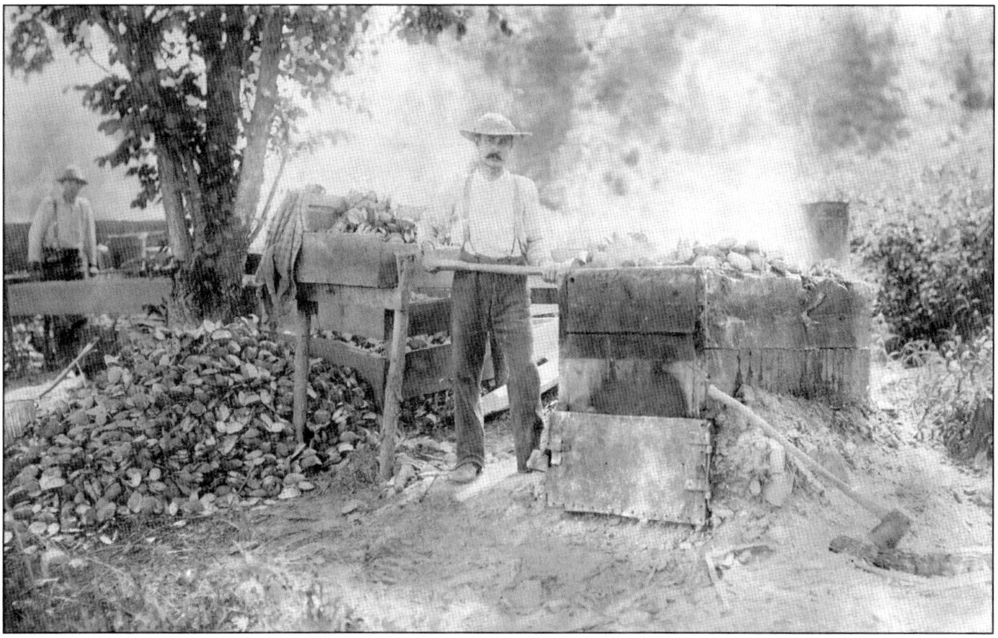

Once ashore, the fisherman and his family cooked the clams to separate the meat from the shells. The shells were bagged to be sold to a button factory. Many of the clam fishermen were descendants of the early French Canadians who still spoke French among themselves. (Courtesy Martner Collection.)

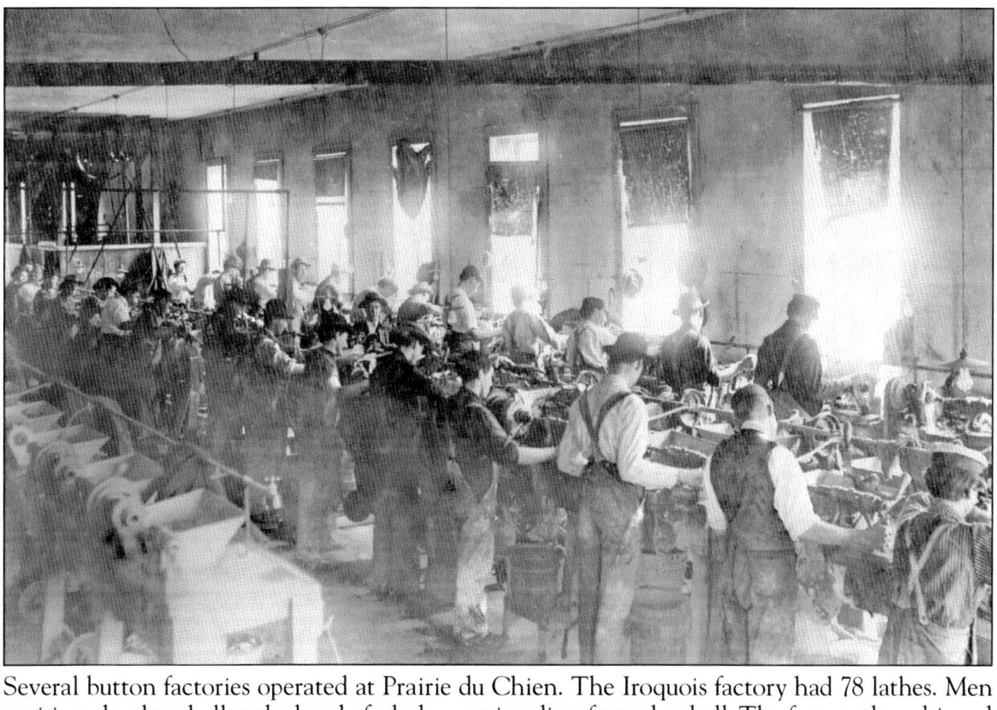

Several button factories operated at Prairie du Chien. The Iroquois factory had 78 lathes. Men positioned a clamshell at the head of a lathe, cutting discs from the shell. The factory then shipped the blanks to Muscatine, Guttenberg, or Lansing along the Mississippi in Iowa to be shaped, carved, and then polished to finished buttons. (Courtesy Martner Collection.)

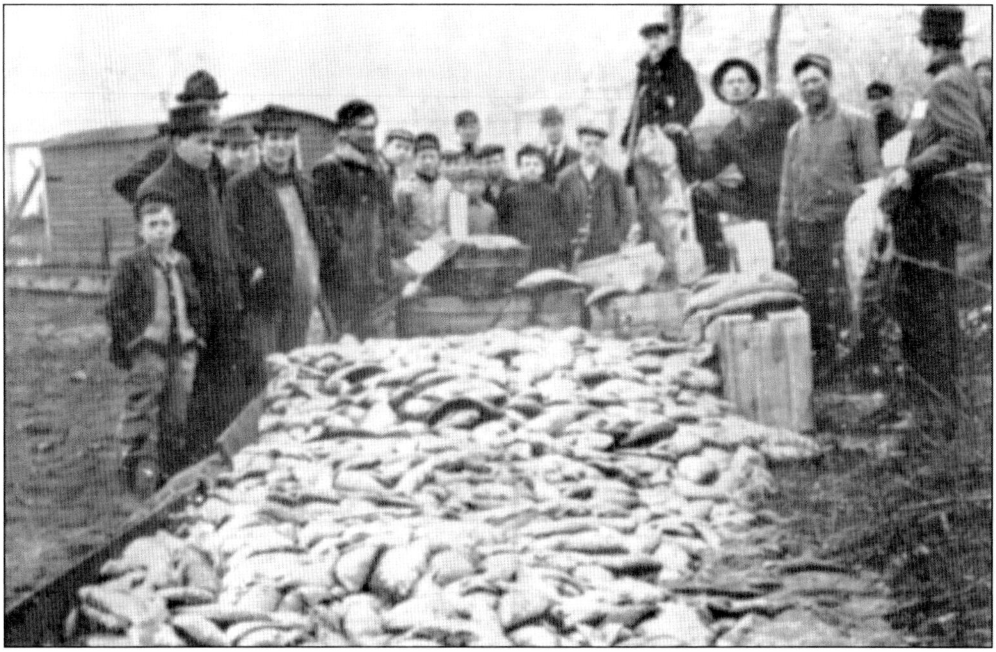

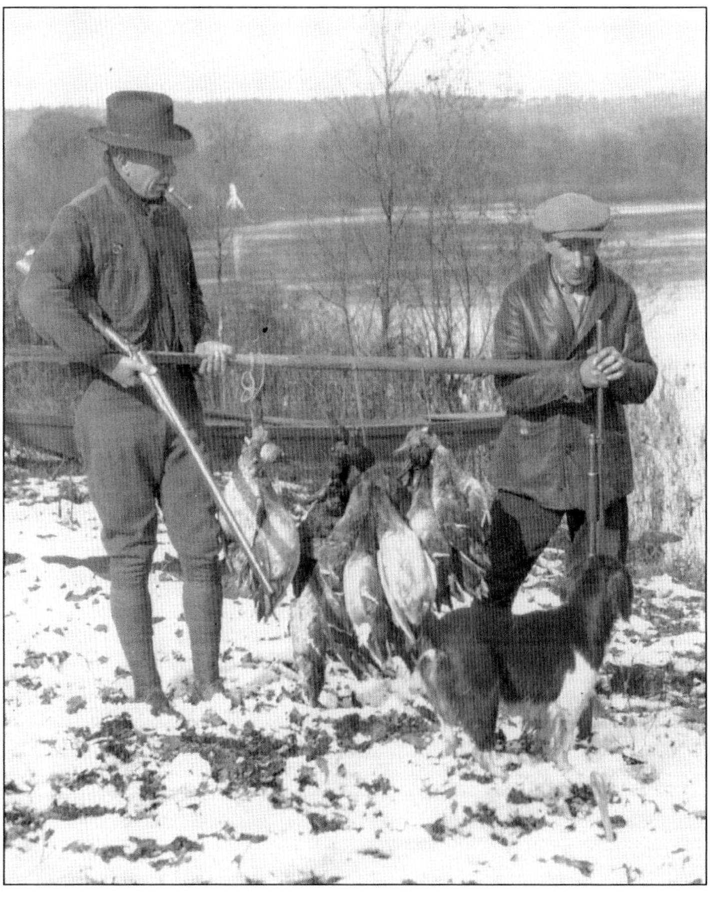

The Mississippi and Wisconsin Rivers teemed with fish. The Gremore Brothers were commercial fishermen. One year, the fish were so plentiful that they netted 80 tons of rough fish, including carp and buffalo. (Courtesy Antoine family.)

In the fall, some who made their living from the river turned to hunting. Waterfowl migrating to warmer climates followed the Mississippi, stopping to feed in the sloughs. Many of the ducks shot were placed on trains bound for Chicago and then to restaurants. (Courtesy Prairie du Chien Historical Society—Howe Collection.)

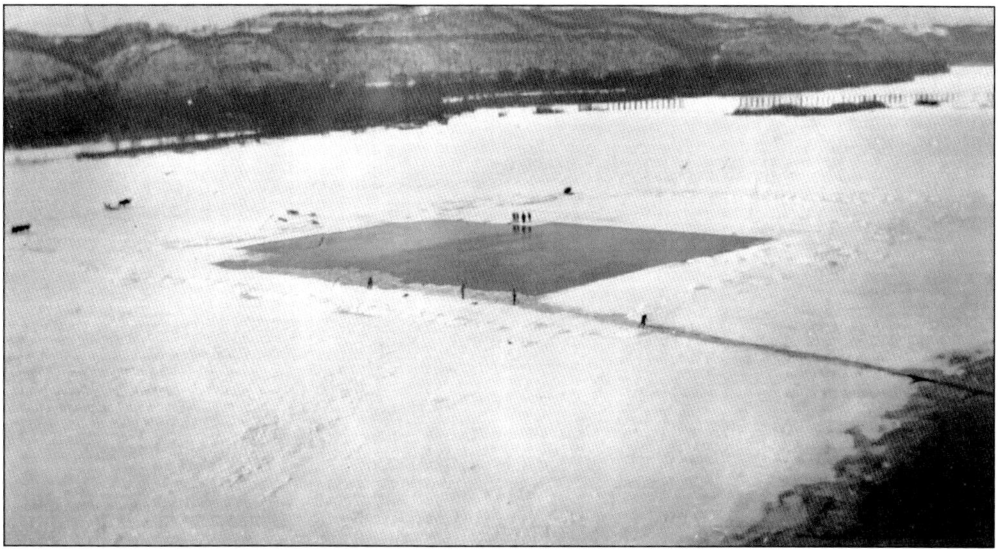

By February, the Mississippi was frozen solid, and the time for harvesting ice began. Men knew the locations where the ice would be clear, so the snow was shoveled away. Using handsaws, they cut the ice into lanes before cutting the lanes into blocks. Some of the ice was sold to the railroads, while the rest was carefully racked and packed with sawdust to be sold to the residents of Prairie du Chien. (Courtesy Martner Collection.)

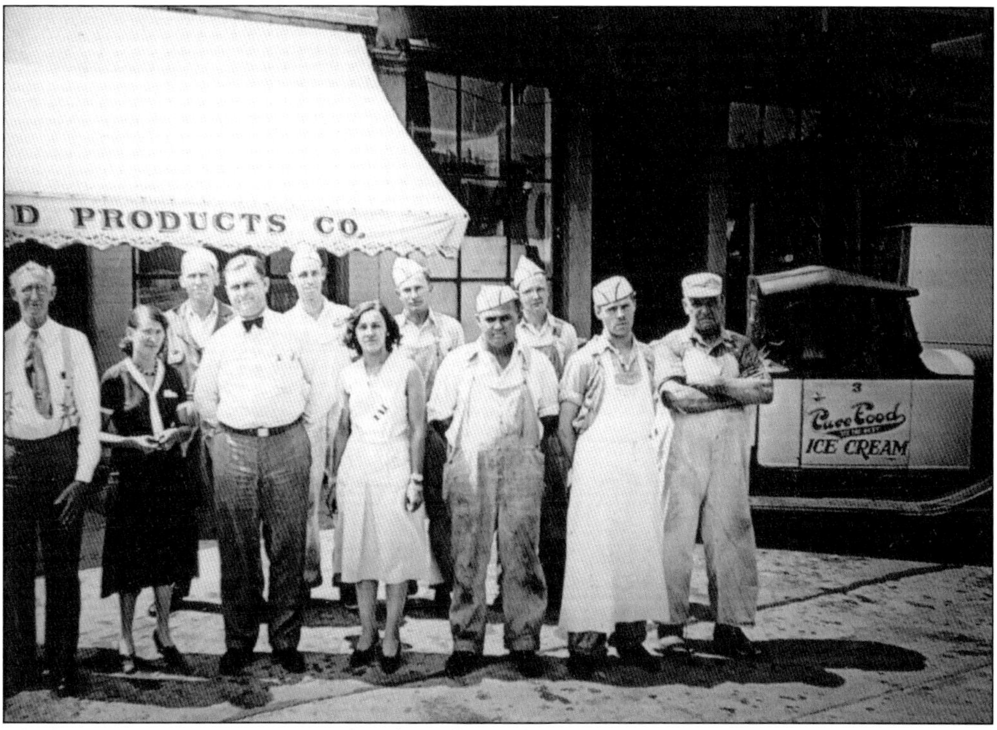

The biggest customer in Prairie du Chien for ice harvested from the Mississippi River was the Prairie du Chien Creamery Company. This business, located in the Case Block, required tons of ice to keep frozen the 3,000 gallons of ice cream it could store. The Zabel family continued to sell fresh ice into the 1950s. (Courtesy Kathleen Novey.)

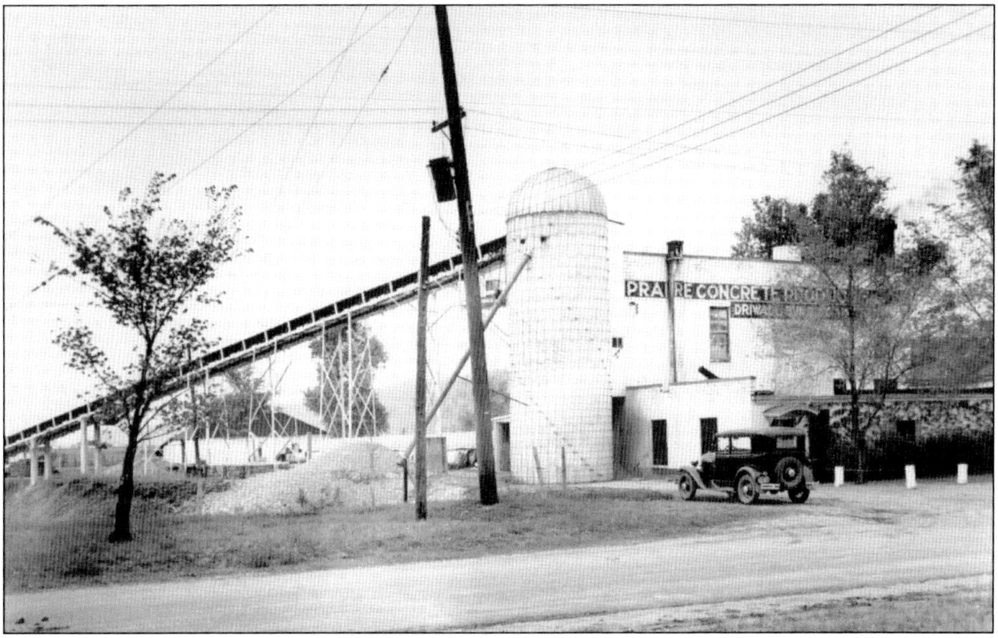

The sand and gravel beds of the Mississippi provided the raw materials to make concrete. Seeing this potential, M. R. Munson organized the Cement Products Company in 1920. Located north of the city, the company made concrete bricks and tile and silo blocks. (Courtesy Prairie du Chien Historical Society—Peckham Collection.)

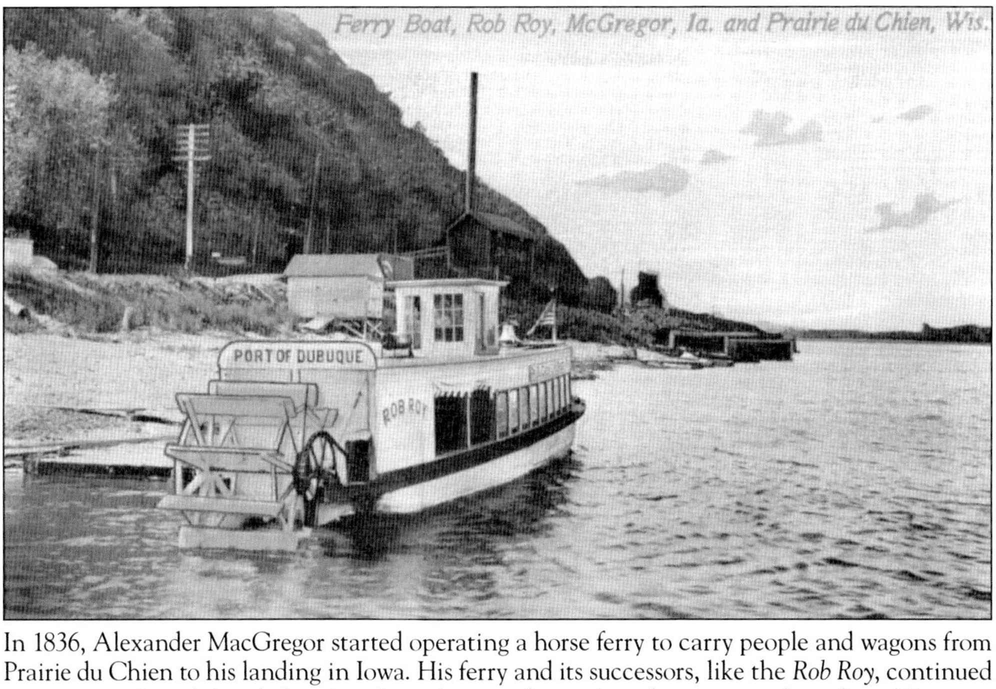

In 1836, Alexander MacGregor started operating a horse ferry to carry people and wagons from Prairie du Chien to his landing in Iowa. His ferry and its successors, like the *Rob Roy*, continued to carry people and their belongings from shore to shore when the river was free of ice. (Courtesy Ken and Louise White.)

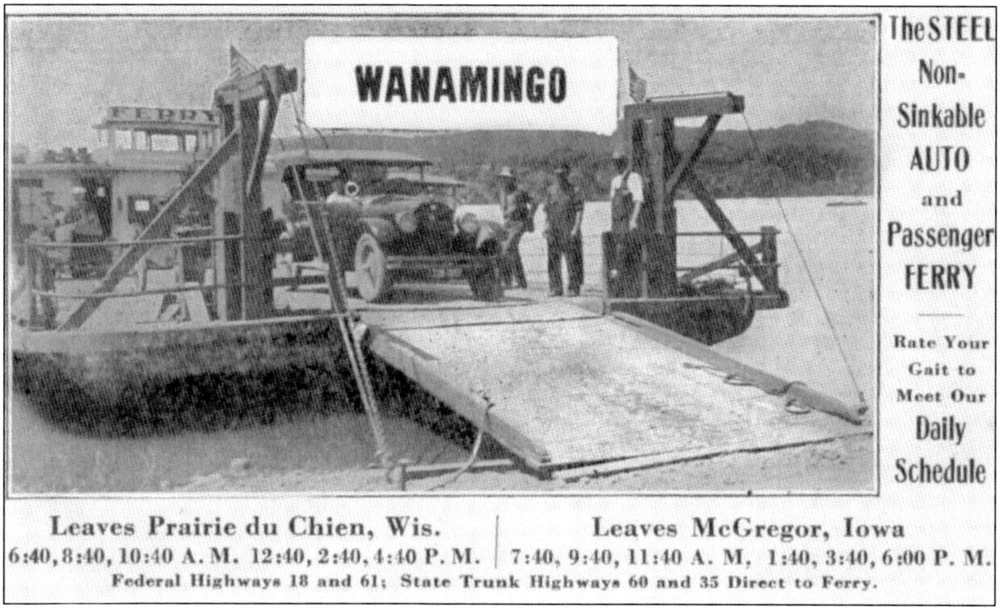

When automobiles began to be a preferred mode of travel, the *Rob Roy II* and the *Wannamingo* offered ferry service. Both carried a five-passenger car for $1 and people for 25¢, assuring all that they carried liability insurance.

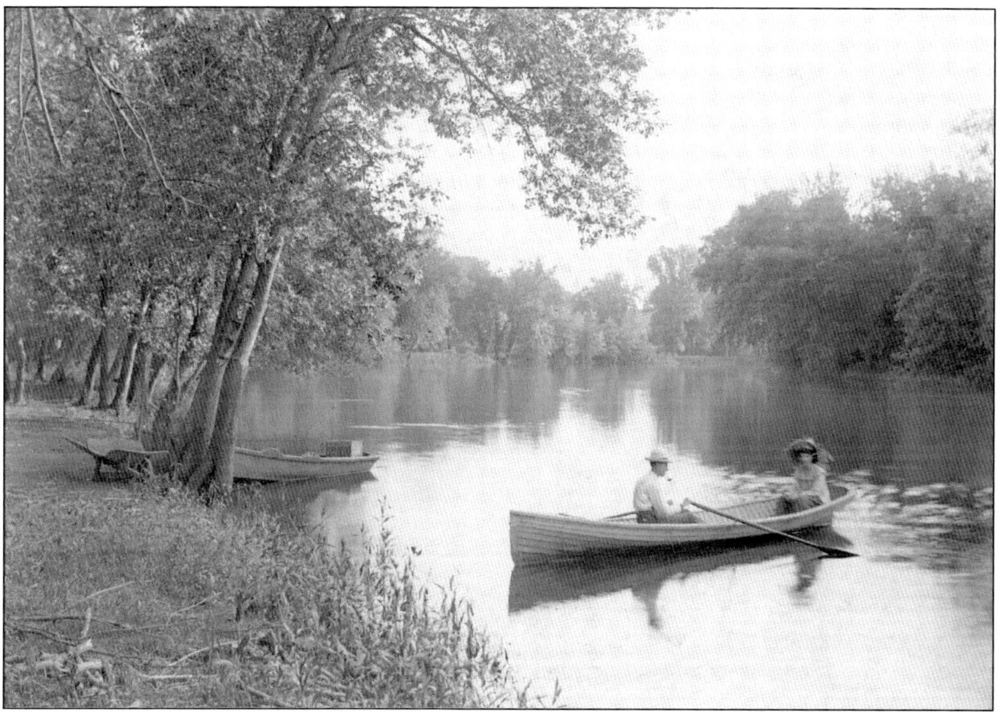

For those who made their living by means other than the river, the Mississippi offered recreational opportunities for residents and visitors. In summer, young men and their young ladies could row among the quiet backwaters. (Courtesy Antoine family.)

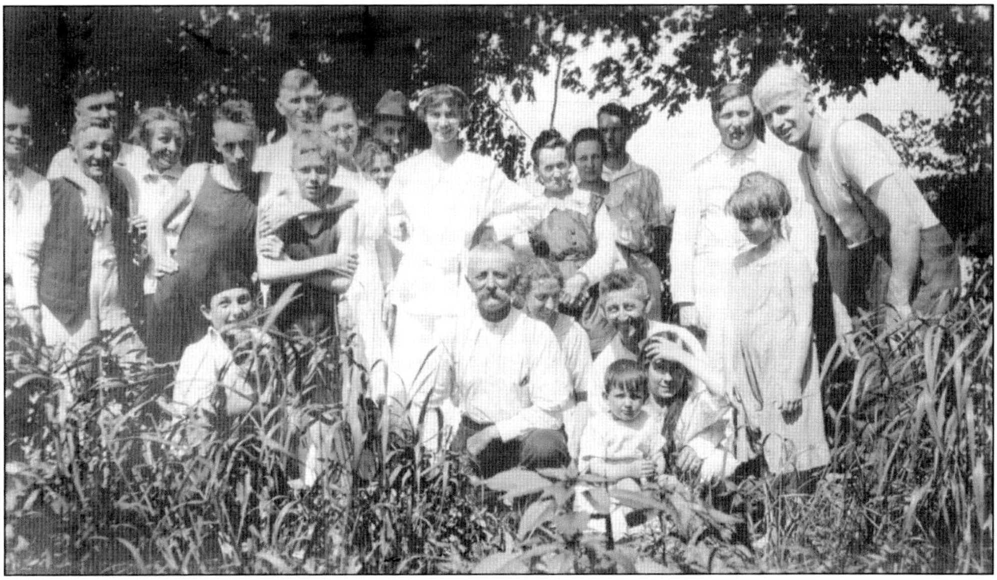

In the 19th century, many residents farmed the grass-covered islands in the Mississippi. They cut the grass for hay and then drove their pigs onto the islands to forage for roots. In time, the islands became a place to picnic and swim. Seen here in 1919, the Prairie du Chien Band is enjoying a day on one of the islands. (Courtesy Kathy Koch.)

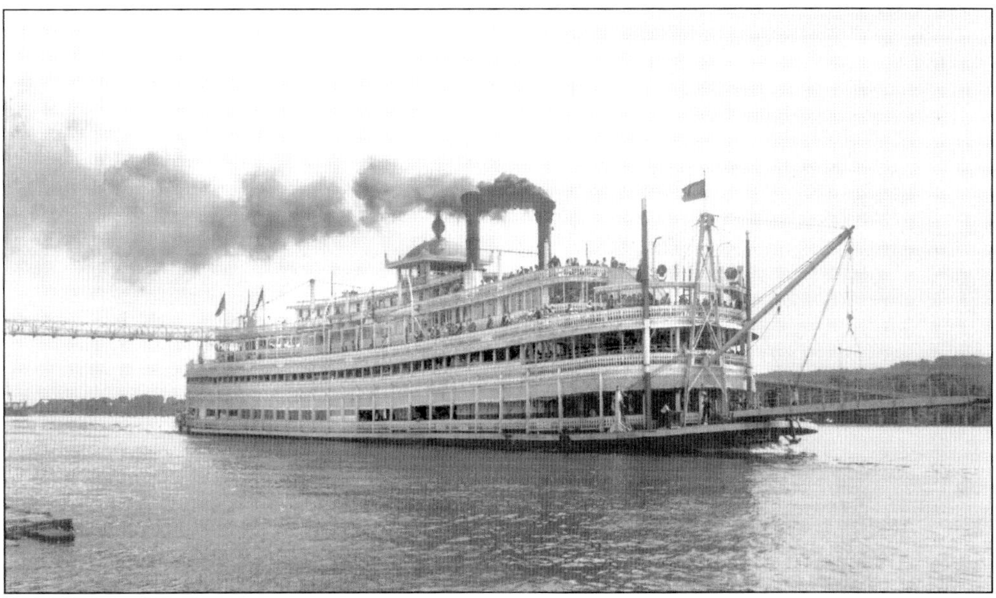

In the first quarter of the 20th century, many of the Mississippi River packet boats were refitted as excursion craft. Headquartered in Dubuque, the *Capitol* regularly stopped at Prairie du Chien between 1925 and 1945. Riders could enjoy a view of the river on a day excursion or dance to a band on a moonlit cruise. (Courtesy Ken and Louise White.)

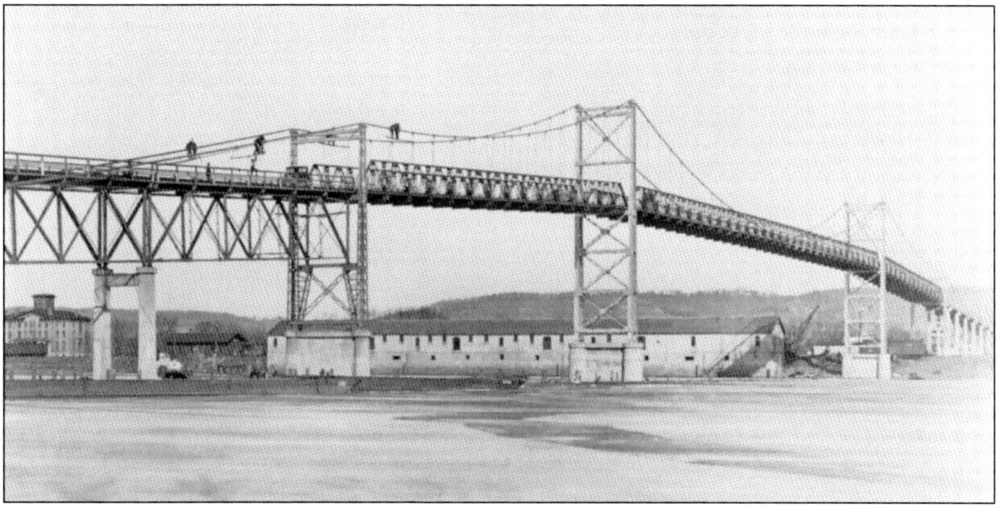

Crossing the river year-round was a struggle, so in 1925 John Frazier, president of the chamber of commerce, appointed a committee "to work in conjunction with other clubs in the interest of a Mississippi River bridge." A suspension bridge was built by F. K. Kether Company and the Pittsburgh-Des Moines Steel Company. It was composed of two metal spans, each approximately 450 feet long. The bridge opened in March 1932. (Courtesy Ken and Louise White.)

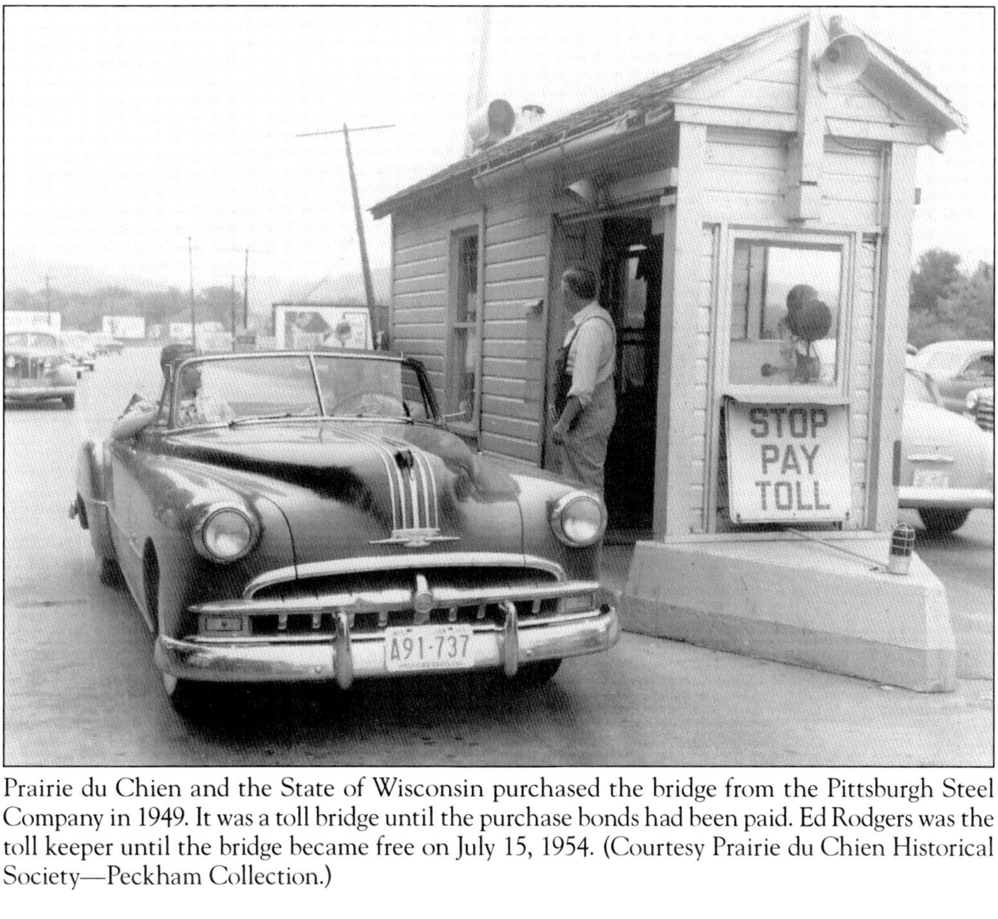

Prairie du Chien and the State of Wisconsin purchased the bridge from the Pittsburgh Steel Company in 1949. It was a toll bridge until the purchase bonds had been paid. Ed Rodgers was the toll keeper until the bridge became free on July 15, 1954. (Courtesy Prairie du Chien Historical Society—Peckham Collection.)

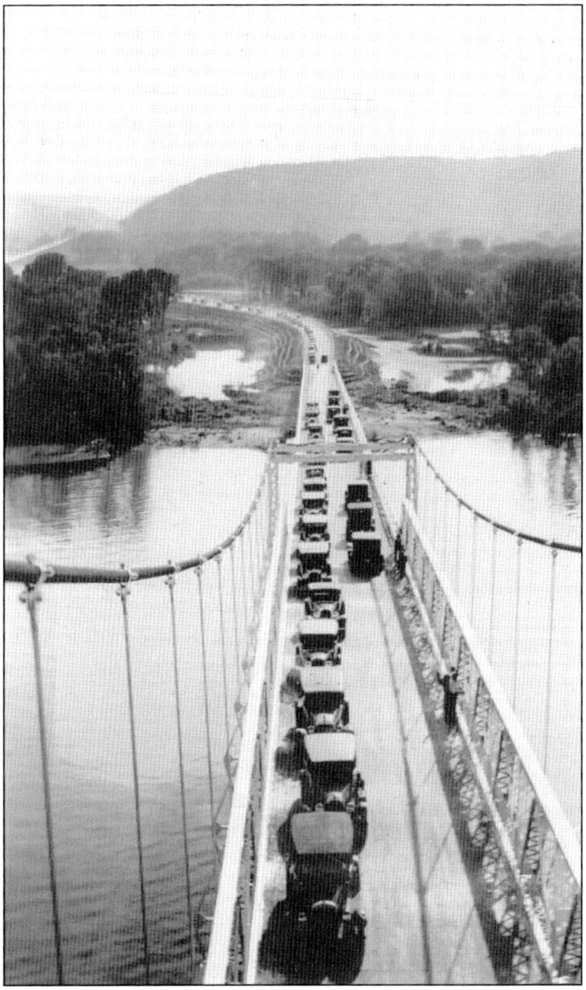

After the repeal of Prohibition in 1933, taverns reopened in Prairie du Chien. Iowa continued to prohibit the sale of alcohol by the drink, so people from Iowa came to Prairie du Chien on weekends. A legend states that during this time, 33 taverns conducted business throughout the community.

George and Emmi McClure's Bar and Cedar Room, located in the Fourth Ward, was a favorite gathering place. George always had chilled bottles of Orange Crush for the children. He would tell stories to the adults while Emmi made chili. (Courtesy Kathy Koch.)

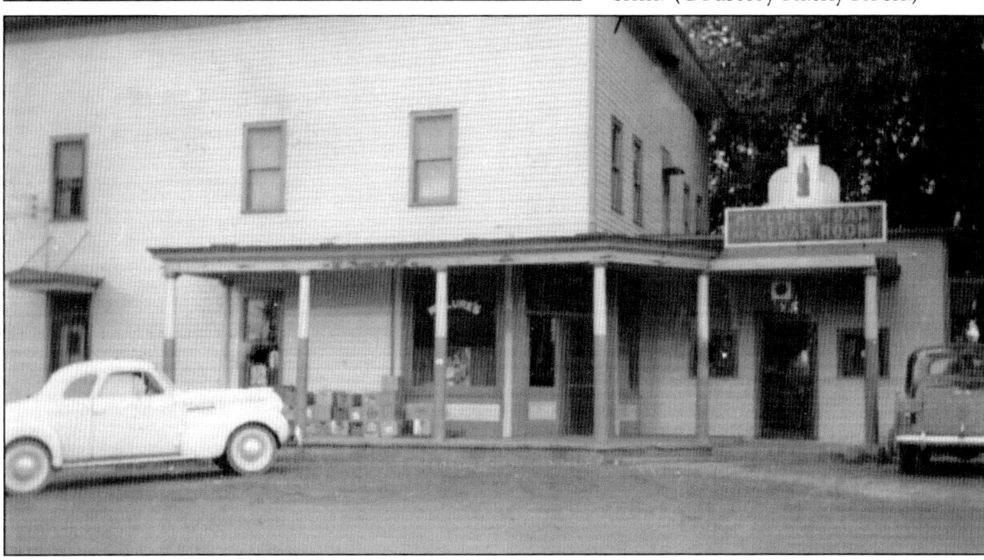

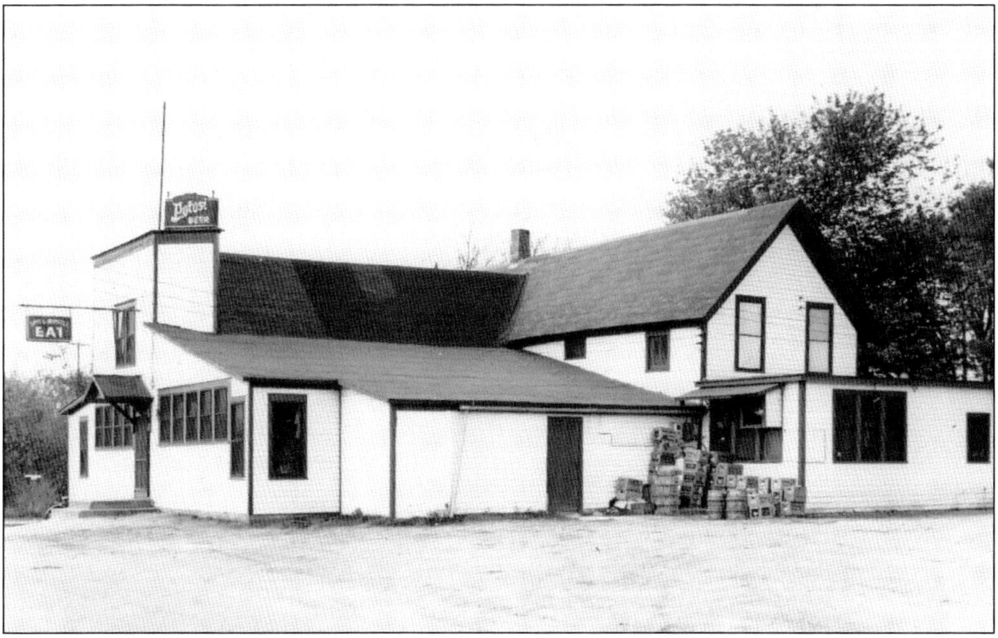

Along South Main Street in Lower Town, the Spit & Whistle had a boisterous clientele kept handily in line by Rose Pitzer. (Courtesy Prairie du Chien Historical Society—Peckham Collection.)

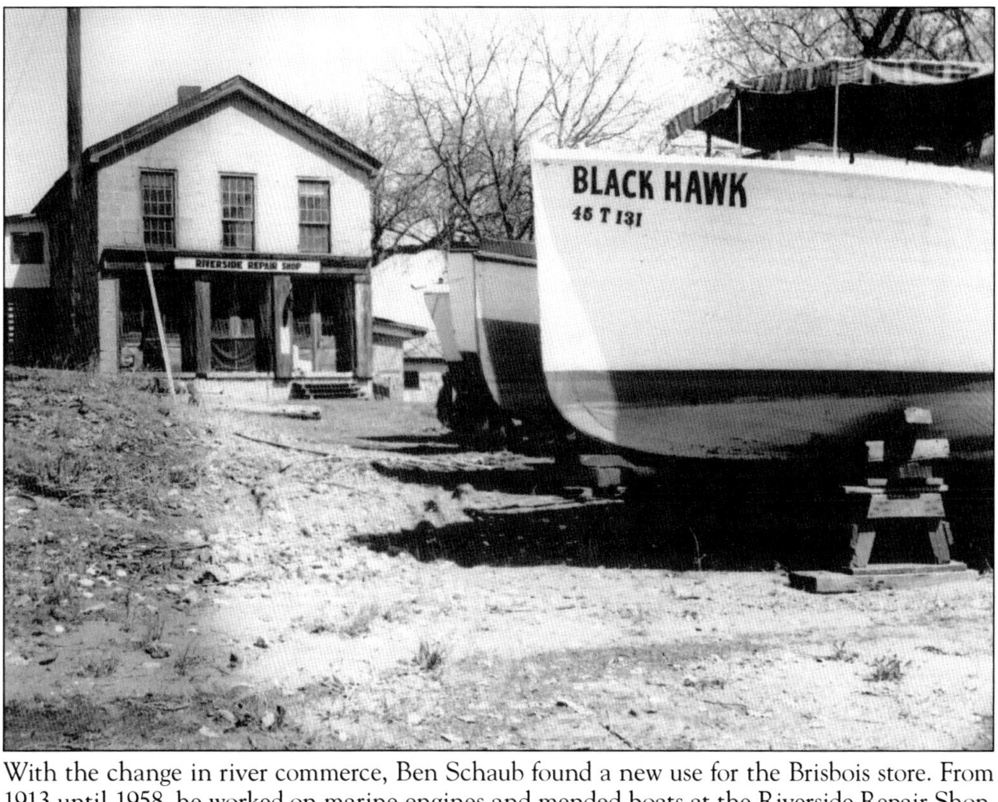

With the change in river commerce, Ben Schaub found a new use for the Brisbois store. From 1913 until 1958, he worked on marine engines and mended boats at the Riverside Repair Shop. (Courtesy Prairie du Chien Historical Society—Howe Collection.)

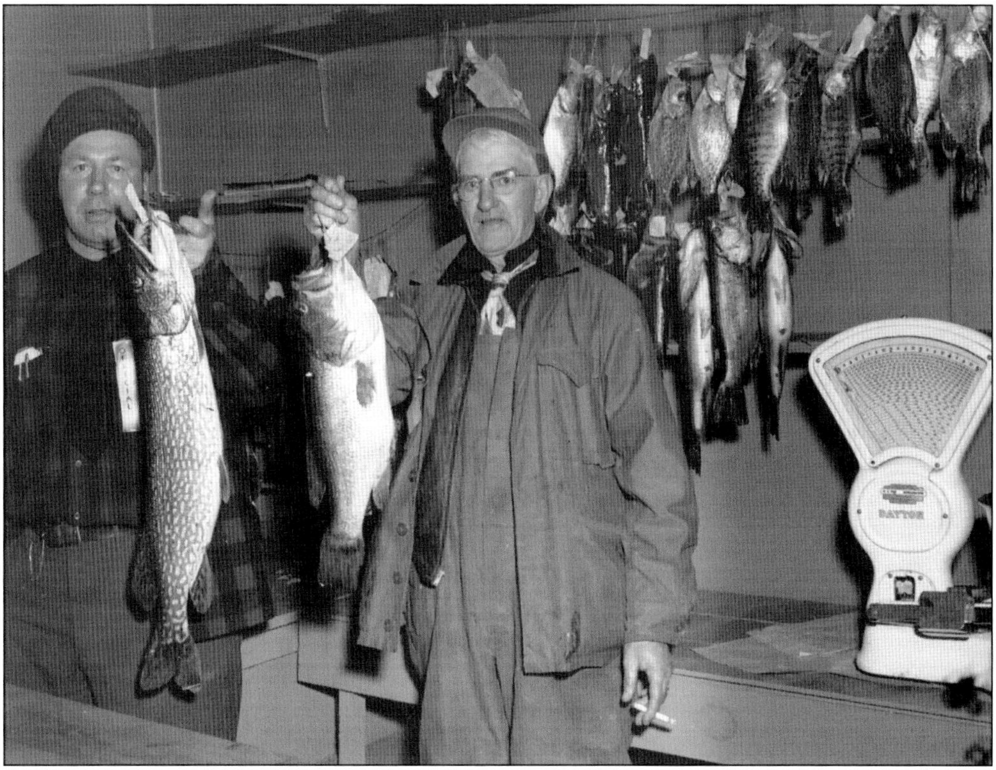

From the Native Americans, residents of Wisconsin learned to chop holes in ice-covered rivers and lakes to angle for fish. In 1950, the chamber of commerce instituted an annual Fisheree on Gremore Lake. Adults and children competed to determine who could catch the largest walleye, bass, perch, bluegill, or crappie. (Courtesy Prairie du Chien Historical Society—Peckham Collection.)

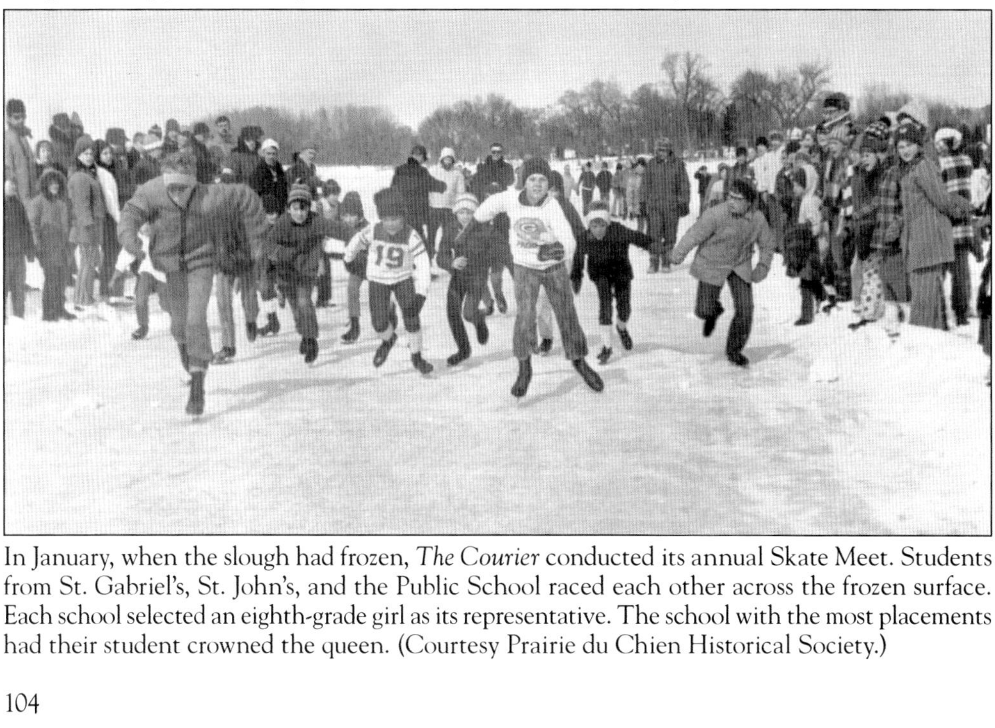

In January, when the slough had frozen, *The Courier* conducted its annual Skate Meet. Students from St. Gabriel's, St. John's, and the Public School raced each other across the frozen surface. Each school selected an eighth-grade girl as its representative. The school with the most placements had their student crowned the queen. (Courtesy Prairie du Chien Historical Society.)

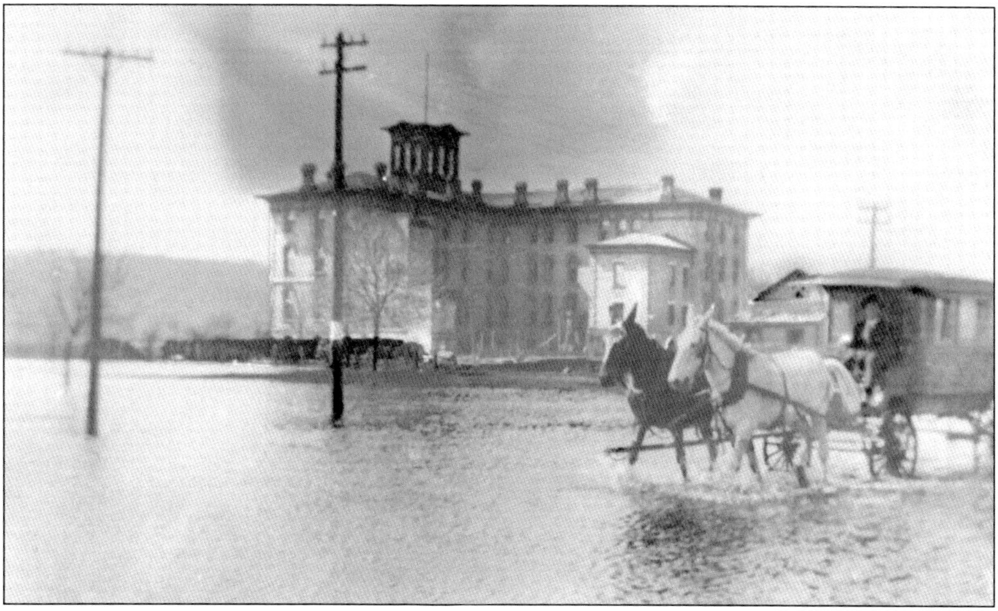

The Mississippi River at Prairie du Chien reaches flood stage at 16 feet. In 1880 and 1888, the Mississippi crested at over 20 feet, with the flood of 1880 being the seventh highest on record. In 1916, with the river at 18 feet, several residents captured the high waters on film. (Courtesy Bob Ziel.)

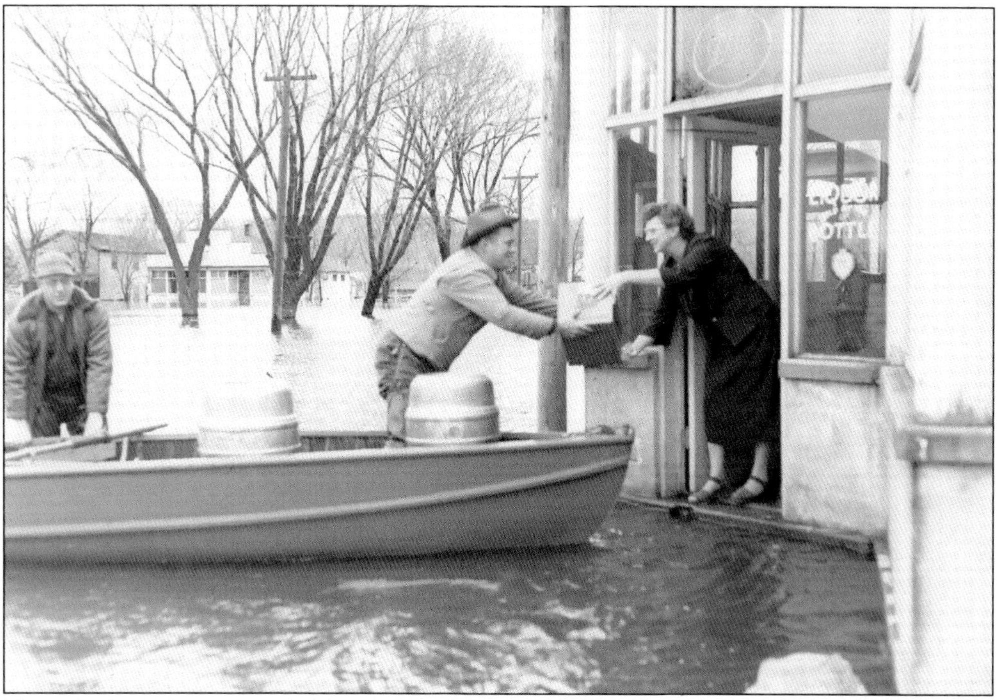

Through the 1920s and until 1938, the upper Mississippi River stayed within its banks. After some slight flooding in the 1940s, the river rose to 21 feet in 1951. The McClures stayed to protect their business, and Barney Morris (left) and Gordy Bower (center) delivered supplies. In 1965, the tavern would not be so lucky. (Courtesy Prairie du Chien Historical Society—Peckham Collection.)

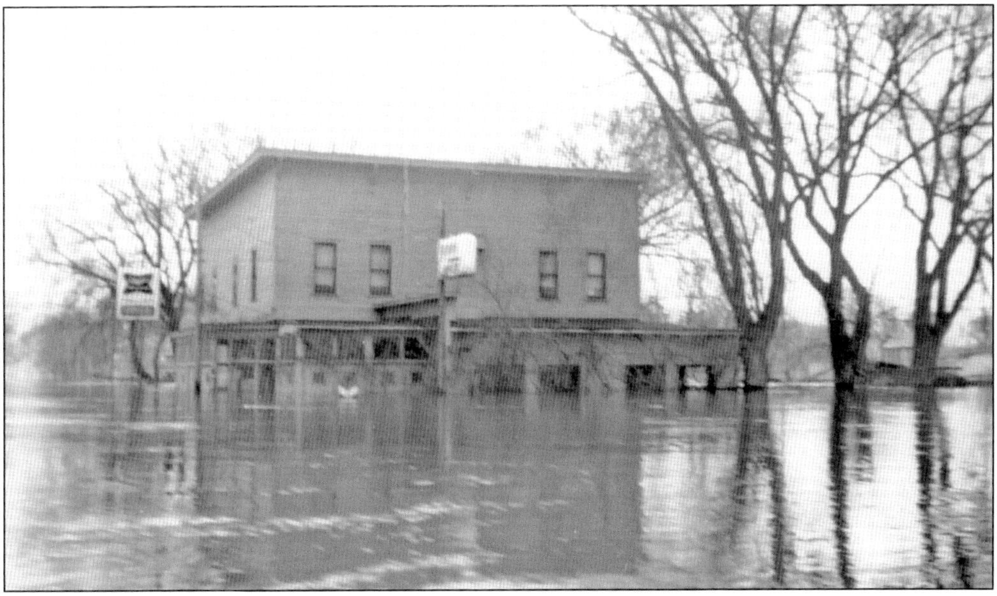

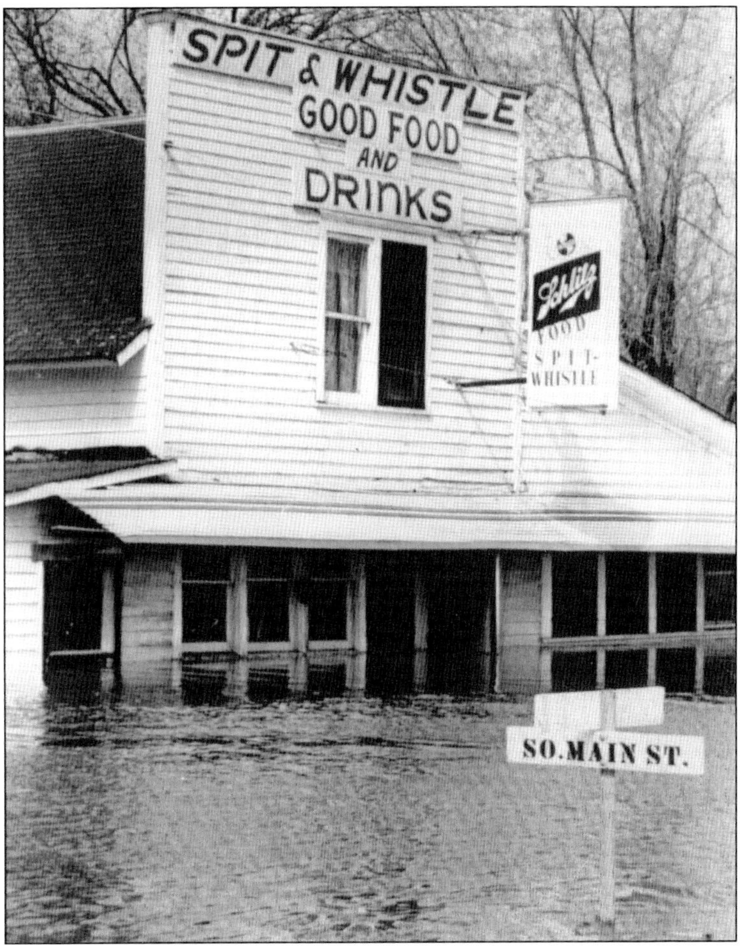

The Mississippi River rose rapidly in early April 1965. Residents of the Fourth Ward began to evacuate homes and businesses on April 9. Shelters were opened in the main part of the city, and massive sandbagging efforts attempted to keep the water out of buildings. (Courtesy Bob Ziel.)

All efforts proved futile. Highways 35 and 18 into Prairie du Chien were closed, as was the bridge to Iowa. Homes and businesses along Main Street also filled with water. On April 24, the river crested at 25.4 feet—the highest on record to this time.

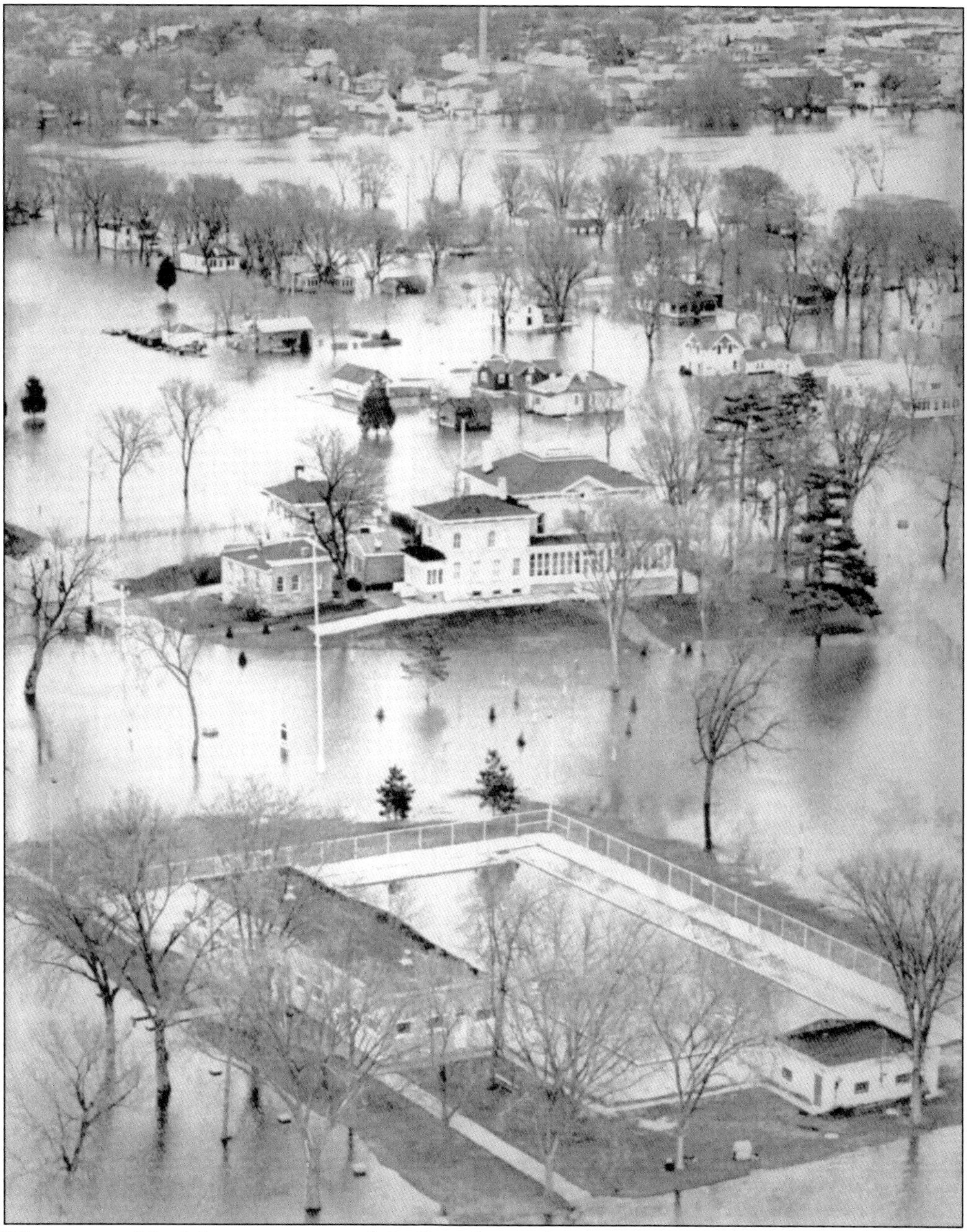

The waters of the Mississippi covered the Fourth Ward in 1969, 1971, 1972, 1973, 1975, 1976, and 1979, reaching 21.12 feet in 1975 and flooding twice in 1973. The cost of the floods in damage and cleanup was staggering.

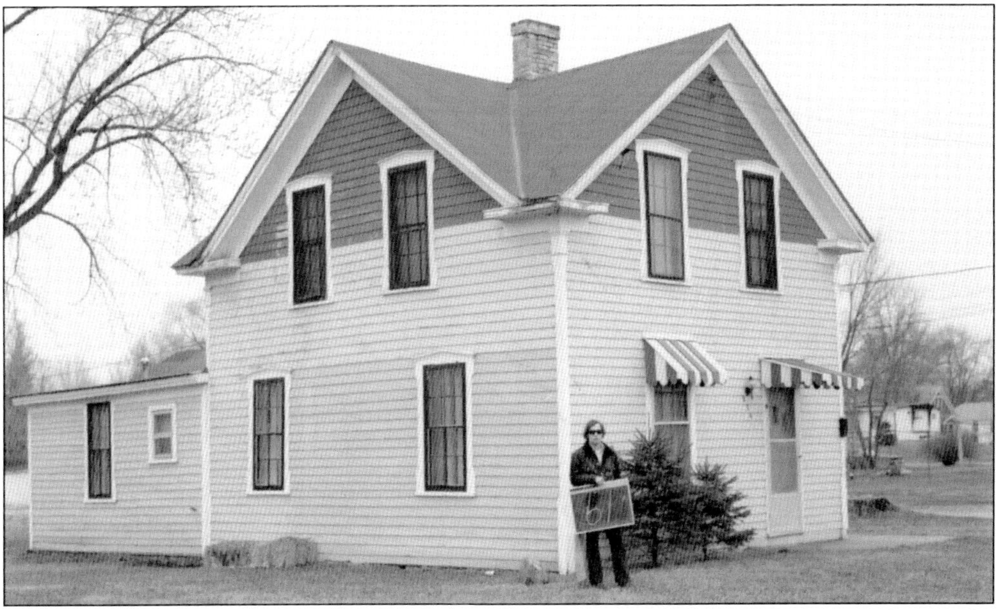

In early 1972, the City of Prairie du Chien and the U.S. Army Corps of Engineers discussed a flood control plan. Building levees around the entire Fourth Ward island required embankments that were too high. The water could not be diverted. Instead, it was decided that people needed to be relocated out of the floodplain. By 1983, eighty-two parcels had been purchased, and 69 families and their homes moved from the island. This was the first and only relocation project undertaken by the U.S. Army Corps of Engineers. (Courtesy the City of Prairie du Chien.)

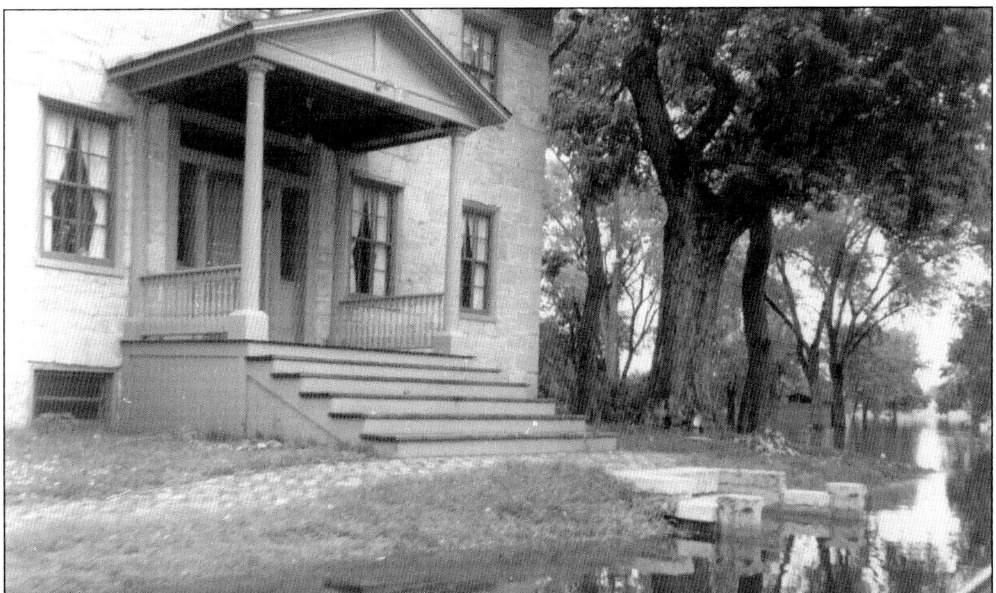

By 1993, all families and businesses had been relocated to higher ground. The winter of 1992–1993 was unusually snowy, and spring rainfall was record-breaking. The entire Mississippi River basin filled with water from runoff caused by snowmelt and rain. The river rose to 21.98 feet at Prairie du Chien and stayed there. For over a week, the Mississippi lapped at the steps of the Brisbois house. (Courtesy Ken and Louise White.)

Six

Natural Beauty and History to Share

Any extended account of the chief points of interest either in the human history or the natural beauty of the region about Prairie du Chien, Wisconsin would fill volumes.

—Althea Sherman, 1919

Post–World War I prosperity brought a sense of introspection to the community, as residents assessed themselves and where they lived. Prairie du Chien lay at the center of a region of immense natural beauty and historic importance. Railroad companies and steamboat lines had promoted the magnificence of the river and bluffs at "one of Wisconsin's oldest settlements." Now the residents began to do the same, encouraging neighbors and visitors to look and stay a while.

Female residents were the first to direct people's attention to the history of Prairie du Chien. The School Sisters of Notre Dame connected St. Mary's Academy to the early history of the area. Members of the Daughters of the American Revolution who lived across the street from the ruins of Fort Crawford saw value in preserving the remains of this important period of U.S. history. The League of Women Voters purchased the Knowlton House, making it their headquarters.

Throughout the Depression, the momentum continued. Laura Case Sherry, a friend of Zona Gale, used her personal experiences and knowledge of Prairie du Chien to write poems, published in 1931 as *Old Prairie du Chien*. Dr. Peter L. Scanlan turned his interest from medicine to history. In 1937, he published *Prairie du Chien: French, British, American*. That same year, Constance Evans and Ona Earll produced *A Short Narrative of the Events at Prairie du Chien*, a history filled with oral tradition.

The City of Prairie du Chien acquired the Villa Louis, the Dousman family estate, in 1935. Under the guidance of archaeologists, historians, and artists funded through the Works Progress Administration (WPA), the Villa Louis and the Fort Crawford Hospital became historic sites.

Grants to the States of Wisconsin and Iowa provided funding to develop and open parks on both sides of the Mississippi River at Prairie du Chien.

Natural beauty and history were now accessible to many. Citizens and visitors could now gaze in awe at the majesty of the Mississippi River, and experience the history of Prairie du Chien, about which they had only read or heard.

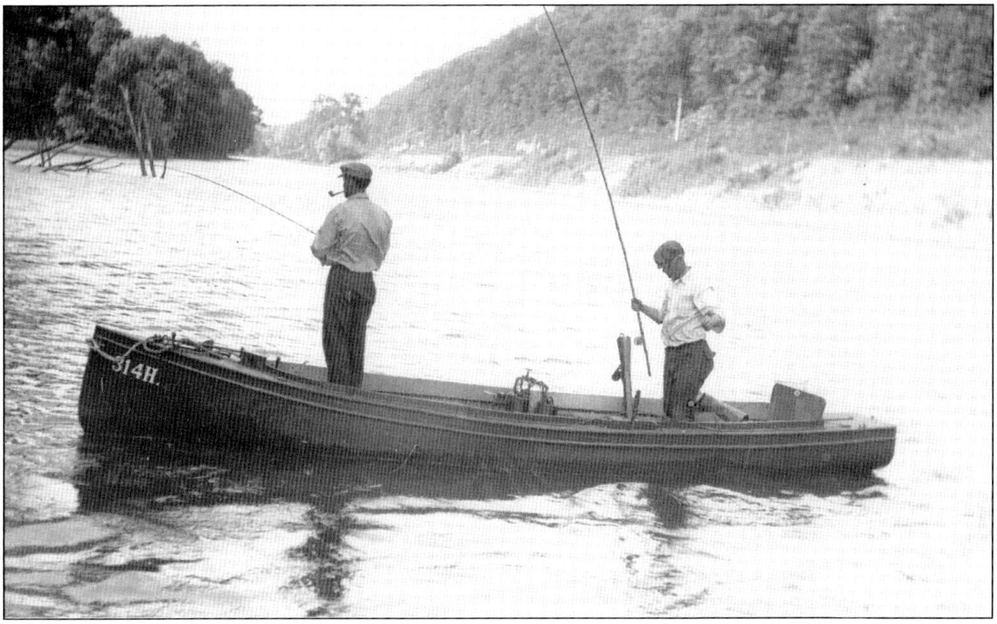

The backwaters had names like Catfish, Winneshiek, and Sturgeon Slough, Roseau Channel and Horseshoe Lake, and through them a person could drift or fish, capturing the history and romantic beauty of the area. Visitors could rent a motor launch, complete with a guide who knew each and every slough and backwater, to take them to the best fishing spot. (Courtesy Prairie du Chien Historical Society—Peckham Collection.)

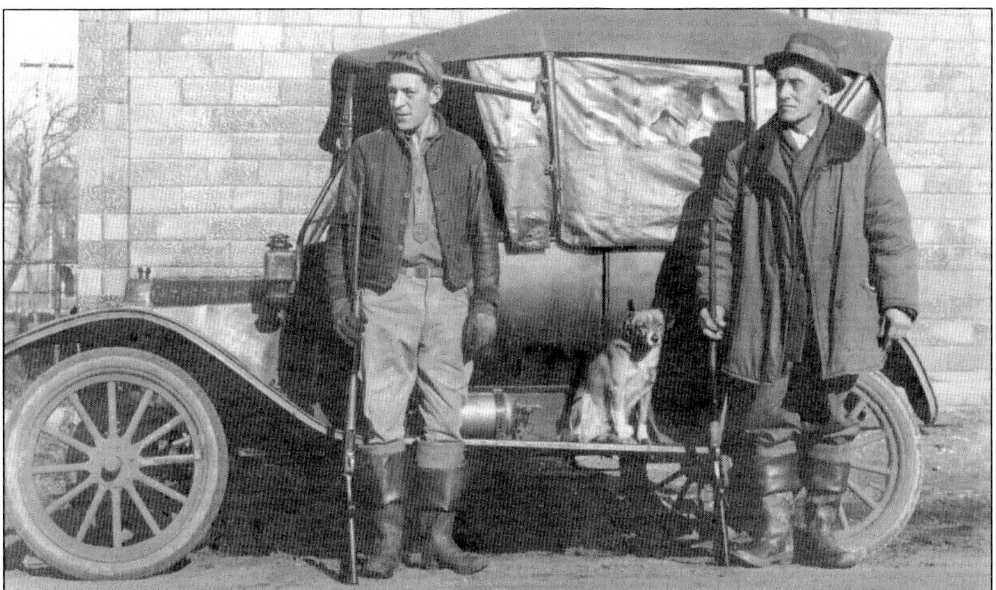

In the fall, local "river rats," such as Denis (left) and Jack St. Jacques (right), guided tourists to prime hunting blinds built where only ducks could land. (Courtesy Bob Ziel.)

From Galena to St. Paul, open outcroppings of limestone bluffs rose 500 feet above the Mississippi. Scaling the faces of a bluff, an intrepid hiker would be rewarded with a panoramic view of the river and the prairie spread below. (Courtesy Antoine family.)

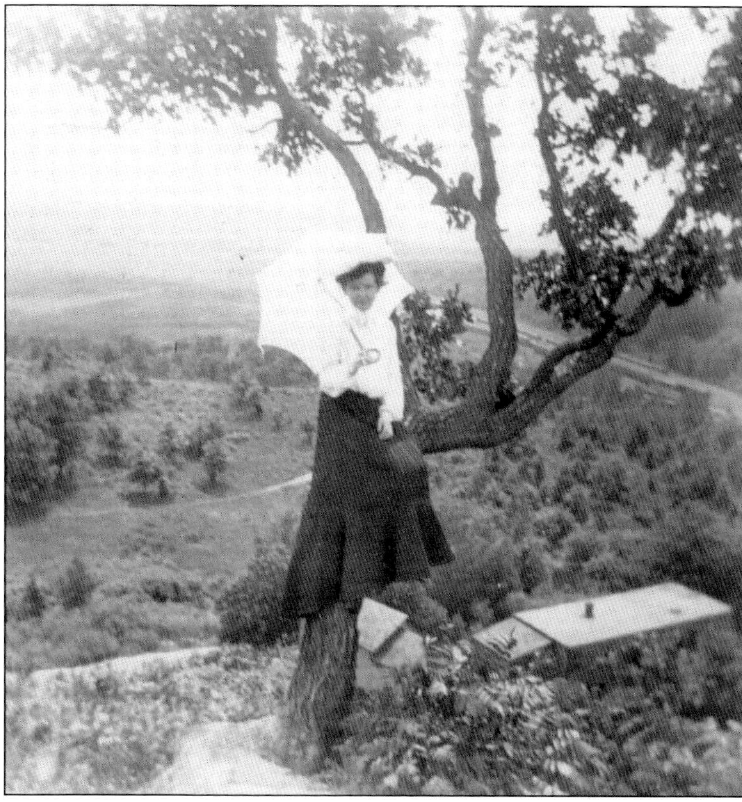

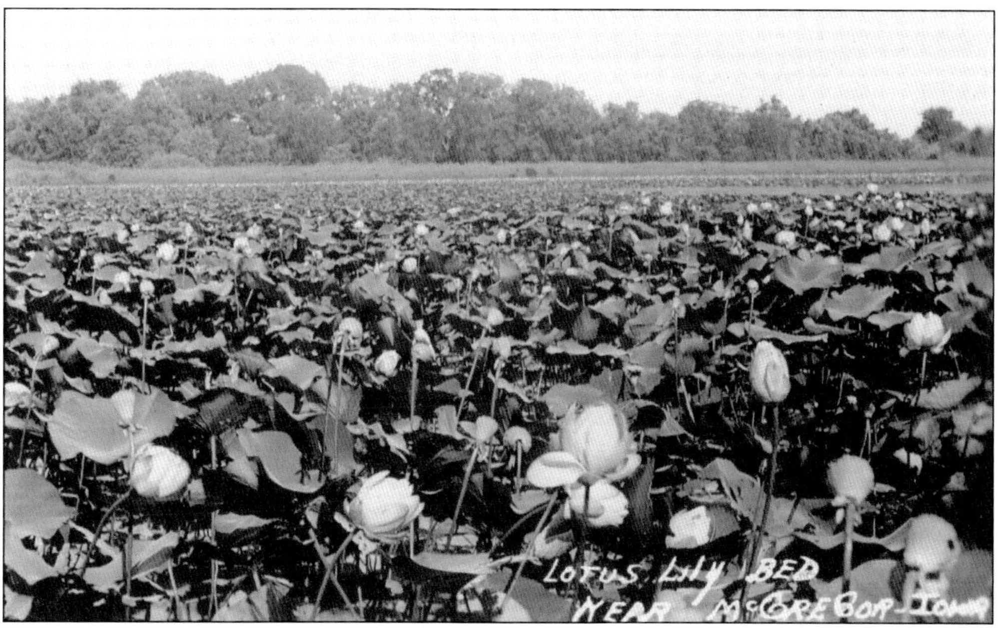

The American lotus thrives in the shallow, still waters of the sloughs with their muddy bottoms. Native Americans harvested the plants as a source of food, while in the 20th century visitors marveled at the yellow flowers in bloom from July to September. (Courtesy Prairie du Chien Historical Society—Peckham Collection.)

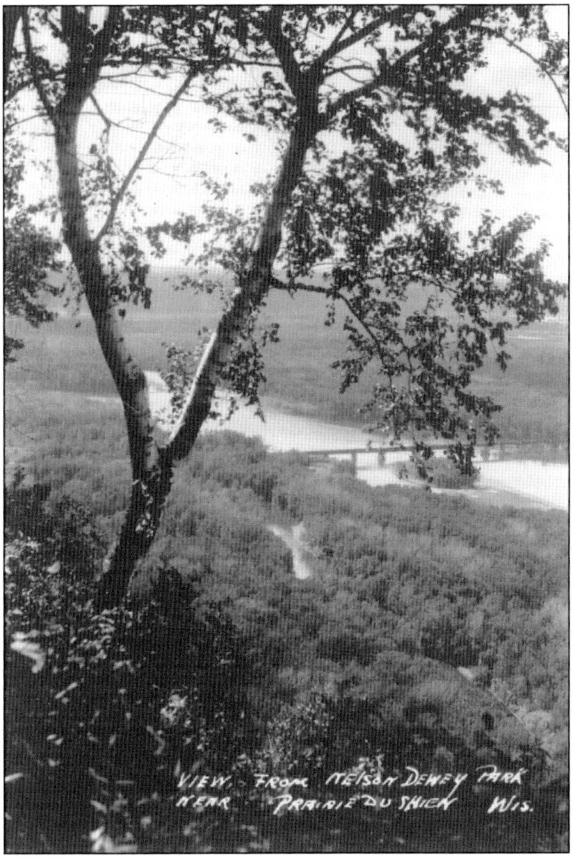

In the early 1900s, the Wisconsin Legislature recommended four sites for state parks. One site overlooked the spot where Marquette and Jolliet had entered the Mississippi River in 1673. This site opened in 1917 as Nelson Dewey State Park, and the confluence of two mighty rivers stretch below the high lookouts built on the edges of the bluffs.

Opposite Nelson Dewey State Park was the point of land on which Lt. Zebulon M. Pike stood in 1804. A descendant of Alexander MacGregor willed the primeval land to be used as a park. Pike's Peak, an Iowa state park, opened in 1935, offering a broad view to the north and south of the river plain.

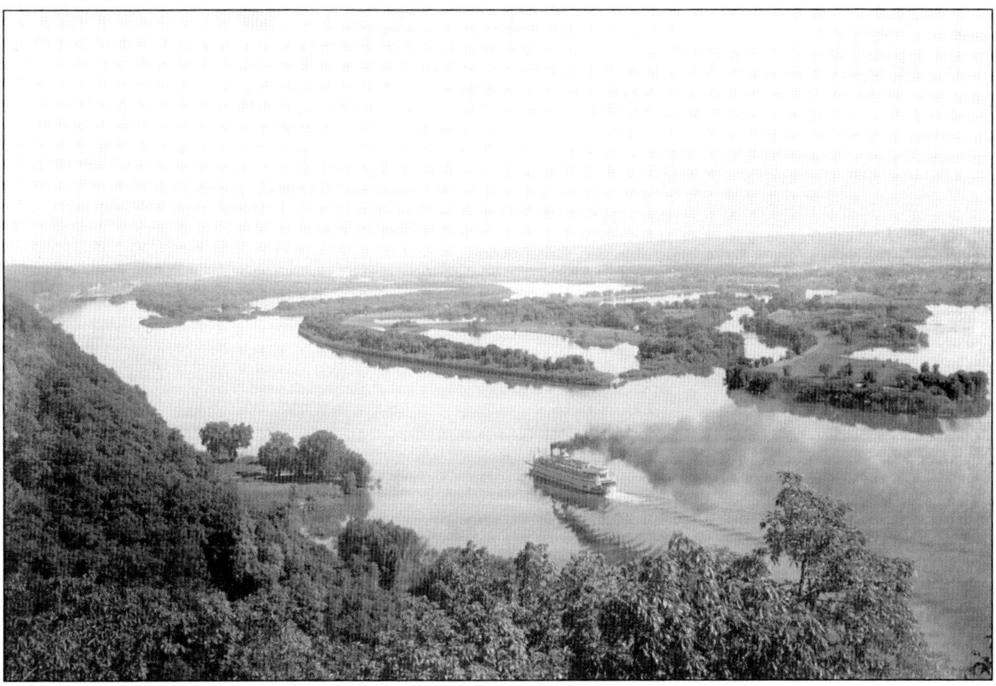

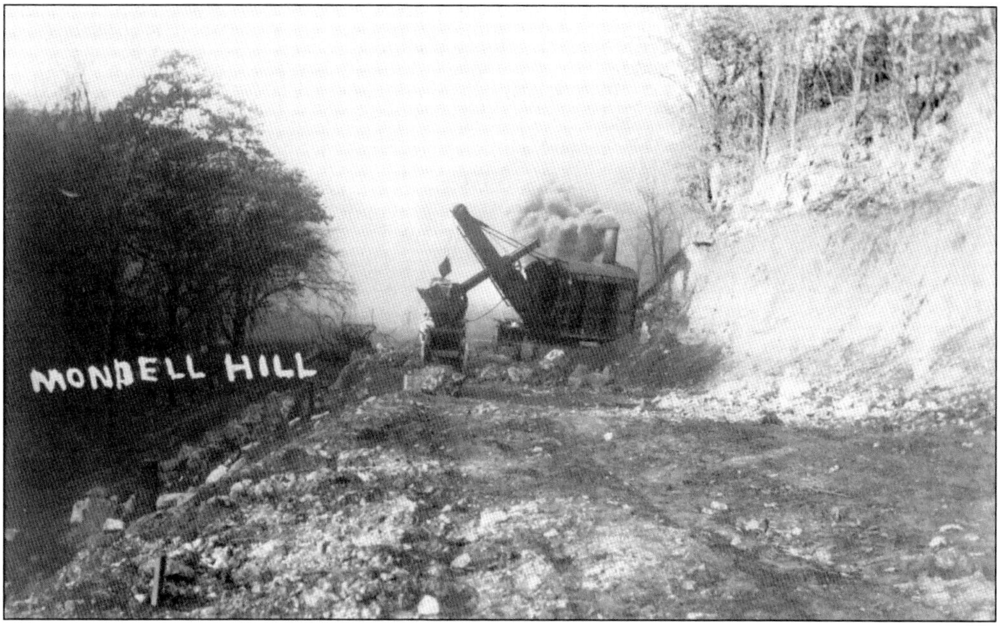

With people traveling by automobile, the dirt road connecting Prairie du Chien to northern Crawford County needed to be widened. This required a cut through the limestone that had been an old quarry on the Mondell Hill. (Courtesy Martner Collection.)

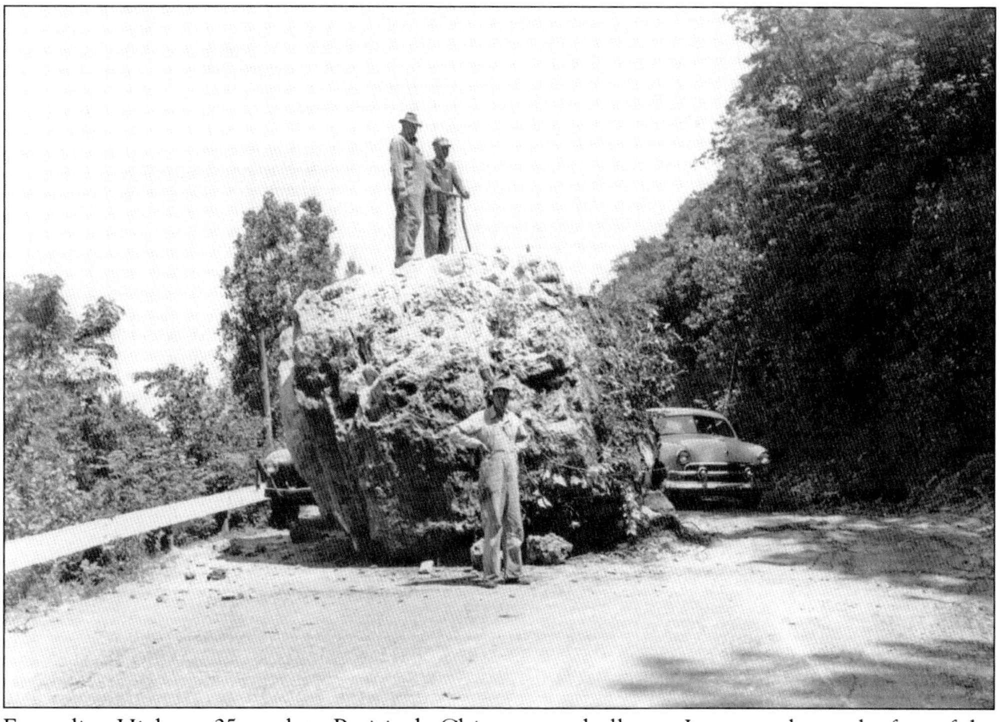

Extending Highway 35 south to Prairie du Chien was a challenge. In many places, the foot of the bluffs touched the waters of the Mississippi. A ledge, safe from flooding, needed to be carved high above the water. Too often heavy rains or melting snows released a portion of a bluff to block man's progress. (Courtesy Prairie du Chien Historical Society—Peckham Collection.)

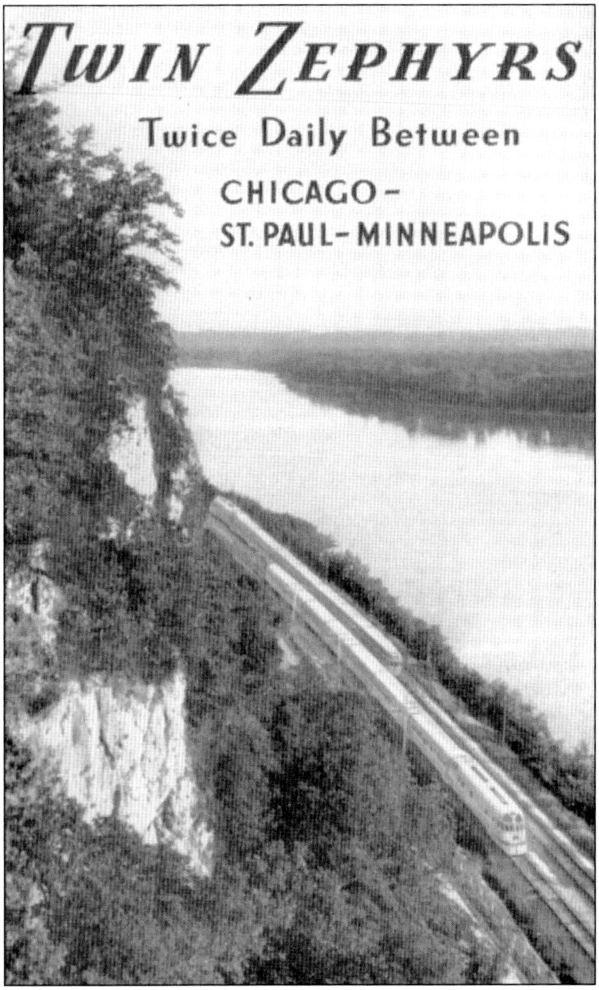

The railroad offered a faster, surer way to travel. Inaugurated in 1935, the *Twin Zephyrs* of the Chicago, Burlington and Quincy Railroad converged just above Prairie du Chien. Along this scenic route between Prairie du Chien and La Crosse, travelers beheld the majesty of the Mississippi while speeding at 85 miles per hour before disembarking to experience what they had seen. (Courtesy Martner Collection.)

The Mattie family built cabins along the eastern shore of Gremore Lake, a prime fishing spot. From here, summer visitors could row up the Ambrough Slough or to Spring Lake and spend the day angling for panfish.

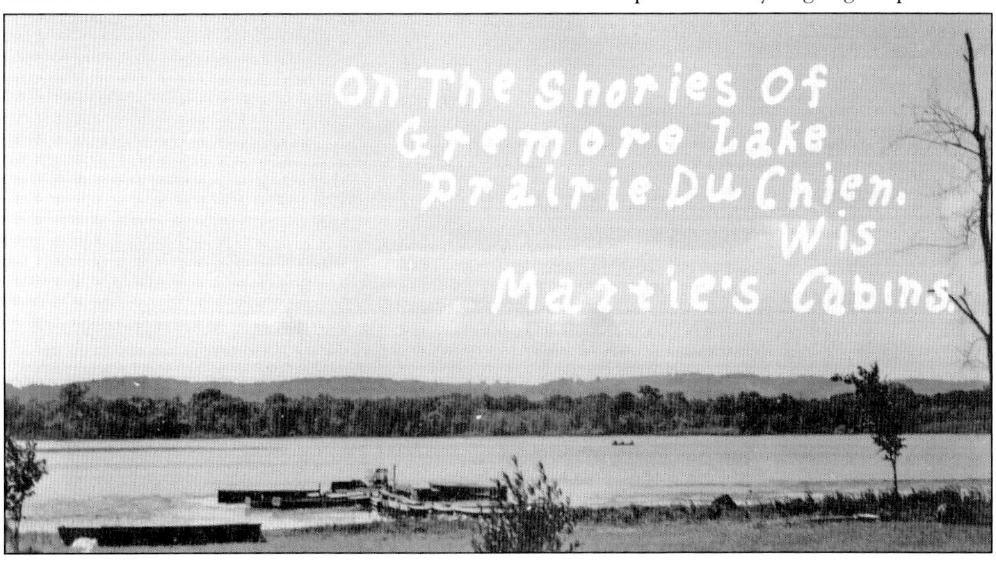

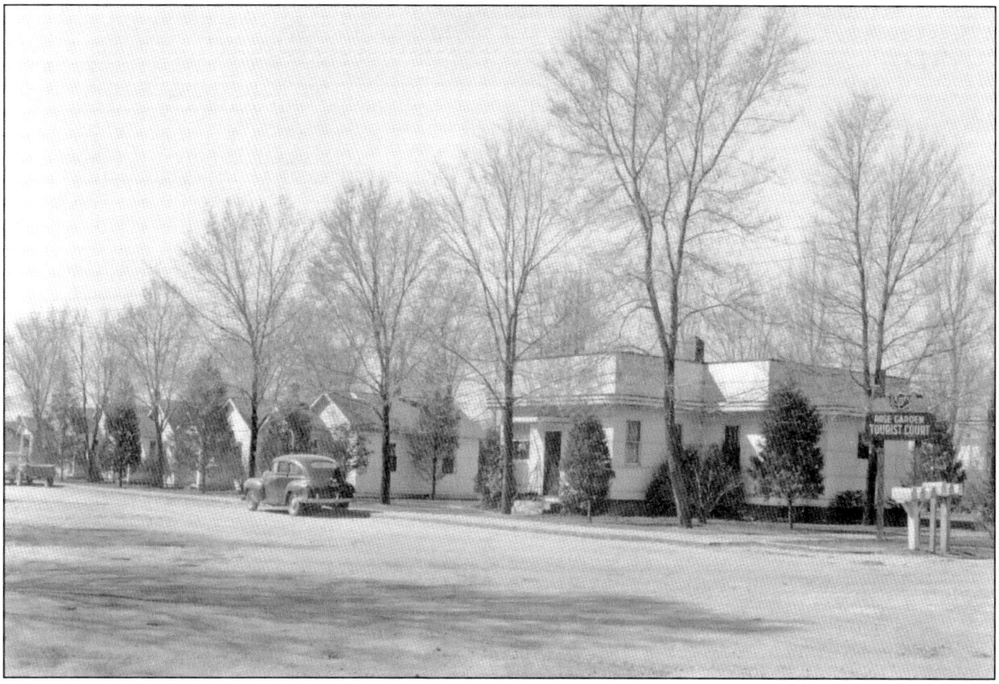

To accommodate visitors arriving at Prairie du Chien by automobile, John Pettera opened the Rose Garden Motor Court. (Courtesy Jim Trentin.)

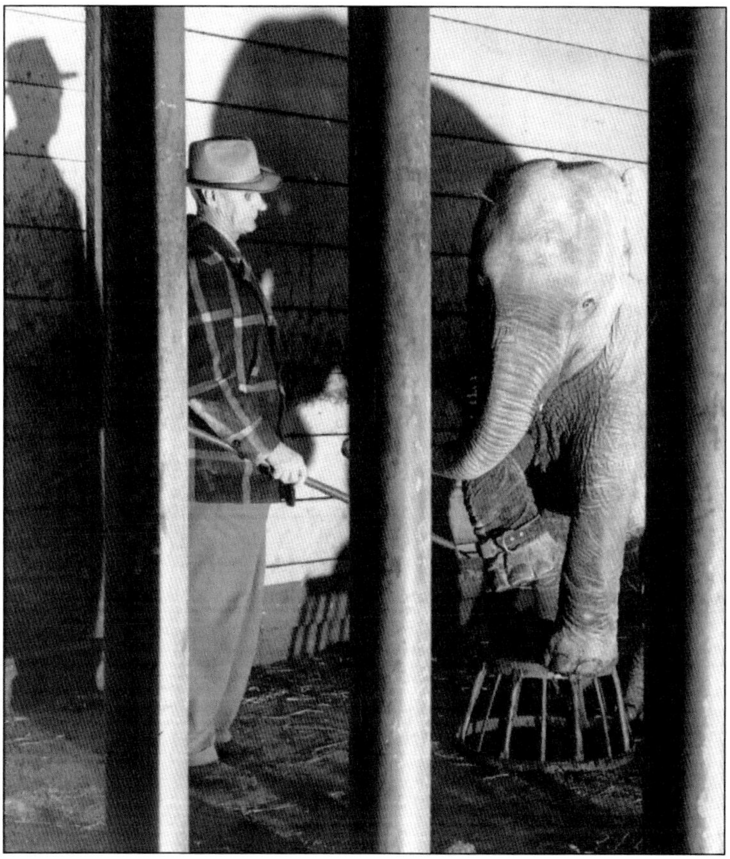

John's interest in breeding pheasants and mallard ducks entertained his patrons. This led to his acquisition of elk and buffalo. Soon he opened Rose Park Zoo. On Sundays, children rode Rosa the elephant as their parents listened to music performed by Leo and His Pioneers. (Courtesy Shirley Machovec.)

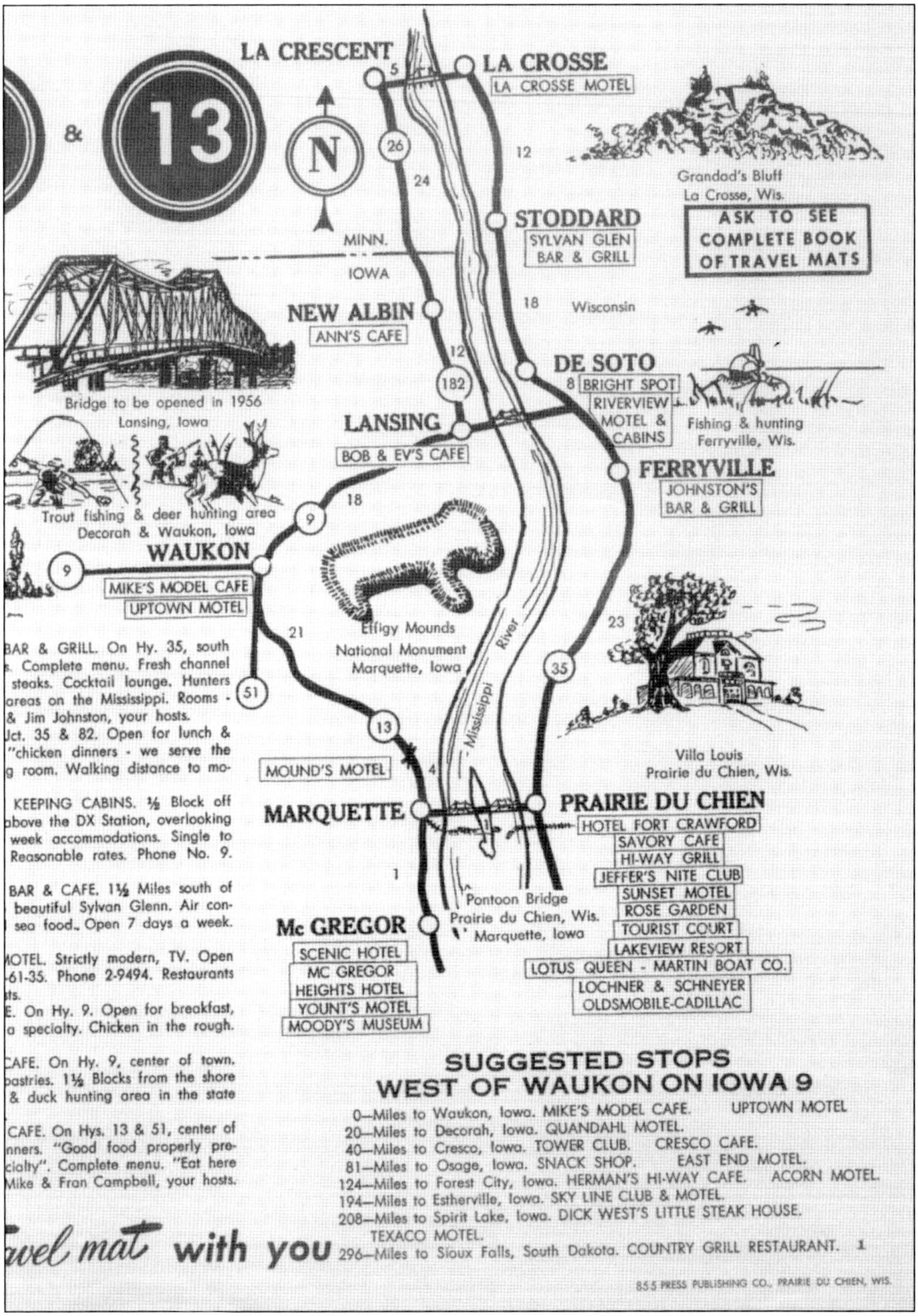

To help the visitor locate points of interest, accommodations, and eating spots, J. Alvin Dru'yor started printing place mats that included a local map and recommended stops. He called them Travel Mats. Beginning with the drive from Prairie du Chien to La Crosse, in time, a person could motor across the United States following Travel Mat recommendations.

For generations, the story was told that after the Battle of the Bad Axe, Black Hawk hid in a large cottonwood tree that grew on the prairie at Prairie du Chien. As the city grew, Bluff Street lengthened. Close to the bluffs, the street parted, passing on each side of the tree. The Black Hawk Tree blew down in September 1922, but residents collected pieces as souvenirs. (Courtesy Antoine family.)

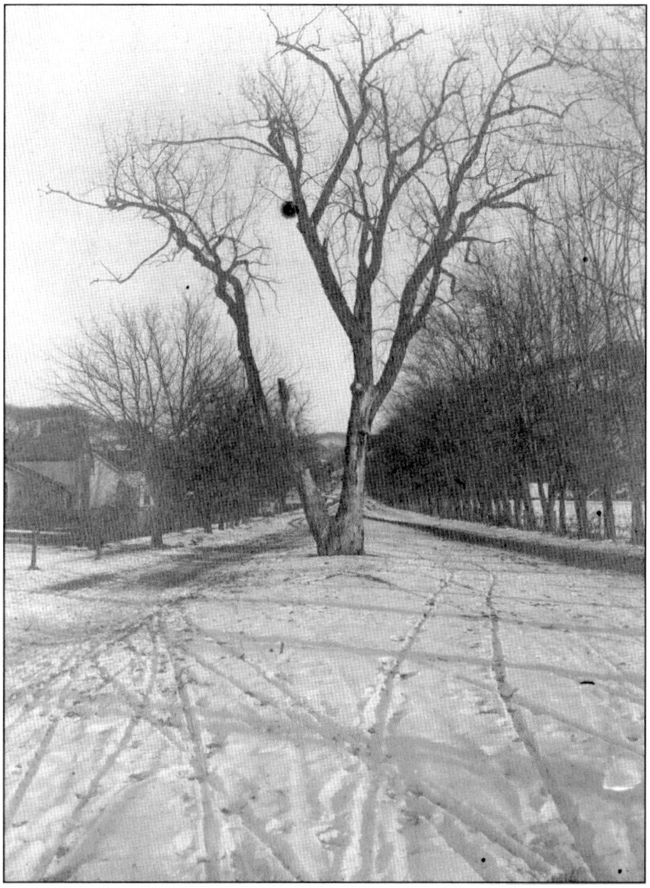

At the same time Fridolin J. Heer designed the new building for St. Mary's Academy, he created a statue of Father Marquette. Set upon a high pillar, the statue defined the new entrance to the school. On June 17, 1910, the anniversary of Marquette and Jolliet's entry into the Mississippi River, the community dedicated the statue. (Courtesy Antoine family.)

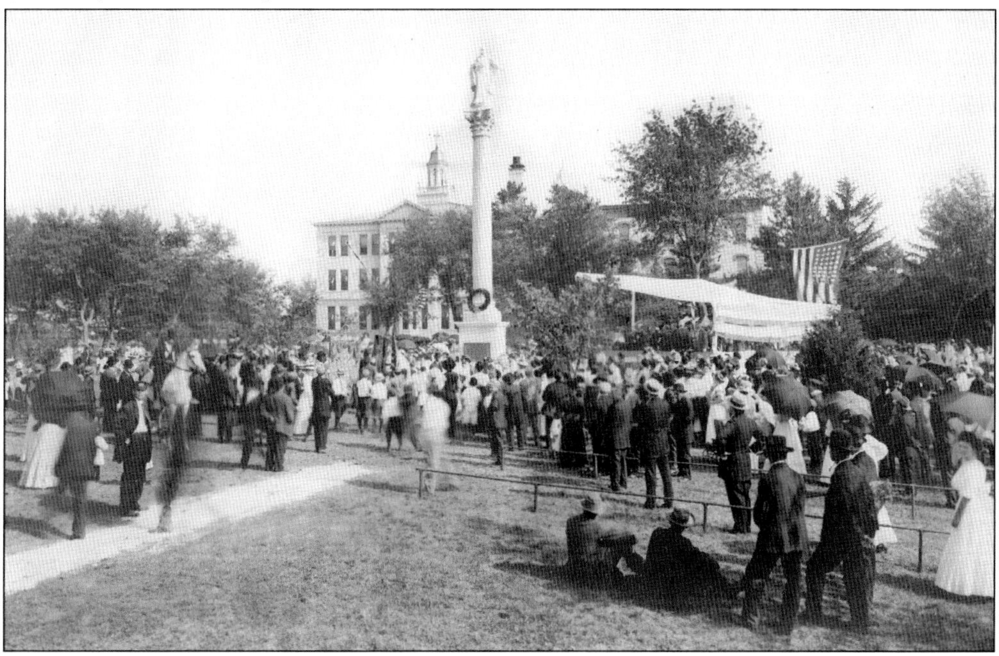

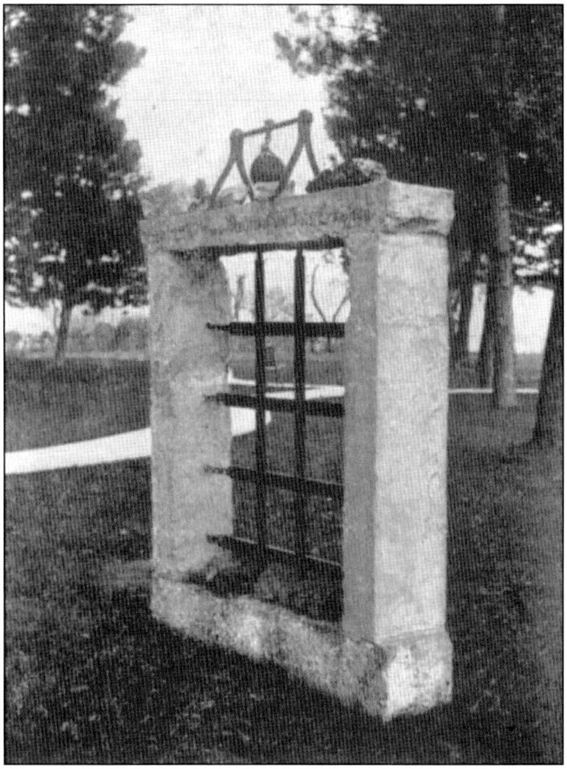

The sisters at St. Mary's Academy salvaged components of Fort Crawford, which they placed at appropriate locations on the campus. A barred window, reputed to have been part of the room in which Black Hawk was imprisoned in 1832, stood on the southwest corner of the school grounds. (Courtesy Antoine family.)

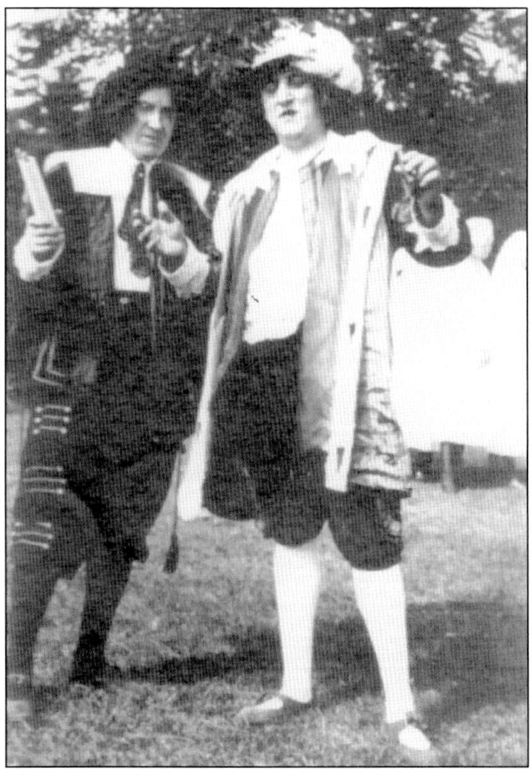

In June 1923, the entire community turned out to commemorate historic events. A pageant depicting the king of France and the governor general of New France charging Marquette and Jolliet with their duties and the subsequent journey to the Mississippi was held on the grounds of St. Mary's Academy. (Courtesy Antoine family.)

Charles Amman complained that the residents were taking away the Fort Crawford Hospital stone by stone. The curious came to see the remains of early Prairie du Chien. Art students at St. Mary's Academy immortalized the ruins on canvas. (Courtesy Prairie du Chien Historical Society—Howe Collection.)

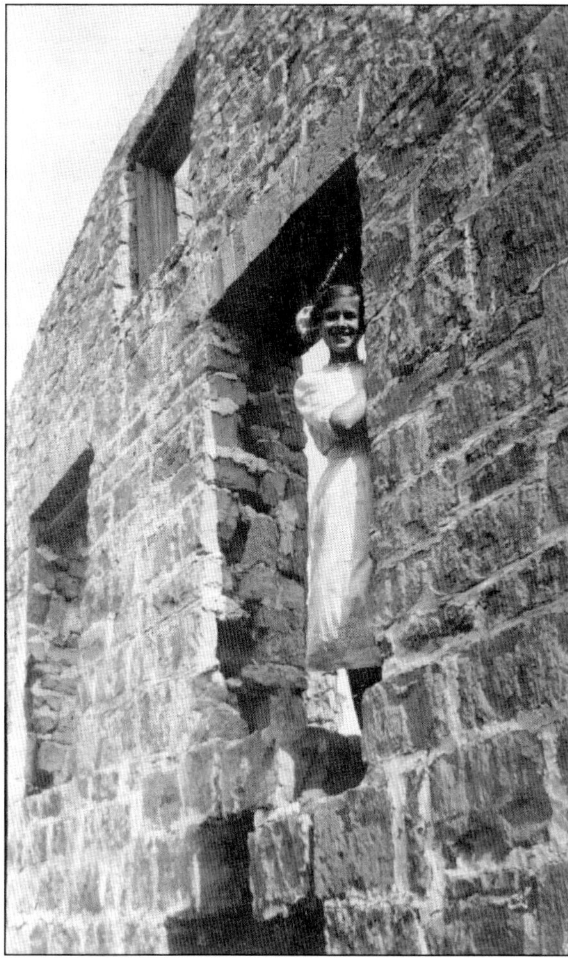

In July 1922, the Fort Crawford chapter of the Daughters of the American Revolution purchased the half-acre of land with the ruins of the Fort Crawford Hospital. (Courtesy Ken and Louise White.)

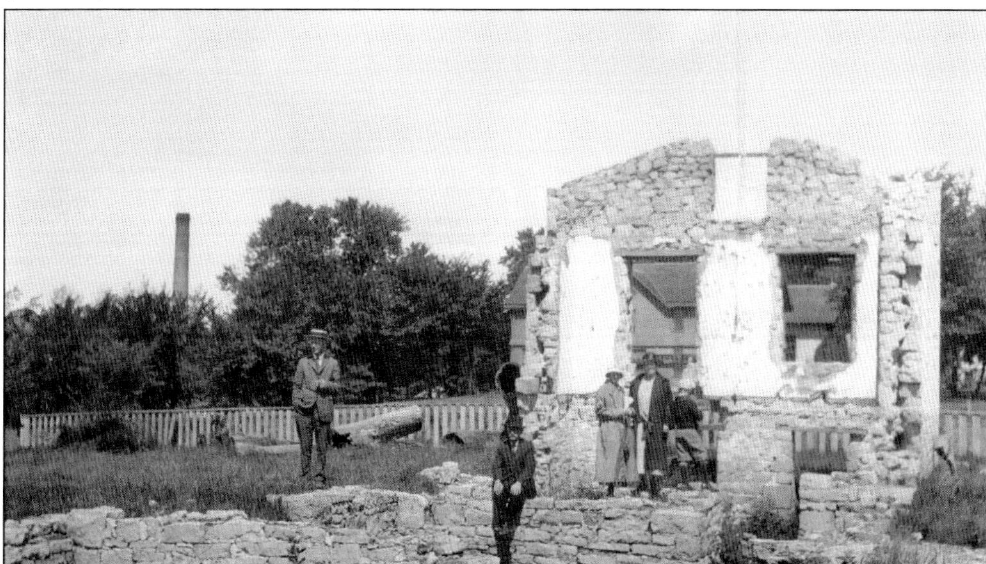

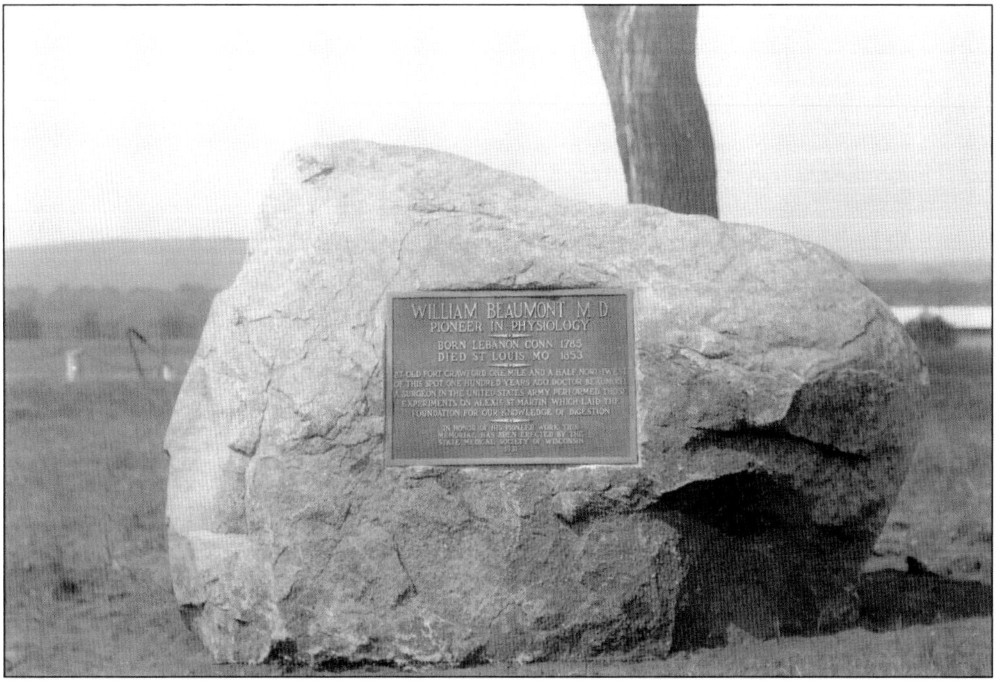

The Fort Crawford chapter then presented a small section of land in front of the Fort Crawford Hospital to the State Medical Society of Wisconsin for a memorial to Dr. William Beaumont. A memorial boulder with a bronze plaque was unveiled on August 30, 1931. (Courtesy Antoine family.)

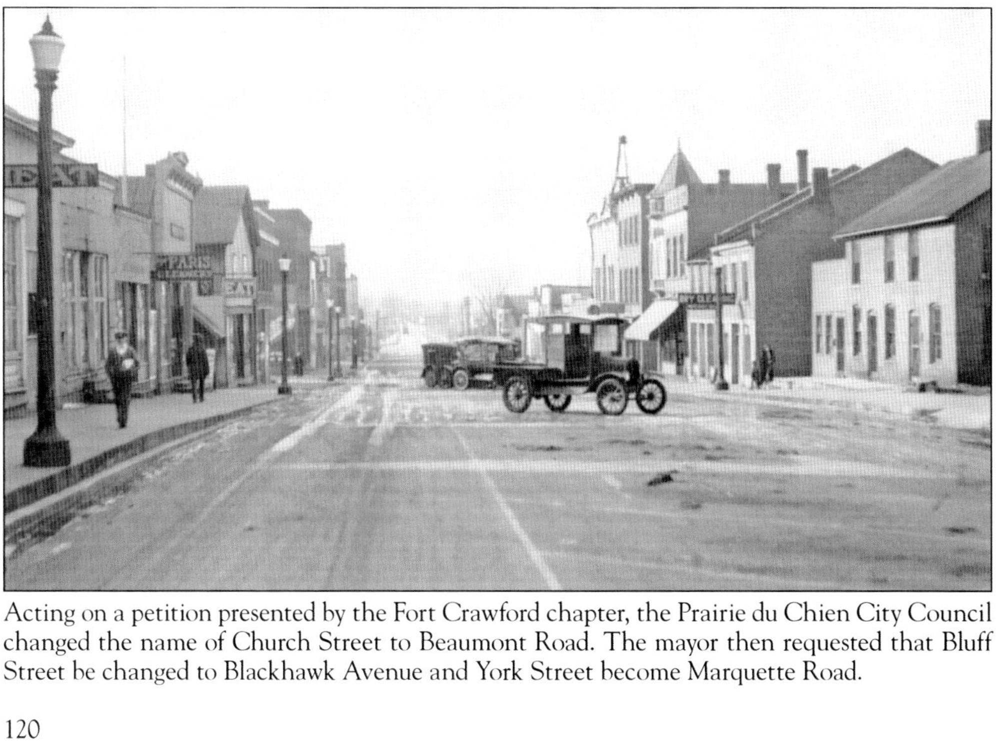

Acting on a petition presented by the Fort Crawford chapter, the Prairie du Chien City Council changed the name of Church Street to Beaumont Road. The mayor then requested that Bluff Street be changed to Blackhawk Avenue and York Street become Marquette Road.

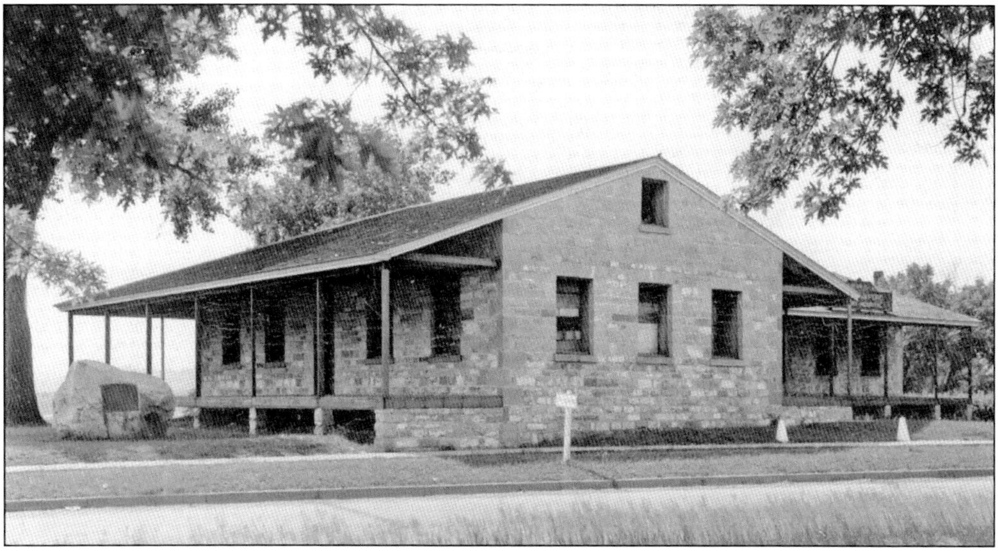

The women of the Daughters of the American Revolution then turned their efforts to restoring the hospital structure. The work progressed slowly, which was limited by funding. So the Fort Crawford chapter gave the hospital to the State Medical Society of Wisconsin. The society completed the restoration, opening a museum dedicated to Dr. William Beaumont and early Wisconsin medicine.

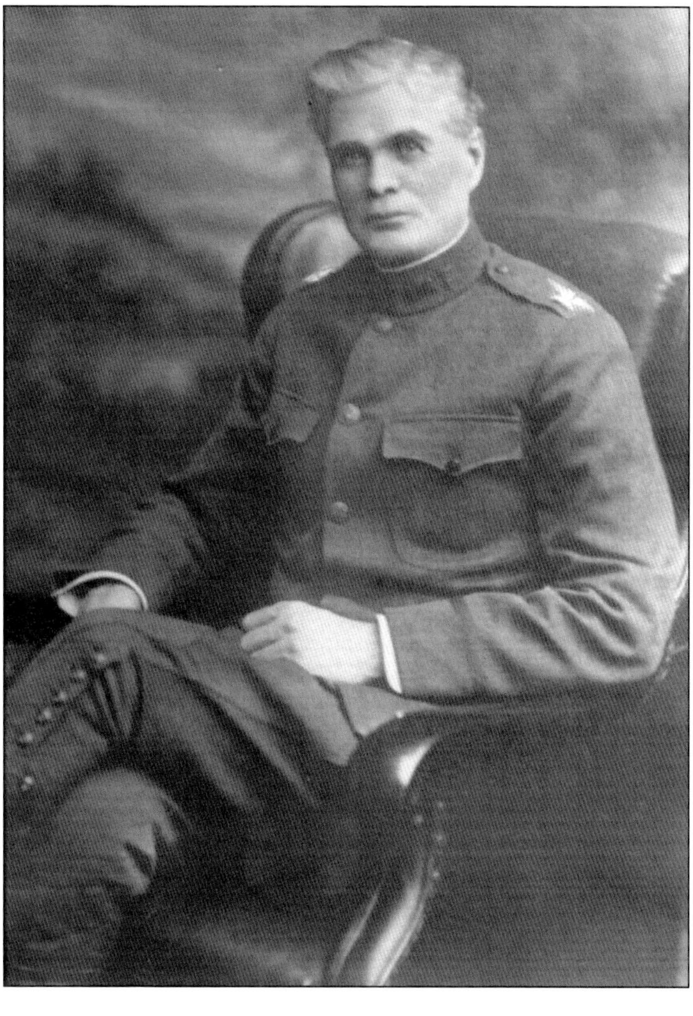

Dr. Peter L. Scanlan gave up the practice of medicine to devote his time to the research of early Prairie du Chien history. He published his book *Prairie du Chien: French, British, American* in 1937 and was working on a second volume when he died. (Courtesy Prairie du Chien Historical Society.)

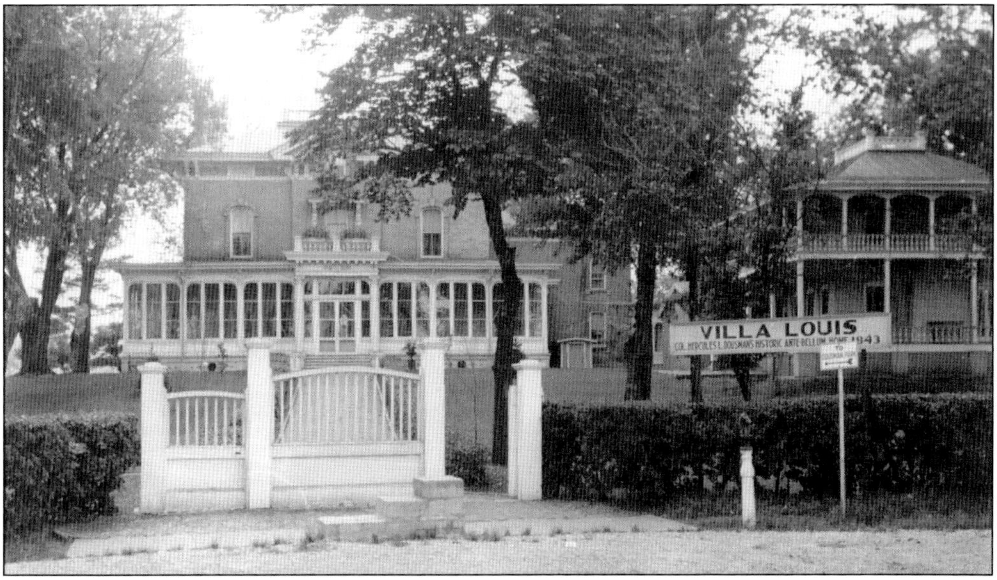

Members of the Dousman family no longer lived in Prairie du Chien, and the Villa Louis property needed care beyond the means of the family. In 1935, the Dousman heirs deeded the family estate to the City of Prairie du Chien, and the Villa Louis opened for tours.

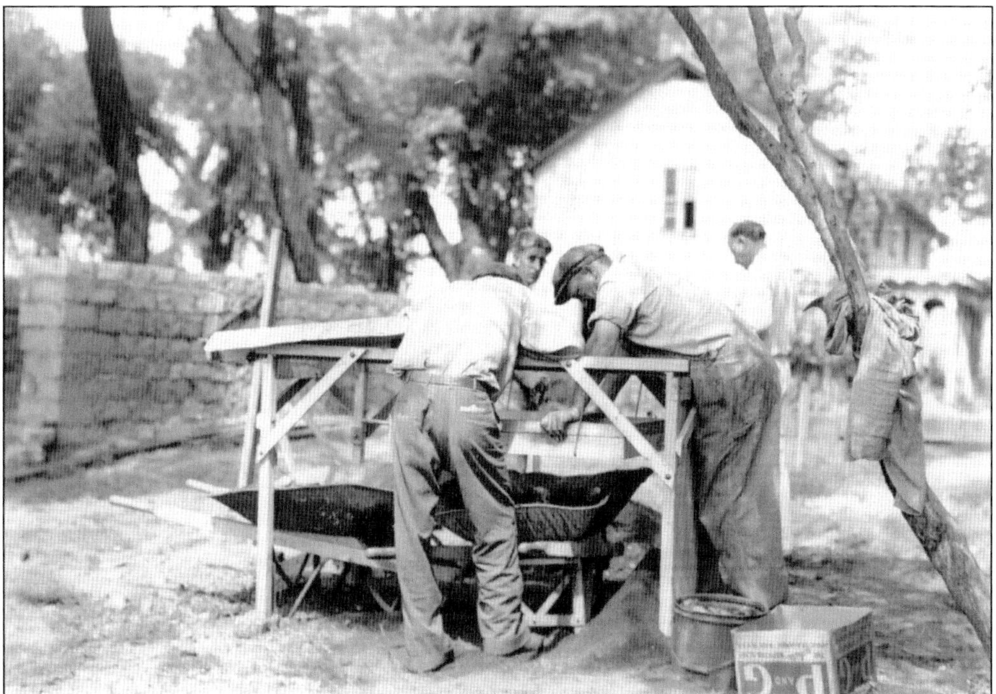

With a grant from the WPA, the city began to develop the property. In the course of the work, men found the foundations from the 1816 Fort Crawford. Rev. Leland Cooper oversaw an archaeological excavation of the fort remains. (Courtesy Prairie du Chien Historical Society.)

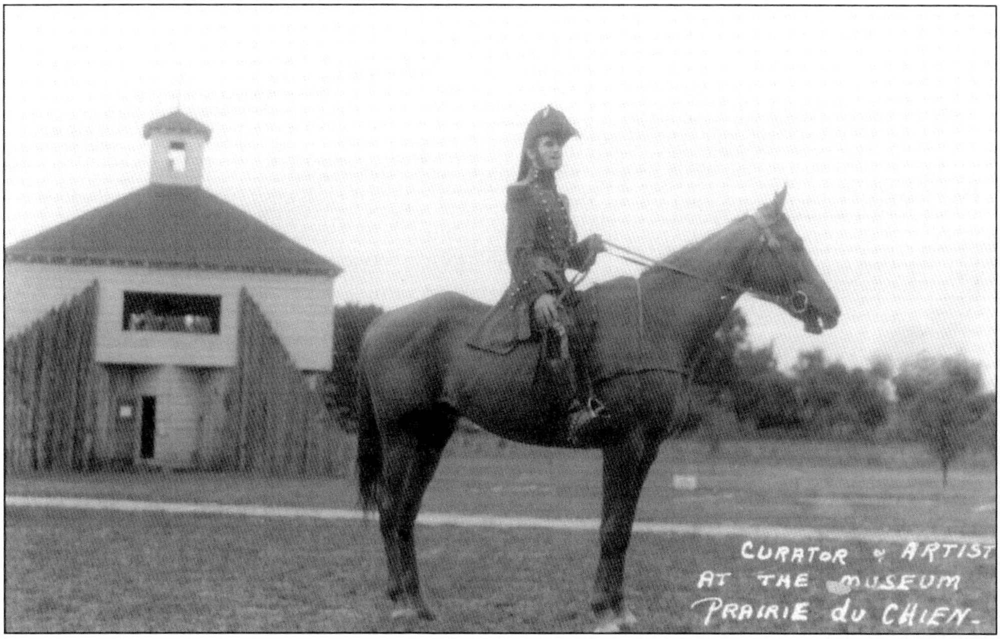

As part of the WPA grant to the City of Prairie du Chien, in 1938 Cal N. Peters was hired as curator of the Museum Prairie du Chien. The museum was installed in a brick building that had been a stable of Louis Dousman's Artesian Stock Farm. (Courtesy Virginia Antoine.)

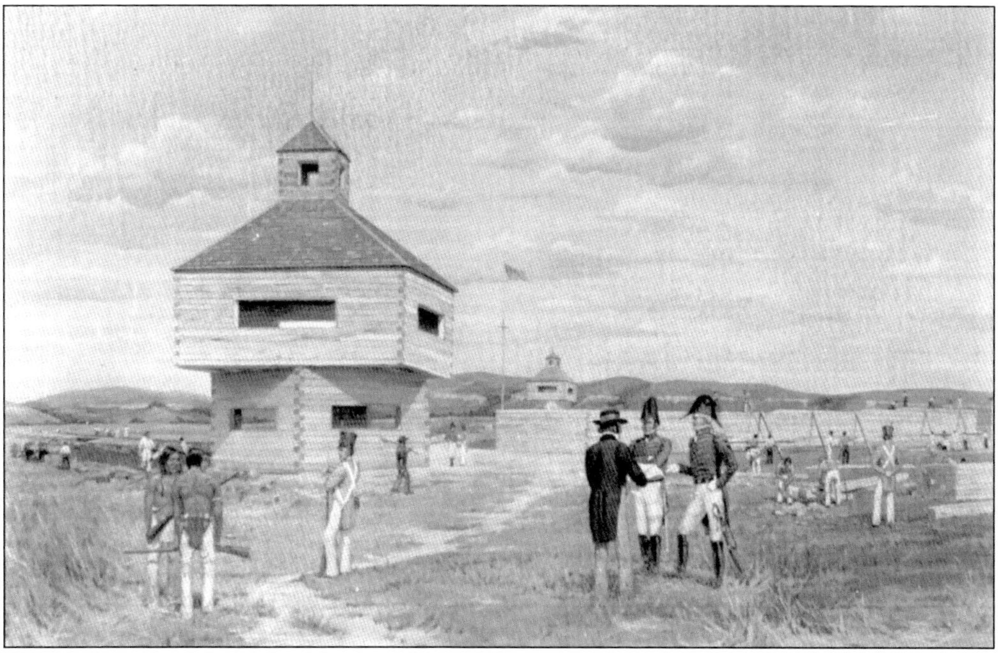
As curator of the museum, Peters created 10 dioramas and painted 11 murals depicting the history of Prairie du Chien (see pages 11 and 23). (Courtesy Ken and Louise White.)

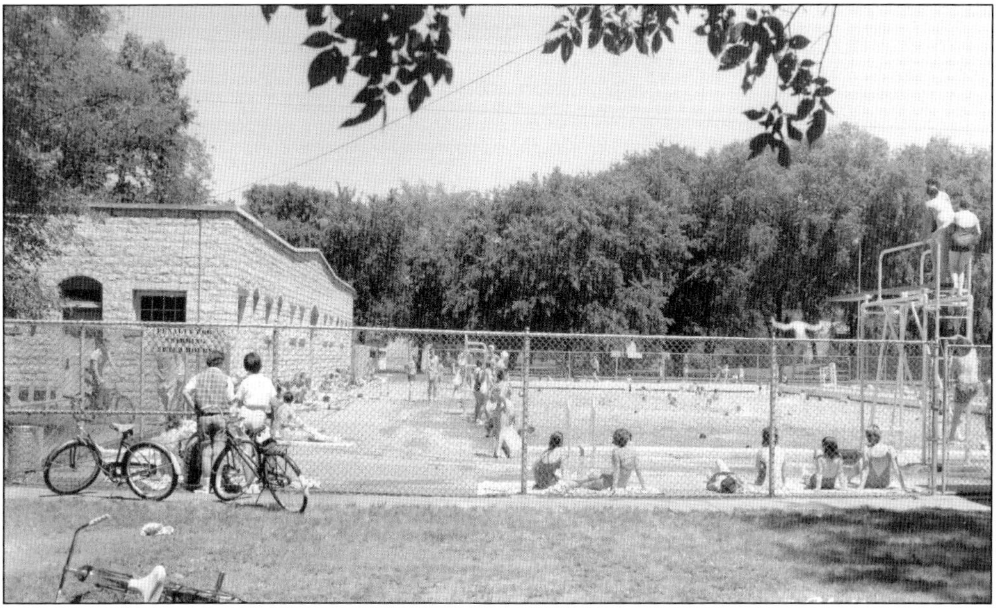

The Dousman property was named Dousman Memorial Park. A nine-hole golf course was laid out east of the house. To the west, the WPA funds were used to build a swimming pool and bathhouse open to all the residents of the city.

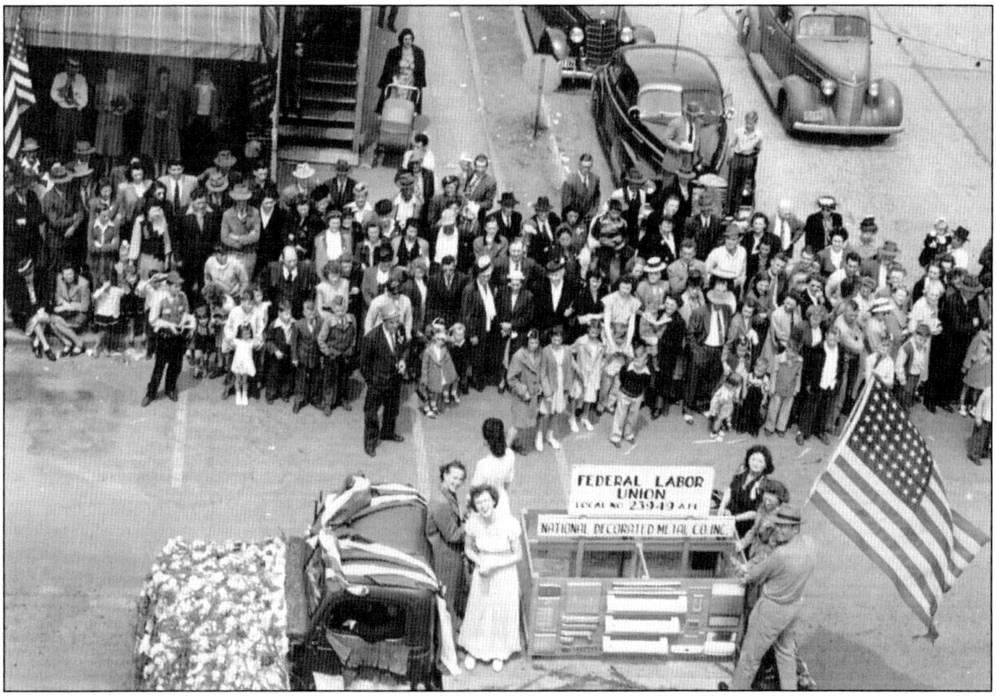

Each year, the Villa Louis opened with a tea, costume ball, and horse show. The highlight of the Villa Louis opening was a parade beginning at 11:00 a.m. on both Saturday and Sunday. The parade wound from the ballpark to the Villa Louis grounds. Bands, pipers, horses, and wagons participated, with ornate floats representing local businesses and organizations. (Courtesy Tony and Chris Trentin.)

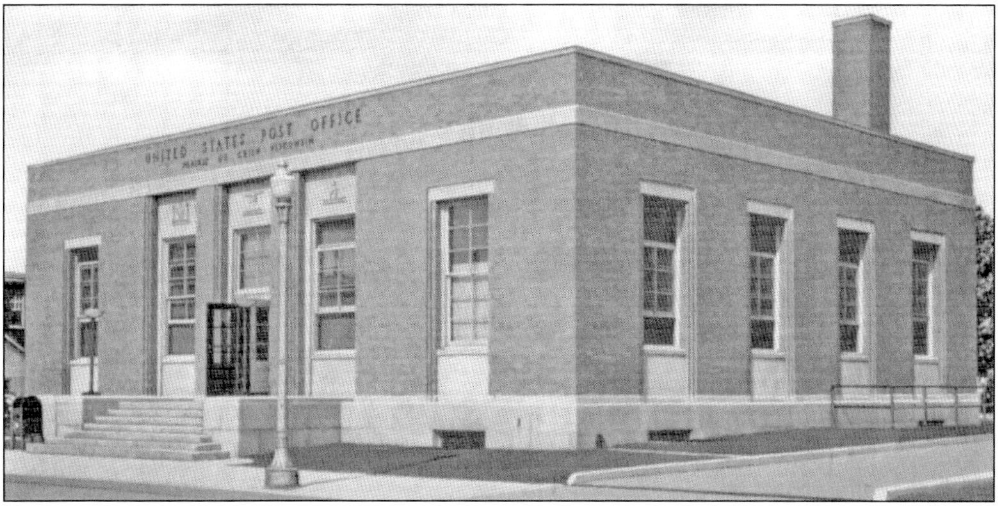

Since its inception, the post office at Prairie du Chien had no permanent location. With WPA money, a building dedicated to be a post office was constructed. Inside a plaster relief sculpture of Marquette and Joliet, created by Jefferson E. Greer, was mounted on the lobby wall. (Courtesy Virginia Antoine.)

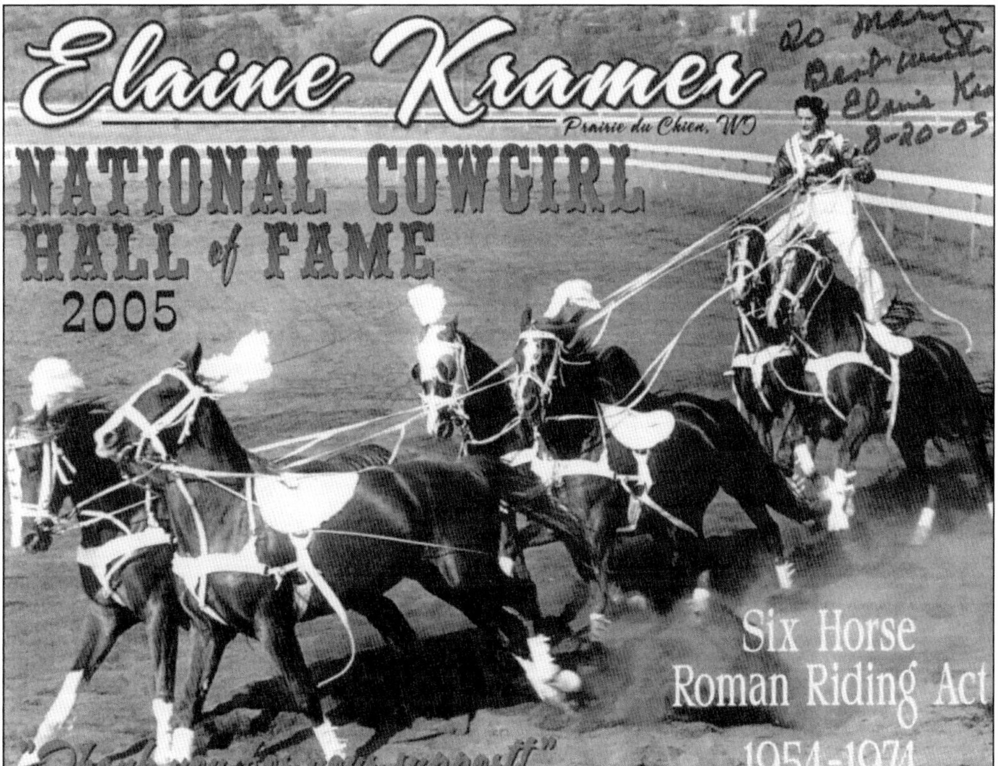

In the 1950s, Rodeo Days replaced Villa Louis Days. Drawing ropers and riders from throughout the Midwest and West, the event starred Elaine Kramer of Prairie du Chien. From 1954 to 1974, Elaine's Roman Riding Act thrilled audiences from New York to San Francisco. (Courtesy Elaine Kramer.)

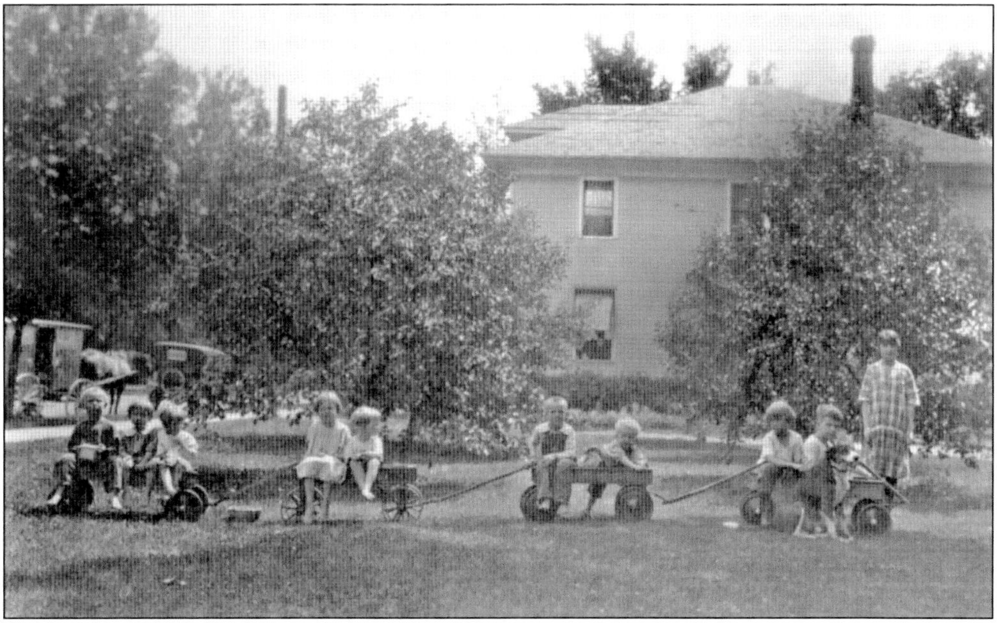

Though it is the 21st century, children still ride coaster wagons and bicycles around the courthouse square, set up corner lemonade stands, and play night games. (Courtesy Antoine family.)

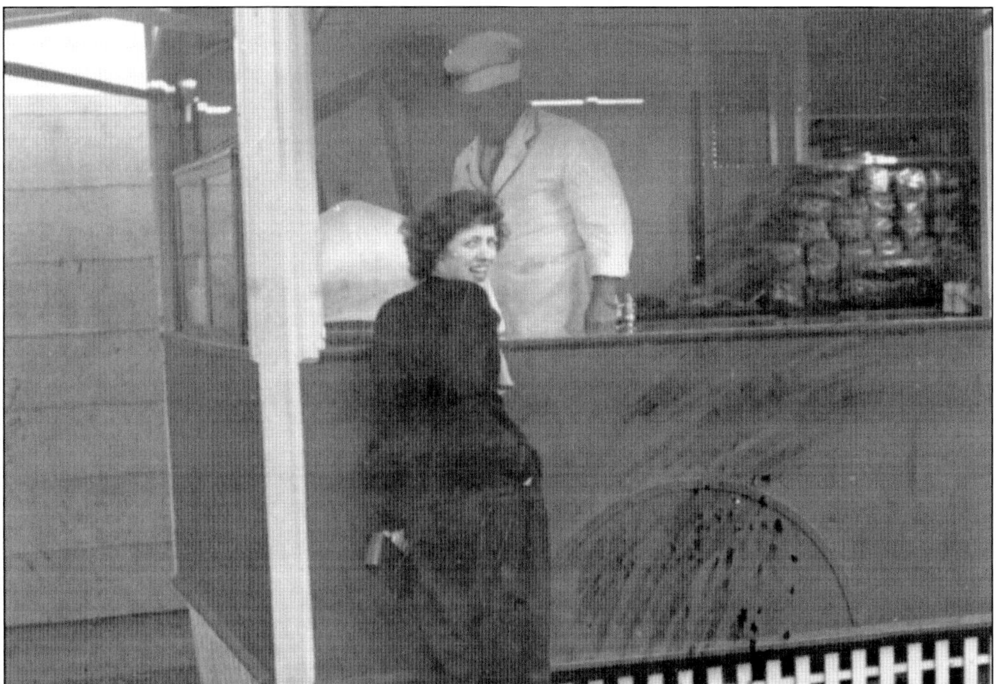

Other traditions of Prairie du Chien also continue. During the summer, Pete Gokey's descendants still sell hamburgers from a stand on Blackhawk Avenue. Mike Valley smokes and sells fish caught in the Mississippi River early that morning. (Courtesy Bob Ziel.)

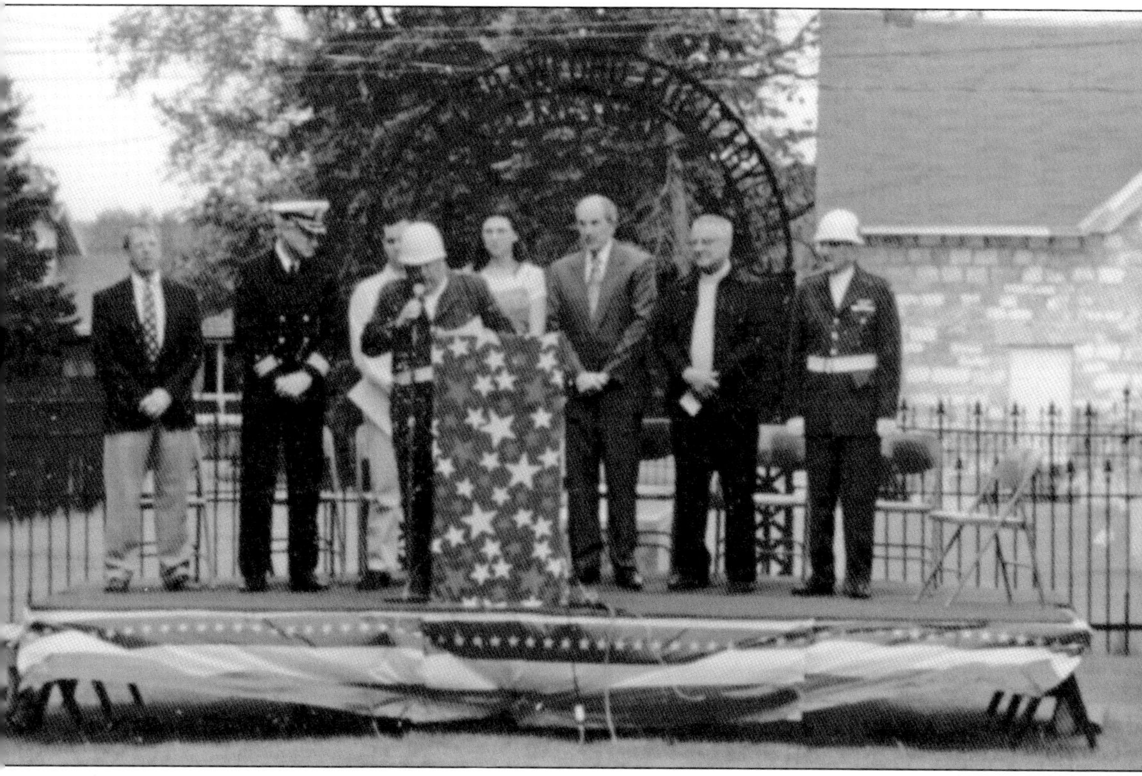

Each Memorial Day, a parade with veterans, the Prairie du Chien school bands, and Boy and Girl Scouts makes its way down Blackhawk Avenue to Beaumont Road to the Fort Crawford Military Cemetery. The ceremony honors the women and men who have served in the military, and Girl Scouts decorate the graves.

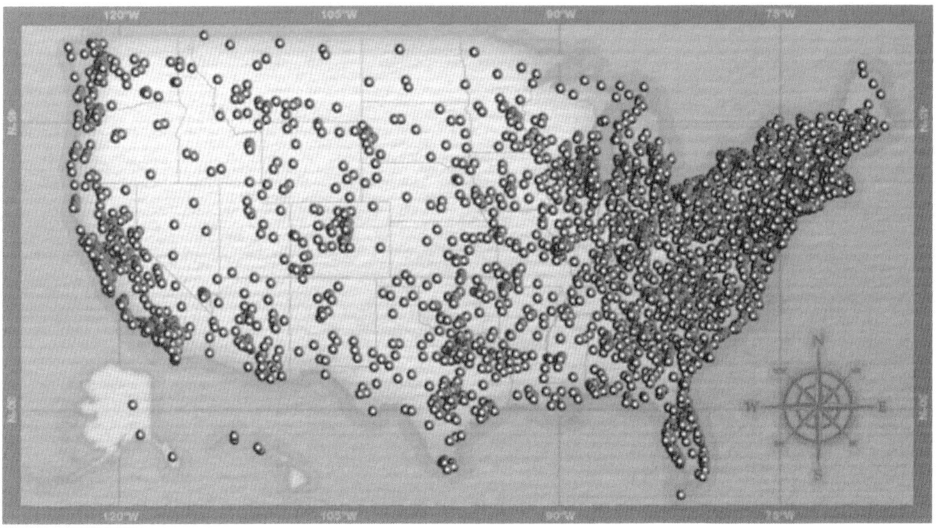

Consistent with our mission to preserve history on a local level, this book was printed in South Carolina on American-made paper and manufactured entirely in the United States. Products carrying the accredited Forest Stewardship Council (FSC) label are printed on 100 percent FSC-certified paper.

MADE IN THE USA